MW00974865

Madrid Inside Out

An Insider's Guide for Living, Working, & Studying in the Spanish Capital

◆

Arthur Howard & Victoria Montero

Editor

David Applefield

Frank

BOOKS

B.P. 29
94301 VINCENNES Cedex
France

45 Newbury Street
Suite 305
Boston, MA 02116
USA

For our parents.
May their visits be long,
and often...

Layout: Cory McCloud
Design conception: Deborah Applefield
Drawings: James King
Cover stamp: Miro, © *Direccion General de Correos y*
Telecommunicaciones, Servicio Filatelico, Madrid.

Achevé d'imprimer en janvier 1992
Sur les presses de l'Imprimerie Fricotel
Many thanks to Claude Briot
Epinal-Paris Tél. (1) 40.23.00.17
Flashage: Compo Rive Gauche Tél. (1) 43.25.33.43
Dépôt Légal N° 2504, janvier 1992

CONTENTS

¡Bienvenido a Madrid!

WELCOME to Europe's fastest-paced city, the capital designated as Cultural Capital of Europe. Spain has pulled out all stops for the celebration of the 500-year anniversary of the European *discovery* of America. Madrid of today continues to surprise and stimulate.

There is no lack of sources and travel guides available for visitors to Madrid. Undoubtedly, even more are on their way. We honor the existing sources and turn to them often to find the forgotten restaurant, the unknown chapel for weekend excursions, and the historic fact on a painting or building....

Those sources belong to the "tourist" in us. There's a place on your bookshelf for them, as there is on ours. *Madrid Inside Out* is no duplication; what we provide here is not so much a guide to your evening stroll as a survival tool for the discriminating newcomer who plans to stay more than a day or week in this often daunting capital. Are you a business person? diplomat? exchange student? professor on sabbatical? entrepreneur? spouse of a Spaniard? We're confident that if you were clever enough to get yourself sent (or to send yourself) to this invigorating city, you'll do well in finding your own favorite restaurants and parks. What you need at the outset though is a bridge to minimize the settling-in process. As cities go, Madrid, for all its real enchantment, is one of the tougher nuts to crack for the newcomer. We know—we were newcomers once ourselves. Now, we can provide the time warp to shorten those difficult initial weeks searching for apartments, running the cultural mine fields with potential gaffes, and taking on the inanimate objects that have it in for you—the telephone booth, the lamp you brought from home with the wrong plug....

Guide books don't always confide to you the charged code words to avoid using when dealing with officialdom, nor tell you the number to call to get the dumpster removed from in front of your house, or the name of the nearest clinic for when your visiting relative suddenly decides to develop a kidney stone. What tourist guide speaks of house pets? Did you know you can cause yourself long delays in Madrid by, even innocently, hitting an ancient cultural nerve?

What we as Madrid editors have in common with you the reader is that we too faced these same barriers and didn't know where to turn. We can laugh now, and wallow in cultural relativism. At the time, though, we were not amused: we could well have skipped the unsuccessful forays down dark, rainy streets, and discouraging taxi rides along polluted avenues on wild goose chases for apartments and drivers' licenses. We'd rather have settled-in quicker and gotten on with our plans and projects, and we assume you'd like to do the same. This is the goal of Frank Books' *Inside Out* guides.

As marvelous and vital a place as Madrid is, dignified and funny as the *Madrileños* are, first impressions count. We want your first impressions to be the best possible because we're fond of this place and want you to be too. The fewer unpleasant surprises, the better.

We hope you'll find *Madrid Inside Out* entertaining and out of the ordinary. More importantly, we want to ease the mechanics of dealing with a complex city, so you can be free to spend more time on what matters: enjoying and getting the most out of your stay.

In the first edition, we've includ-ed special sections on Barcelona and Seville, essential in the landmark year of 1992. The Quincentennial marks Spain's entry into the European Inner Market, the Olympics and Expo 92 as well as Madrid's début as the Cultural Capital of Europe. We assume that unless you've just won the lottery, you prob-ably won't be seeking to establish residence in these places; however, you'll at least want to visit them during this unique time in Spain's history. Thus, we've prepared essential information in the hope that such visits will complement your experiences. After all, Spain is no more Madrid than Great Britain is London alone or the United States is New York City. Madrid has become a city of immigrants from Spain's incredibly varied provinces, and often you'll find you need to see the latter in order to read between the lines and truly understand this upstart capital. So let's get going. *¡Adelante!*

Arthur Howard &
Victoria Montero

MADRID of the 1980s was a city of breakneck speed and prodigious growth. It increased in population, wealth and cultural offerings at a pace unknown in Europe in this century. What the mid-1990s will bring is unforseeable, but as of this writing there is no sign of any slackening in the city's pace or grandiose intentions for itself. *La movida*, they used to call it, but now even that term implying exhilaration and the breaking of old forms has fallen into obsolescence.

The visitor arriving during the 1980s found almost none of the old stereotypes of slow austerity, severe signs of authority, ponderous introspection broken with occasional fits of exuberation. Instead, Madrid underwent the greatest sustained binge of its history, going yet once more for the prosperity that has remained so often out of reach, and this time finally hitting pay dirt. Backing the binge was Europe's fastest growing and most diversified economy.

Madrileños couldn't quite believe their good fortune; they were more intent on experiencing it to the hilt than in taking a good look at it, for fear it might go away if they took stock of it. Pollution got out of hand, the traffic became something between a joke and a daily media scandal. Prosperity came at the expense of Europe's highest rates of unemployment and drug addiction.

The difference from before was that people stayed, hoping to cash in on the Spanish miracle. What had once been a city producing an urban proletariat for export now was transformed into the reverse — a magnet attracting immigrants from the Maghreb, Sub-Saharan Africa, even Asia. Prices skyrocketed, discouraging tourism; formerly gracious, tree-lined avenues became screaming speedways or else monumental traffic jams in Europe's officially noisiest city. (According to figures from the World Health Organization, Spain is the noisiest country in Europe, second in the world only to Japan, the noisiest. The WHO sets 65 decibels as the highest a human being ought to be subjected to in the daytime, 45 at night. In Madrid, Barcelona and Valencia, the decibel level often goes up to 85 in the daytime.) Literacy plummeted while the world's second largest university, the Complutense, became a holding pen for masses of unemployable youngsters. With one of Western Europe's most troubled telephone systems, Spain took up to a year to install people's private phones, got lines crossed, then charged rates four times that of the leading telephone companies in the U.S. and U.K.

But despite its manifest problems, Madrid continued to attract people by the thousands, because it was, well...Madrid. Something was on the move; stories abounded of rags-to-riches empires made overnight; people remained funny and genuine despite the urban adversity they lived in; clear days at the 667-meter altitude continued to invigorate, and whole sections of the old city were somehow allowed to survive and carry on as they had for centuries. In a survey conducted in 1990 by the Washington-based Population Crisis Committee, Madrid, nonetheless, received 73 out of a possible 100 points for *livability*, ranking *ahead* of Paris and Berlin, and close behind Washington, D.C.

Something dynamic was compensating for Madrid's infrastructural problems, and people sensed it. The compensation was the Culture — maddening sometimes in its irrational attachment to old values, garish at its worst, but holding its own with a confident smile and visible in the basic decency of its folk. It's why you're in Madrid in the first place, so make the best of it.

Unless you've been following the city closely over the years, Madrid will undoubtedly surprise you. Consider these:
• Madrid is as expensive as any European capital.
• Madrid has almost as many banks as *tapas* bars.
• Madrid considers itself cosmopolitan, while to a high degree the cosmopolitanism consists of Spaniards from the other regions of Spain, moving to the capital from Murcia and Galicia (the way U.S. government employees move to Washington from Nebraska and Georgia).
• Madrid isn't particularly warm or even sunny all the time; one recent year it rained from November to March almost without letup.
• *Madrileños* are lighter in hue than you might expect,

more Teutonic in fact than Andalusian for good historical reasons.

• *Madrileños* are immensely hard-working on the days when they *do* work (no country has more legal and religious holidays), and they generally make it to their appointments on time. Quite the contrary of the Anglo-Saxon image of the *mañana* ethic, you'll be surprised at times with the promptness and smiles proferred by the plumber, the bureaucrat or the shop-keeper.

Madrid hosts a people united against its own infrastructure. *Madrileños* will tell you that they reserve a special place in hell for the directors of their telecommunications system or traffic circulation. The frustrations are more an aspect of what you're up *against* together than a general indifference or lack of helpfulness which you might encounter elsewhere.

Madrid's greatest appeal is its people — as honest and sweet-natured as any on earth, while tough as nails when it comes to competing for diminishing resources such as a few square meters in a traffic lane or a moment of the cheese-seller's attention. Somehow it all works; it has so far. If you can find out how — quickly — you'll be far ahead of the game in feeling at home in Madrid.

Form of Government • Constitutional Monarchy. King Juan Carlos I, Head of State as of 1975. Felipe González Márquez (Socialist), President of Government from 1982. Spain is a member of NATO and the EEC.

Area • 194,884 square miles (504,750 sq kms), about the size of Colorado and Wyoming together. Western Europe's second largest country, after France.

Topography • High interior in Europe's second highest country after Switzerland. Madrid elevation 667 meters (2,188 ft). Heavily watered in the north, arid in the center, Mediterranean climate to the south and east.

Population • 39,784,000 (1990). Density 204 per sq mile, about the same as New England.

Ethnic Groups • Spanish (Castilian, Andalusian, Asturian) 72.8%, Catalan 16.4%, Galician 8.2%, Basque 2.3%.

Capital • Madrid (4,137,000 — 7,000,000 with suburbs)

Other Major Cities • Barcelona (3,842,000); Valencia (720,000) Seville (600,000).

Languages • Castilian Spanish (official), Catalan, Basque, Galician. Only Basque is not a Romance language.

Religion • Roman Catholic 94%. (No official State religion has existed since promulgation of new Constitution in 1978.)

Time • GMT + 1. Daylight savings time does not coordinate with the U.S., so for three weeks in the fall there are five hours difference from East Coast time instead of the usual six; three weeks in the spring, seven hours.

Business Hours
•Banks Mon-Sat 9:00-1:00p.m.
•Offices Mon-Fri 9:00-6:45 p.m.
•Shops Mon-Sat 9:00-1:30p.m. 4:30-8:00p.m. Summer hours tend to go straight through to 15h (3p.m.) and end then for the day.

Average Temperatures for Madrid • January 41 F (5 C), July 76 F (24 C).

Currency • Peseta. Varies around 100 pesetas to the U.S. dollar (to convert, just lop off two zeros). There are approximately 180 pesetas to the £ Sterling, 90 pesestas to the Canadian dollar, 60 pesetas to the German mark, 18 pesetas to the French franc, 8 pesetas to 100 liras, 70 pesetas to the Swiss franc, 55 pesetas to the Dutch guilder, and 80 pesetas to 100 Japanese Yen.

Weights
1 kilo = 2.2 pounds

Lengths
1 centimeter = .394 inches
1 meter = 3.28 feet
1000 meters = 1 kilometer = 0.62 miles
(to calculate miles quickly multiply kilometers by .6)

Measurements
1 liter = 0.265 gallons
1 gram = .033 ounces

Temperatures
Converting Celsius to Fahrenheit:
Multiply Celsius temperature by two and add 32

Fahrenheit		Celsius
0		-17.8
32	(freezing)	0
50		10
68	(room temperature)	20
77		25
86		30
98.6	(normal body temp.)	37
100.4		38
104		40

Clothing Sizes

Women's dresses

Spain	36	38	40	42	44	46	48
US	6	8	10	12	14	16	18

Men's pants

Spain	42	44	46	48	50
U.S.	32	34	36	38	40

Shoes

Spain	37	38	39	40	41	42	43
U.S.	6	7	7.5	8	9	10	10.5

Men's shirts

Spain	37	38	39	40	41	42	43
U.S.	14.5	15	15.5	15.75	16	15.5	17

Dates: In Spain, 1/3/65 is March 1, 1965, not January 3, 1965.

Time of Day: Generally expressed by the 24-hour clock. Thus, 8 am = 8h00 and 8 pm = 20h00. Midnight = 24h or 24h00, Noon = 12h or 12h00

Electric Current: Spain's system is 220 volts, 50 cycles. To use standard North American 110 volt, 60 cycle appliances you will need an adapter plug and a transformer that is appropriate for the wattage of the appliance. Some 220 volt appliances have a combination 50/60 cycle motor that allows them to operate in Spain without any problems.

Holidays	
January 1	New Year's Day
January 6	Epiphany *(Día de los Reyes)*
March 19	St. Joseph *(San José)*
Easter Thursday and Good Friday	*(Jueves y Viernes Santo)*
May 1	Labor Day *(Primer de Mayo)*
May 2	Feast of Madrid Community *(Día de la Comunidad)*
May 15	St. Isidro/Patron Saint of Madrid
July 25	Feast of St. James *(Santiago)*
August 15	Assumption *(Asunción)*
October 12	National Day *(Día de la Hispanidad)*
November 1	All Saints' Day *(Todos los Santos)*
November 9	Almudena (Madrid only)
December 6	Constitution Day *(Día de la Constitutión)*
December 8	Immaculate Conception *(La Inmaculada)*
December 25	Christmas *(Navidad)*

New Year's Eve *(Noche Vieja):* Includes the custom of eating one grape for each of the twelve chimes of midnight, representing the twelve months of the year; if you succeed, it brings good luck.

January 6, (Epiphany or *Los Reyes):* Celebrated in remembrance of the Three Wise Kings, competes with Christmas as an occasion for giving gifts. Processions *(cabalgatas)* depict the original epic.

March 19, St. Joseph or San José: One of the most common names in Spain (Josés are also Pepes, *P.P. = Padre putativo,* the putative father of Jesus.) In the Valencia region, San José is celebrated with satiric cardboard sculptures (towns compete with one another) before being burnt during *la nit del foc* (the night of the fire), accompanied by impressive fireworks.

Easter: The week prior to Easter *(Semana Santa)* is important. Spain shuts down and everyone goes somewhere.

May 1, Labor Day: Though decreasing in importance in recent years, May 1 remains a day of demonstrations of labor/minorities/student organizations.

May 2, Feast of the Madrid Community: Commemorates the uprising of the people of Madrid against the Napoleonic regime of 1808.

May 15, San Isidro: The organ grinder accompanies dancing in the streets *(chotis)* by the boys and girls *(chulos y chulas).*

July 25, Santiago: Celebrated mostly in the northwestern city of Santiago de Compostela, traditional burial site of St. James and destination for pilgrims from all over Europe.

August 15, *Día de la Virgen*: Day devoted to the Madonna. All Spaniards named María celebrate their name day, receiving presents from family and friends — as is the custom on their birthday.

October 12, National Day, *Día de la Hispanidad* and Columbus Day: Also serves to honor *La Virgen del Pilar,* one of Spain's most celebrated Madonnas whose pilgrimage leads to the *Basílica del Pilar* in Zaragoza. During the Franco years, the National Day was July 18, in commemoration of the nationalist uprising of 1936. Since the Franco period, much discussion has ensued over just when Spain's national day ought to be, given that each province has its own version of the important days on the calendar. The discovery of the New World is an event of interest to all Spaniards, but each Autonomous Community has its own important day; for Madrid it is May 2.

November 1, All Saints' Day *(Todos los Santos):* Families visit cemeteries to lay flowers and spruce up the area around the graves of the deceased. They eat traditional bone-shaped biscuits, *Huesos de Santo*.

November 9, Almudena: Almudena is the Madonna to whom Madrid's unfinished cathedral is dedicated (it looks as if it never will be finished). A good occasion to have a *chotis* dancing contest on the Plaza Mayor while spectators have an *agua, azucarillo y aguardiente*, similar to the French pastis. Dinner is postponed over the traditional *barquillos* (waffles).

December 6, Constitution Day: A newly established holiday as of 1978. People rejoice over the day off, though almost no one has any idea how the Constitution works.

December 8, *Día de la Inmaculada Concepción:* Yet another holiday devoted to the Madonna, in which all Spaniards named Conchita,

Concha and Inmaculada receive presents and buy drinks on the occasion of their name day.

December 24-25, Christmas Eve *(Noche Buena):* Tends to be a more significant holiday than Christmas *(Navidad)*. A family dinner usually precedes the *misa del gallo*, Midnight Mass. People eat *turrones*, sweets made of ground almond and honey, with marzipan. The menu served on *Noche Buena* is a closely studied affair, differing according to the region of the country. Christmas carols are called *Villancicos*. A word of advice: prices rise dramatically during the weeks prior to Christmas, so good planners buy their food before and freeze it.

December 28, *Día de los Inocentes:* Beware — This day functions like April Fools, and *Madrileños* love to victimize gullible newcomers.

Climate

"Ten months of winter [*invierno*]; two months of hell [*infierno*]."

The adage isn't far from the truth, though you have to take the *invierno* part with a grain of salt. Curiously, travelers from cold climates record Madrid winters as the coldest they remember — including the Nordic Hans Christian Andersen in his travelogue on Spain.

As for *infierno*, we submit without further comment the fact that a friend of ours registered 50° C one summer afternoon on his terrace — comparable to the most extreme temperatures in the Persian Gulf.

True enough, Madrid is favored by more sunlight than your average European capital. On the other hand, don't come to Madrid expecting year-round lawn parties. As reflected below, for reasons of extreme heat or cold, average temperatures prohibit outdoors lounging over half the year. Seasonal changes can occur overnight. Winters over the past ten years have grown progressively warmer — due, some say, to Madrid's own greenhouse effect, a self-inflicted plague of heating by soft coal.

Don't be scared off, because in spring and autumn at least, Madrid is blessed by weather of incomparable beauty; during the other seasons there are always the hills north of the city to escape to, closer to Madrid than the Berkshires are to Boston, the Castkills to New York, or the Cotswolds to London. Do, however, prepare for extremes if you plan to live in Madrid — including daily temperature fluctuations of ten to fifteen degrees Celsius (20° Fahrenheit) between 2:00 am and 4:00 pm.

Summer temperatures are unbearable only for a six-week period from late June to early August. Mid to late August can be a delightful time to be in Madrid; the heat slackens and the city is cleared of a good third of its population, making it possible to drive, park, breathe, and conduct other human activities you wouldn't want to undertake a month earlier.

Note: Madrid's elevation of 650 meters (2000 feet) and dryness most of the year can provoke respiratory problems among those prone to them.

Average Madrid Afternoon Temperatures											
	Jan.	Feb.	Mar.	Apr.	May	June	July	Aug.	Sept	Oct.	Nov.	Dec.
°F	47	51	57	64	71	80	87	86	77	66	54	48
°C	8	11	14	18	22	27	31	30	25	19	12	9

TRAVELLING to and from Madrid is relatively easy from all corners of Europe and the rest of the world. If you are coming from the United States or Canada, there are a number of reduced-rate travel possibilities available to students. Reduced rates are also possible for those under 26. The Council on International Educational Exchange (C.I.E.E.) issues international student and youth cards which allow substantial discounts on flights. Otherwise, you should consult your travel agent for the most recent rates on scheduled airlines serving Madrid. (See Air Travel).

Council on International
Educational Exchange
205 E. 42nd Street
New York, NY 10017
Tel • (212) 661-1450

Council on International
Educational Exchange (C.I.E.E.)
Doménico Scarlatti 9
28003 Madrid
Tel • 594-1886 / 594-1976

Other U.S. Locations: C.I.E.E./Council Travel

ARIZONA
• Tempe
120 E. University Drive
Suite E
Tempe, AZ 85281
Tel: (603) 966-3544

CALIFORNIA
• Berkeley
2486 Channing Way
Berkeley, CA 94704
(415) 848-8604
• La Jolla
UCSD Price Center
Q-076 9500 Gilman Drive
La Jolla, CA 92093
(619) 452-0630

• Long Beach
1818 Palo Verde Avenue
Suite E
Long Beach, CA 90815
(213) 598-3338
(714) 527-7950
• Los Angeles
1093 Broxton Avenue Suite 220
Los Angeles, CA 90024
(213) 208-3551
• San Diego
953 Garnet Avenue
San Diego, CA 92109
(619) 270-6401
• San Francisco
312 Sutter Street
Suite 407
San Francisco, CA 94108
(415) 421-3473

• San Francisco
919 Irving Street
Suite 102
San Francisco, CA 94122
(415) 566-6222
• Sherman Oaks
14515 Ventura Blvd.
Suite 250
Sherman Oaks, CA 91403
(818) 905-5777

COLORADO
1138 13th Street
Boulder, CO 80302
Tel: (303) 447-8101

CONNECTICUT
• New Haven
Yale Co-op E., 77 Broadway
New Haven, CT 06520
(203) 562-5335

DISTRICT OF COLUMBIA
• Washington
3300 M Street
Washington, D.C. 20007
(202) 337-6464

GEORGIA
• Atlanta
12 Park Place South
Atlanta, GA 30303
(404) 577-1678

ILLINOIS
• Chicago
1153 N. Dearborn Street
Chicago, IL 60610
(312) 951-0585
• Evanston
831 Foster Street
Evanston, IL 60201
(312) 475-5070

LOUISIANA
• New Orleans
Danna Student Center
6363 St. Charles Avenue
New Orleans, LA 70118
(504) 866-1767

MASSACHUSETTS
• Amherst
79 South Pleasant Street
(2nd floor rear)
Amherst, MA 01002
(413) 256-1261
• Boston
729 Boylston Street
Suite 201
Boston, MA 02116
(617) 266-1926
•Boston
156 Ell Student Center
Northeastern Univ.
306 Huntington Avenue
Boston, MA 02115
Tel: (617) 424-6665
• Cambridge
1384 Massachusetts Ave, Suite 206
Cambridge, MA 02138
(617) 497-1497
• Cambridge
Stratton Student Center
M.I.T., W20-024
84 Massachusetts Ave
Cambridge, MA 02139
(617) 225-2555

MICHIGAN
1220 S. University Ave., Rm. 208
Ann Arbor, MI, 48104
Tel: (313) 998-0200

MINNESOTA
• Minneapolis
1501 University Ave, SE, Rm. 300
Minneapolis, MN 55414
(612) 379-2323

NEW YORK
- New York
356 West 34th Street
New York, NY 10001
(212) 564-0142
- New York
205 W. 34th Street
New York, NY 10017
Tel: (212) 661-1450
- New York
35 West 8th Street
New York, NY 10011
(212) 254-2525

NORTH CAROLINA
- Durham
703 Ninth Street, Suite B
Durham, NC 27705
Tel: (919)286-4664

OREGON
- Portland
715 S.W. Morrison, Suite 600
Portland, OR 97205
(503) 228-1900

PENNSYLVANIA
- Philadelphia
3606A Chestnut Street
Philadelphia, PA 19104
Tel: (215) 382-0343

RHODE ISLAND
- Providence
171 Angell Street, Suite 212
Providence RI 02906
(402) 331-5810

TEXAS
- Austin
2000 Guadalupe Street
Austin, TX 78705
(512) 472-4931

- Dallas
6923 Snider Plaza, Suite B
Dallas, TX 75205
(214) 350-6166

WASHINGTON
- Seattle
1314 NE 43rd St, Suite 210
Seattle, WA 98105
(206) 632-2448
- Seattle
219 Broadway Avenue East
Alley Building, Suite 17
Seattle, WA 98102
Tel: (206) 329-4567

WISCONSIN
- Milwaukee
2615 N. Hackett Ave
Milwaukee, WI 53211
(414) 332-4740

ELSEWHERE
- **France**
49, rue Pierre Charron
75008 PARIS
Tel: (33) (1) 45.63.19.87
1, Place de l'Odéon
75006 PARIS
Tel: (33) (1) 46.34.16.10
- **England**
28A Poland Street
London W1V 3D
Tel: (44) (71) 437-7767
- **Germany**
18, Graf Adolph Strasse
4000 DÜSSELDORF 1
Tel: (49) (211) 32.90.88
- **Japan**
Sanno Grand Building
Room 102
2-14-2 Nagata-cho
Chiyoda-ku
Tokyo 100
Tel: (81) 581-7581

If you're going to live in Spain for any length of time, you'll need to take certain steps in order to comply with local law. Here's a short list of the essentials:

Tourists, *Touristas*

An American or EC passport entitles you to stay in Spain without special permission for up to six months. Tourists are entitled to special tourist bank accounts. For a longer stay on tourist status, you need only exit the country and have your passport stamped, then reenter the country; this turns over the clock for another six months. (As of 1993, EEC passports will entitle holders unlimited stays in Spain.)

Residents, *Residencia*

For *residencia* of a year or more, the foreigner must have either money in the bank, income from abroad, a work permit, or be the dependent of someone else. Residents may bring their furniture from abroad (tourists may not), and open a regular bank account in Spain. For a work permit, address your questions to the Ministry of Labor. A *gestoría* can help you with this. Artists, writers, and others who work at home need not have a work permit in order to obtain resident status.

If you chose to become a legal resident of Spain, you'll be subject to the same laws as a Spanish citizen: you must close your tourist bank account and open a regular one, using your Spanish ID number; if you want to drive, you must get a Spanish driver's license, etc. If you are a legal resident, you must have your *Tarjeta de Residencia* with you at all times.

Residents' Visa, *Visado de residencia*

Before leaving home, you should get this document from your Spanish embassy or consulate, the visa you'll need if you're going to live and work in Spain for over 90 days. If you are retiring to Spain or are to be employed, you'll need the residence visa, even if you're an EEC citizen. The only exception is for individuals planning to be self-employed, or to set up their own business. This visa is not needed. For a list of Spanish embassies and consulates around the world, see page 70.

Residents' Authorization, *Autorización de residencia*

Once you are actually living in Spain and plan to spend a long time there, it's to your advantage to convert your *visado de residencia* into an *autorización*. This entitles you to borrow money from a bank, receive Spanish health benefits in some circumstances, retain a work permit. The principal advantage of *not* becoming a resident is the greater ease in dealing with foreign currencies (sending or receiving them). However, you do need residency in order to import your household effects. (You can avoid this by declaring *vivienda secundaria* in Spain for your vacation or retirement residence. Then, you may import household goods if you haven't been a resident in Spain during the two previous years; if your goods enter the country within three months of your arrival in the country; and if your goods are at least six months old.)

To get residency status as an EEC citizen, you need to demonstrate sufficient means for supporting yourself, evidence of having health insurance, and a home to live in. If you're working on getting residency status, go through a *gestor* to minimize the headaches.

Identification Number, NIE

Spanish banks are directed as of 1991 to require a *Número de Identificación de Extranjero* for each foreigner seeking to establish a bank account. The *NIE* echoes the *NIF (Número de Identificación Fiscal)* required of Spanish citizens and resembles in function the American Social Security number. Some 18 million Spaniards have an *NIF.* You'll need the *NIE* not only to perform bank transactions, but also to buy or sell property, receive earnings on stocks and bonds or take out an insurance policy. To get an *NIE,* report to any local police station that has a department for foreigners *(extranjeros),* with a photocopy of the front page of your passport.

A non-resident does *not* need an NIE to open or use a bank account, but does need one to hold a Spanish insurance policy, pay taxes or take out a loan. A resident needs an NIE for any of the above.

If you remain on non-resident status, you may import a car and certain other belongings. For information, contact the Spanish Ministry of the Economy and Treasury, Office of the Director General for Customs. Guzmán el Bueno, 137, 28003 Madrid. Tel: 554-3200 or your local Spanish embassy or consulate.

Work Permit

Spanish authorities both require and easily grant work permits for non-Spanish citizens working in the country. Almost half a million foreigners work legally in Spain (in addition 300,000 — mostly Africans and Latin Americans — work illegally, generally for wretched wages).

A *gestoría* can help you get papers, and you are advised to go through the process in order to avoid misunderstandings and complications. The gamut of possibilities is as follows:

Permit A is valid for nine months; Permit B is valid for one year only in a given profession and in one geographical area, with possibility of renewal; Permit C allows you to work in any geographical or professional area for five years. If you're self-employed, Permit D permits you to work in a certain place; Permit E, for any type of activity in any part of Spain. Apply to the *Dirección Provincial del Ministerio de Trabajo*. Required documents for non-EEC citizens may include a letter from the employer; a visa or residence permit; documents proving your qualifications for working in Spain; evidence of having paid income tax. Requirements for EEC citizens are considerably less, but the paper work will remain after the rules are changed.

Foreign Workers' Rights & Obligations

All labor laws applying to Spaniards (hours, holidays, pay...) apply to foreign workers as well in possession of legal work permits. Whether you are setting up a business or working for someone else's, you must make social security payments. Doing so entitles you to health insurance, unemployment benefits, retirement, etc. With respect to money and banks, residents come under the same set of rules as Spanish citizens — with limits to the amount of money that can be removed from the country. Spanish citizens or residents may open bank accounts and take out cash cards, but they are not allowed to have convertible peseta accounts.

Taxes

If you spend over 183 days a year in Spain, you're considered a resident for tax purposes, and will be taxed on *all* your income regardless of where it comes from. Non-residents (those who stay fewer than 184 days) still must pay taxes on property owned in Spain and income earned there. In the case of residents paying taxes elsewhere, Spain has treaties with some countries to avoid double taxation. Scandinavians, Dutch and Belgians benefit from this arrangement, as their home countries' taxes are higher than those of Spain. A peculiar U.S. law requires American citizens to pay U.S. tax, regardless of their place of residence. Americans living in Spain will then be levied the difference between their low American tax and the somewhat higher Spanish taxes.

Note: non-residents are subject to a 35 percent tax on the sale of property — the *incremento de patrimonio* or capital gain. Everyone pays the VAT or IVA *(Impuesto sobre el Valor Añadido)* on individual purchases. This tax is usually built into the retail price of goods and services, and ranges from 6 to 30%, with most consumer goods taxed at 12%.

Property, Rentals, Investments

This can be tricky. We refer you to David Searl's *You and the Law in Spain* (Lookout Publications, Fuengirola), or John Reay-Smith's *Living in Spain* (Robert Hale, London).

Air Travel

Iberia, the Spanish national airline, has direct connections throughout Western Europe, Latin America and the U.S. (New York, Chicago, Indianapolis, New Orleans and Los Angeles). It also services Tokyo, Cairo, Tel Aviv and a half dozen cities in West Africa, and, of course, all major domestic cities. In turn, most of the major carriers fly into Madrid's Barajas International Airport.

Customs

You may bring in 200 cigarettes, 100 small cigars, 50 cigars, 250 grams of pipe tobacco; two liters of spirits up to 44 proof, or one liter of higher proof; 50 ml. of perfume and one-quarter of a liter of *eau de toilette*. There are no restrictions on the amount of pesetas or foreign currency you may bring into the country, though foreign currency in excess of the equivalent of 50,000 pesetas is required to be changed into

Spanish currency within 15 days.

You may leave Spain with up to 100,000 pesetas, or up to 350,000 pesetas in foreign currency. Larger sums must be approved by the *Dirección General de Transacciones Exteriores.*

Airport buses and taxis

Frequent yellow buses connect the airport with the Plaza del Descubrimiento (formerly the Plaza Colón), for 250 pesetas. Taxis are plentiful from the airport; the average fare to downtown Madrid ranges from 1000 to 2000 pesetas.

Iberia runs telephone information lines for all flights on (91) 411-2545. For domestic flight reservations, 411-1011. For international flights, 563-9966.

Madrid Tourist Office

Torre de Madrid
Plaza de España
Open Monday-Friday, 10 a.m. - 1:30 p.m., 4 p.m.-7 p.m.
Saturday 10 a.m. - 7 p.m.

Municipal Tourist Office
Plaza Mayor 3
Open Monday-Friday, 10 a.m.-1:30 p.m., 4 p.m. - 7p.m.

Major Airlines Serving Madrid

• Air France
Gran Vía, 53
Tel: 247-2000
• Avianca
Gran Vía, 88
Tel: 248-7303
• Alitalia
Aeropuerto Madrid s/n
Tel: 205-4335
• British Airways
Serrano, 60
Tel: 431-7575
• Iberia
Velazquez, 130
Tel: 585-8585
• KLM
Gran Vía, 59
Tel: 247-8100
• Lufthansa
Po. Castellan, 18
Tel: 577-3741
• PanAm
Gran Vía, 88
Tel: 541-4200
• Sabena
Gran Vía, 88
Tel: 541-8903
• SAS
Gran Vía, 88
Tel: 247-1700
• SwissAir
Sta. Cruz de Marcenado, 31
Tel: 247-9207
• TWA
Plaza de Colón, 2
Tel: 410-6010
•United Airlines
Rosario Pino, 18-2
Tel: 570-1011
Toll free from Spain: (900) 983-386

The Spanish railway system, RENFE, serves all regions of the country with connections to Portugal and France. In addition, there are regional networks (FEVE) with narrow-guage tracks. In general, Spanish trains have come a long way since the rickety, romantic wagons you've seen in films about the Civil War and Dr. Zhivago (filmed in Spain). However, if you're used to the precision and cleanliness of the French or German trains, don't expect the same from RENFE.

Different categories of trains make different claims to punctuality: in order from top to bottom, TALGO, Inter-City, TER and Expreso. Night trains have *couchettes* for six, sleeping compartments for one, two, three or four passengers, with bathroom and other facilities. The latter are prohibitively expensive, sometimes twice the price of air fares.

Currently, the Spanish government is working on a fast train, TAV *(Tren de Alta Velocidad)*, between Madrid and Seville, comparable to the French TGV or the Japanese Bullet. The TAV is due for inauguration sometime in 1992.

You can save about 15% by traveling on *Días Azules* (Blue Days), avoiding rush periods or holidays. Four people traveling together on a Blue Day can get their automobile included for free on the Express Train routes. Special weekend round-trip rates also exist. You're well advised to avoid travel of any sort on *puentes* (three-day weekends), when the entire Spanish nation seems to make it a point of honor to go *somewhere*.

Special discounts also exist for young people under the age of 26. For this, you must first obtain the *Tarjeta Joven (Dirección General de la Juventud*, Fernando el Católico, 77, Tel: 244-2290). In addition, other reductions are offered to families under certain circumstances, or travel vouchers *(Chequetren)* which get 15% discounts. When you buy a train *bono* or coupon, your rides are checked off as you travel. For details call RENFE (429-0202) or one of the municipal train stations:

• Charmartín
Tel: 733-6561 / 733-6362
• Príncipe Pío
Tel: 247-0000
• Atocha
Tel: 227-3160 / 429-0202

You can reach the three stations above through *feeder* lines at special stations at Paseo de Recoletos, and Castellana *(Nuevos Ministerios)*.

RENFE has a home delivery service (9:00 am to 9:00 pm). For information call 501-3333.

Special tourist circuits service certain areas — such as the Al-Andalus to Andalucía, the Transcantabria to the northern section of the country, and the Strawberry Train, which simulates Spain's first rail transport from the time of Isabel II, between Madrid (*Delicias*) and Aranjuez. Most overnight trains will transport an automobile for an extra fare.

The Spanish Rail Pass, like Eurail, must be purchased outside of Spain before being used for travel in Spain. First or second class, one or two week passes, are available.

Spanish Tourist Offices in the U.S.
- New York
Tel: (212) 759-8822
- Chicago
Tel: (312) 642-1992
- Los Angeles
Tel: (213) 658-7188
- Miami
Tel: (305) 358-1992

Spanish Tourist Offices Around the World
- Paris
Tel: (33) (1) 720-9059
- London
Tel: (44) (71) 499-1169
- Sydney
Tel: (61) (2) 264-7966

| Abidjan | 3915 | 2433 |

Distances in Kilometers & Miles from Madrid to Foreign Cities

City	Km	Miles	City	Km	Miles
Amsterdam	1458	906	Lisbon	515	320
Athens	2359	1466	London	1244	773
Bogota	8026	4987	Los Angeles	9378	5827
Brussels	1314	831	Manchester	1433	890
Buenos Aires	10079	6263	Marseilles	798	496
Casablanca	868	539	Mexico City	9060	5630
Copenhagen	2058	1279	Miami	7100	4412
Chicago	6739	4188	Milan	1178	732
Dublin	1453	903	Montreal	5563	3457
Cairo	3349	2081	Moscow	3149	1846
Istanbul	2712	1685	Munich	1478	918
Stockholm	2598	1614	New York	5758	3578
Frankfurt	1420	882	Paris	1031	641
Geneva	1009	627	Rio de Janeiro	8140	5058
Havana	7457	4634	Rome	1330	826

Tel Aviv	3541	2200	Vienna	1804	1121
Tokyo	10764	6689	Zurich	1238	769
Toronto	6057	3764	Alicante	355	220

Distances in Kilometers & Miles
from Madrid to Spanish Cities

Arrecife	1574	978	Mallorca	546	339
Barcelona	483	300	Santiago	486	302
Bilbao	319	198	Seville	395	245
Ibiza	458	284	Valencia	285	177
Las Palmas	1764	1095			
Malaga	432	268			

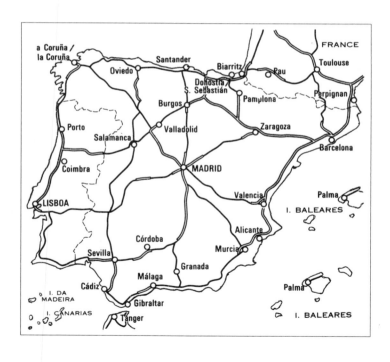

A RCHAEOLOGICAL remains from the eighth century have been found along the *calle de Segovia*. In the ninth century, Arabs under Mohamed I built fortifications in the present Madrid to repel attacks of the Christian *Reconquista*. The city's name is derived from the Arabic *Magerit* (plenty of water).

By 1085 the military fortress was conquered by King Alfonso VI. The inhabitants gathered along two hills with a small valley between, along what is now the calle de Segovia. The Christians lived by the hill where the Royal Palace now stands; the Arabs remained along the other hill, today the Vistillas district.

In 1561 King Felipe II brought the Royal Court to Madrid, making it the *de facto* capital of Spain. Before then, the site had been little more than a military settlement; afterwards, Madrid's growth took off, and it tripled in size within a few years. In 1600, the shy Felipe III transferred the Court to Valladolid, then returned to Madrid in 1606, and officially made it his capital. He gave the *Madrileños* the *Plaza Mayor* (1619) along with his apologies for having tried to put his capital elsewhere. The Madrid of the period of the Hapsburgs *(los Austrias)* solidified in

appearance and size, remaining its recognizable self until the nineteenth century.

During the War of Spanish Succession (1701-14), Madrid changed hands a number of times but remained predominantly under the rule of Bourbon sympathizers. With Felipe V, the Bourbons strived to leave their mark on the capital, particularly under Carlos III, whose reign saw the construction of neoclassical buildings and monuments such as the *Puerta de Alcalá* and the *Paseo del Prado*.

During the Napoleonic period, the French Emperor installed Joseph (José) Bonaparte as King of Spain. *Madrileños* bridled at the French reign, and rose up in the War of Independence May 2, 1808, at the *Plaza Mayor* and *Puerta del Sol*. The French withdrew in 1813, repulsed by British troops.

Queen Isabela II celebrated her wedding in 1846 at the

Plaza Mayor with enormous pomp. After her reign went sour (she abdicated in 1868, fleeing to France), Madrid dug in for the Industrial Revolution, some decades after England, France and Germany. Spain's railroad system branched out in spokes from the capital, with the construction of Atocha Station in 1892. The Salamanca district was carved out and built, and the famous cafés (*Gijón el Comercial*...) were opened.

By 1900 Madrid had a million inhabitants. The air service between Barcelona and the capital was inaugurated in 1919 as Spain sat out World War I; the Metro began operation in 1921, with the *Telefónica* building reaching completion in 1929.

Madrid was a Republican stronghold during the Civil War of 1936-39, enduring nightly bombing raids by German planes. The Nationalists destroyed large sectors of the city both before and after their takeover in 1939, when Franco made it his capital.

Years of diplomatic isolation under Franco following World War II saw quiet growth and the expansion of the capital to areas previously under the legal aegis of the suburbs. All traces of destruction from the Civil War were removed.

In 1981 Picasso's *Guernica* was moved to Madrid from the MOMA in New York — an act symbolizing the new, freely breathing Spain following the death of Franco in 1975. In keeping with Spain's entry into NATO and the EEC in the 1980s, and President Felipe González' internationalist policies, Madrid was the venue of a nearly three-year long CSCE meeting (1980-83).

Madrid has been named in 1992 the Cultural Capital of Europe.

Pre-Spain
1,500,000 B.C.: Earliest human remains on the Iberian peninsula.
40,000-15,000 B.C.: Altamira cave paintings.
1200-800 B.C.: Indo-European penetration. Phoenicians and Greeks on the Iberian peninsula.
218 A.D. - 409 A.D.: Roman Hispania.
272-710: Visogothic Kingdom. Germanic invasions.

Muslim Spain 710-1492
756-929: Umayyad Dynasty.
929-1009: Caliphate.
1009-1090: Ta'ifas (Petty States).
1090-1146: Almoravides.
1146-1224: Almohads.
1224-1232: Banu Marins' invasion.
1232-1492: Nasrid Kingdom in Granada.

Christian Spain 710-1492
Offensives 1065-1214 by Alfonso VI, VII and VIII; reign in 13th century of Alfonso X *The Wise* — astronomer, poet, codifier of the law.
803: Kingdom of Navarre.
1137: Kingdom of Aragón and Catalonia.
1143: Kingdom of Portugal.
1230: Kingdom of Castile and León.
1479: Fernando and Isabela unite Castile and Aragón through marriage.
1492: Conquest of Granada. Columbus to America.
1535-45: Viceroyalties of Mexico and Peru.

Hapsburgs 1517-1700
1517-1556: Carlos I of Spain (Charles V to everyone else).
(Cortes in Mexico. Pizarro conquers Peru 1531).
1556-1598: Carlos abdicates in favor of his son Felipe II.
(Dutch revolt begins 1567. Spain defeats Ottomans at Battle of Lepanto 1571. Spanish Armada, sent to defeat English Protestantism after the execution of Mary Stuart, defeated 1588 off the English coast).
1598-1621: Felipe III.
(Don Quixote, 1605. 1618-48: Thirty Years War).
1621-1665: Felipe IV.
1640: Secession of Portugal.
1665-1700: Carlos II, last of the Spanish Hapsburgs.

Bourbons 1700-1808
1700-1746: Felipe V installed.
(War of Spanish Succession, Treaty of Utrecht 1713, ceding Gibraltar to England).
1746-1759: Fernando VI.
1759-1788: Carlos III.
1788-1808: Carlos IV.
(England defeats Spain at Trafalgar 1805).

1808-1814: Disintegration of the *ancien régime* and Peninsular War. Joseph Bonaparte enters Madrid, *Madrileños* rebel May 2, 1808. British fight the Napoleonic French in Spain.

1814-1833: Reaction and liberal revolution. Restoration with Fernando VII. *Pronunciamiento* of 1820 brings liberal rule, followed by second absolutist restoration in 1823.

1833-43: Fernando deprives his brother Don Carlos of direct succession to the throne in favor of his infant daughter Isabela, her mother, Maria Cristina, becoming Regent upon Fernando's death. Regency under Maria Cristina, forced into exile by Baldomero Espartero. Monarchist Carlists rebel, favoring Carlos over succession by a woman.

1843-68: Isabela II. Liberals force out Isabela, draft Constitution of 1869.

1868-74: Revolutionary period, Regency of General Serrano. First Republic proclaimed 1873. Carlist uprisings continue.

1875-1923: Restoration under Alfonso XII. Regency under another Maria Cristina. Loss of the Spanish-American War. Reign of Alfonso XIII.

1923-31: Dictatorship of Primo de Rivera and fall of the Monarchy.

1931-39: Second Republic and Civil War.

1939-75: Regime of General Francisco Franco.

1975: Death of Franco and proclamation of Juan Carlos I as King of Spain. Spain cedes Spanish Sahara to Morocco.

1977: First general elections in 40 years. Adolfo Suárez (center-right CDS Party) appointed President (Prime Minister) by Juan Carlos I.

1978: Constitution.

1979: Basque and Catalan autonomy. Resurgence of Basque terrorist (ETA) activity. Calvo Sotelo forms a new UCD government.

23 February 1981 (23F): Attempted coup by Colonel Antonio Tejero fails. King Juan Carlos enters parliament and disbands military rebels on his authority as Commander-in-Chief.

1982: Spain enters NATO. Felipe González voted in as Prime Minister, with Socialist Party (PSOE).

1986: Spain becomes full member of EEC and confirms NATO membership in national referendum. González reelected with PSOE absolute majority.

1992: Entry into European Inner Market; celebration of the Quincentennial of Columbus' voyage to America; Expo 92; Olympic Games in Barcelona; Madrid Cultural Capital of Europe.

Political Affairs

Spain is a constitutional monarchy. King Juan Carlos I was proclaimed king in 1975 after Franco's death. He saved Spanish democracy single-handed on February 23, 1981, when as Commander-in-Chief he disbanded a group of military leaders under Lt. Col. Antonio Tejero, who had taken over the *Cortes* (Parliament) at gunpoint.

While no one questions the validity of recent elections, Spain is an imperfect model for true pluralism. Since coming to power in 1982, the Spanish Socialist Party (PSOE) has dominated Spanish politics, moving the country in the direction of one-party rule. More than once, comparisons have been made between the PSOE and Mexico's PRI, which operates generally unopposed. Many of the PSOE's original

supporters continue to vote for their party's leaders only because there are no centrists they can switch to. Some political analysts from outside Spain believe that the party ultimately is the only real political mechanism in place, with the judicial and legislative branches of government serving a mainly decorative function.

In 1990 Adolfo Suarez' CDS (centrist — formerly UCD) party faded almost entirely from the scene, after once being the only show in town when Suarez served as King Juan Carlos' first Prime Minister in 1975. In the late 1980s the conservative *Partido Popular* (PP), took on young leader José Maria Aznar in order to try to rid itself of the old Franquist image under Franco's Tourism and Communications Minister Manuel

Fraga. The PP won a plurality in Madrid in the elections of 1989, but remained at only a little over half the PSOE in terms of national representation. A number of regional parties (including Herri Batasuna, the Basque party with direct links to the ETA terrorist group) achieved representation in the *Cortes*, but remained scattered and politically insignificant in terms of national strength. The same was true for the communists under the *Izquierda Unida* and their able spokesman, Julio Anguita.

The PSOE, dominating national politics from their solid base in Andalusia, suffered an identity crisis as they became the Establishment they had originally campaigned to combat. Their leader Felipe González made powerful statements in the *Cortes* and backed the U.S. initiative in the Persian Gulf. González' *brains*, however, was generally believed to be his friend from his Andalusian childhood, the former Vice President Alfonso Guerra. When Guerra was accused of taking over a period of many months influence money indirectly through his rags-to-riches brother Juan, González defended him publicly, threatening that if

Guerra went, so would he. The affair was dubbed *Waterguerra* by conservative opposition newspaper *ABC*. When Guerra's estranged wife, about to testify against him in the *Waterguerra* affair, died under mysterious circumstances, rumors circulated of foul play. The rumors were never followed up with evidence or open accusations.

Internal leadership battles broke out, with Economy Minister Carlos Solchaga and former Defense Minister Narcís Serra (now Vice President) making noises that the time had come for González to step aside; but González used the Party Congress in 1990 to shore up his power and remains the undisputed leader of the PSOE. Contrary to his previous promises, he stayed put when Alfonso Guerra finally stepped down in January, 1991. A cabinet reshuffle two months later put the matter on the sidelines, with the new cabinet generally affirming the faces and politics as before, only with the noticeable absence of Guerra himself, and Narcis Serra in his stead.

The Church
Gone are the days of Church dominance of Spanish political affairs. In a 1976 Gallup Poll

almost two-thirds of the Spanish public described themselves as practising Catholics. A decade later, only two-fifths did. In a recent controversy over a campaign to encourage the use of condoms for birth control and the prevention of AIDS, the Church, opposing the campaign, was laughed off the stage by 85 percent of the Spanish public. *Opus Dei*, the older lay group on the fringes of the Church which is sometimes associated with Franco but which actually was persecuted under the *Generalísimo*, has lost the influence it once had on public policy. On the other hand, its membership has almost doubled since 1975 to about 25,000.

The Family

The birth rate fell by half in Spain between 1975 and 1986, to an average of 1.5 children per woman (compared to 1.8 in France). This was the steepest decline in Europe during that period. Women outside of the rural areas of Andalucia tend not only to have fewer children, but also to work: four out of five new job-seekers today are female. After a decline in the early 1980s the marriage rate is now rising, hovering at around five per 1,000 population.

Though there is more sex before marriage, and although abortion was legalized in 1985, births out of wedlock are still taboo, accounting for only seven percent of the total born (compared to 20% in France).

Political Geography

Spain is made up of 17 political subdivisions called Autonomous Communities (*Comunidades Autónomas*). The divisions are based on historic, cultural and economic rationale. The squeaky wheels of Catalonia and the Basque Country receive the greatest degree of local autonomy, the other *Comunidades* correspondingly less. Each has its own government, working in conjunction with the central government in Madrid. The transfer of responsibilities is no trivial matter, but on occasion makes up the stuff of domestic political debate.

• *Galicia:* The northwest corner of Spain, with geographic, linguistic, cultural and historical links to Portugal. One of Spain's poorest regions, its mainstays are agriculture and fisheries. Ancestral home of Francisco Franco and Fidel Castro.

• *Asturias:* A principality (the Prince of Asturias is the Heir-Apparent, as the Prince of Wales is in England). Rugged terrain, a region of mines, metallurgy and some industry.

• *Cantabria:* A geographic continuation of Asturias, rural in character with a beautiful, rugged coast. Tourism on the rise.

• *Basque Country* (Euskadi): Prosperous region of the north, though with a high rate of unemployment. A region developed in heavy industry. Home of Spain's strongest separatist movement, though the population generally eschews the terrorism associated with the movement. As of September 1991, according to a Sigma Dos survey 68% of Spaniards opposed independence for the Basque Country or Catalonia. 25.7% supported independence.

• *La Rioja:* Rural area with agriculture, agro-industries, and excellent and abundant wines.

• *Navarra:* Culturally and geographically close to the Basque Country, home of agriculture and light industry.

• *Aragón*: One of Spain's main industrialized areas, also rich in agriculture. Sports resort center, particularly for winter sports as practised in the Pyrenees.

• *Catalonia:* Spain's most highly industrialized area, also has a highly developed tourist industry throughout the region as well as on the Costa Brava. Barcelona, traditionally a more sophisticated cultural center than Madrid and more European in feel, still rivals the capital in commerce and culture.

• *Balearic Islands:* One of the world's most sought-after tourist areas. In the month of August, the airport at Palma de Majorca is said to be the busiest in the world.

• *Valencia:* Agricultural and citrus production in one of the world's most fertile and productive areas. Valencia is an industrial center as well.

• *Murcia:* Valencia's poorer sister; mainly agricultural; home of an important military port at Cartagena.

• *Castilla-León:* The heart of Spain, now developing new industries. Beautiful countryside in the area around Segovia.

• *Castilla-La Mancha:* Poorer than Castilla-León, scene of Cervantes' fiction. Now mostly agricultural.

• *Extremadura:* One of Spain's poorest regions, arid and almost lunar in its topography. The Conquistadores came from Extremadura, chiefly to get away from it. Site of some magnificent medieval cities and monasteries.

• *Madrid:* A region as well as a

city. Highly developed, and almost completely devoted to the administration of Spain. Scene of new industrial development in the city's outskirts.

• *Andalucía:* The region that most typifies the world's image of Spain — one of sun-flooded patios, dark, captivating women and macho duellists. Andalucía is Spain's poorest region, now receiving special attention and investment, particularly in Seville for *Expo 92.*

• *The Canary Islands:* As much north African in climate as they are Spanish, these volcanic islands are an important tourist center; they also produce tropical vegetation and exotic fruits.

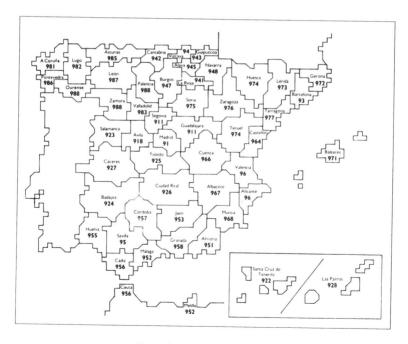

S p a i n ' s   R e g i o n s
indicated with telephone prefixes

Spain has the fastest-growing economy in Western Europe (around five percent in recent years), and one of the most diversified. Agriculture was Spain's success story of the 1970s and 1980s, with production growing by six to seven percent a year, and large tracts of land in the south being put under the plow after centuries of inactivity.

At the same time, Spain has Europe's highest rate of unemployment, 17 percent. Prime Minister Felipe González has been accused of engineering these results deliberately, and of abandoning the orthodox Socialist approach he brought to Spanish politics in the 1970s.

Entry into the Common Market in 1986 brought a rash of foreign investment, to the tune of $10 billion a year. There has been some concern that this investment may slow as capital is redirected to Eastern Europe. A consumer binge over the past five years has spurred inflation, partly responsible for a serious dip in tourist revenue in the late 1980s. Tourism, Spain's largest industry, accounts for nine percent of the GNP and employs one worker out of ten. The number of visitors dropped by four percent in 1990 (down to a mere 52 million visitors!).

More critically, hotel residency was down by 25 percent. Thus, the main brunt of tourism losses was borne by hotels.

At present, U.S. firms have important investments in the automotive, banking, and electronics industries and are active in a wide range of other sectors, mainly manufacturing and real estate. Nevertheless, European investments (with British) caught up with American ones in 1987 and overtook them.

In an end-of-year article in 1990, the *Wall Street Journal* said Spain's economy was entering "into rough waters." Following tremendous growth from 1985 to 1989, the economy had begun to falter, though not nearly so much as doom-sayers claimed. Per capita income continued to rise, hitting $8,620 in 1989, over double that of 1985. Nevertheless, car sales were down 20 percent after stunning years like 1985, when one adult out of 25 bought one. Company failures increased by two-thirds in 1990 as compared to 1989. Though consumption remained high, the investment needed to keep it propped up dropped sharply; gross fixed capital formation fell by five times, compared to the previous year.

With unions bargaining each year for seven to eight percent raises (twice the European average), Spanish competitiveness will decline and even fewer investments will come in.

Spain is literally banking on the year 1992 to reverse its problems and solidify its advances. There will be a dizzying rate of activity leading up to that date, including the appearance of millions of visitors to the various events planned, and major investments in infrastructure to make it all possible. A Gold Rush spirit continues to reign, with Spaniards as well as foreigners lining up to get part of the action. What happens after 1992 is anyone's guess.

Note: New rules require foreigners to obtain a *Número de Identificación Extranjero* (Foreign Identity Number) from their local police stations, in order to maintain bank accounts, take out insurance policies and perform other financial transactions. The Spanish government has imposed the requirement in order to be able to levy taxes on foreigners, thus ending *de facto* tax shelters previously enjoyed by real estate owners, etc. If you fail to get an *NIE,* your bank account can be frozen.

**Felipe González goes
to work in a suit now**

In their work rhythms, contemporary *Madrileños* have mixed a strong northern work ethic with a southern languor and pleasure principle. You may be surprised at how productive *Madrileños* are when they are at work: if you expected to find a *mañana* mentality in Madrid, you'll soon see how wrong you were. While the people in Madrid do face horrific infrastructure problems at times, their willingness and skillfulness in tackling them on an individual level is impressive.

Madrileños take every opportunity to play instead of work, and enjoy a full panoply of legal and religious holidays, plus truly humane amounts of summer vacation, maternity leave, etc. Some would say they've figured out life's dilemmas and found a correct balance. We could all well learn from them.

Before taking them as adepts at the *dolce far niente* mastered by their cousins across the water, however, you should consider their high output and motivation when they *are* on the job. As good Spaniards, *Madrileños* put a high premium on competence at all levels of endeavor; while they accept and respect social and economic castes, they also give frequent and abundant signals of respect to one another up and down the ladder. People strive to perform services competently and quickly; when they succeed in doing so they expect and receive praise from others.

The famous long Madrid lunch is not really time off from work; despite appearances, and notwithstanding the chit-chat you'll overhear at the lunch table, the midday break is one of the most important elements in the *Madrileño* work day: deals are conceived and delivered, partnerships formed, vital information exchanged. The buoyant and efficient manner in which *Madrileños* do their business over lunch is one of the enviable marks of their civilization. Observe, imitate, enjoy.

The typical work schedule at an office runs from 9:00 a.m. to 6:00 p.m., with an indeterminate lunch lasting from about 2:30 to 4:30 or longer. This now ritualized procedure has largely replaced the siesta in a city too modern and sprawling to sustain the old habit of going home at midday. While the *Madrileño* lunch seems to start later and later — 3:00 is not exceptional — this is by no means obligatory; restaurants are delighted to start you off *early* at 2:00 or even 1:30, so don't feel you have to follow some unwritten rule on the subject.

Likewise the late dinner can run from 10:00 or 11:00 to midnight and beyond, but restaurant owners will cheerfully seat you at 9:30 or even earlier. Don't be daunted by empty rooms, as they'll fill up in time. Also, if you find you can't talk your alimentary tract out of a 7:00 pm dinner schedule, remember you can *cheat* and take appetizers (*tapas*) with the *Madrileños* at 6:00 to 8:00, eating a bit more than they might and then calling it dinner. No one will ever know.

Different theories have been advanced for why Madrid has the latest eating hours in Europe; one theory is that *Madrileños* like all other humans simply adapt to their physical surroundings; located at the western-most end of their time zone, they get the sun late into the night in the warmer months, and the heat can be a bad mixture with early eating. The late dinners necessitated by their climate in summer push back the lunch hour in turn, and so forth. This is only a speculative theory.

Note: business lunches are frequent, business dinners rare. *Madrileños* will often meet business associates for *tapas* immediately following the working day at 6:30 or 7:00, but dinner is generally reserved for close friends. Thus you may be stepping out of bounds by proposing dinner to a potential client.

Punctuality

Madrileños are punctual but not annoyingly precise; they'll expect the same from you. To explain: if you set a meeting for 11:00, *Madrileños* will consider they were *on time* to arrive at 11:15. Later than that is *late*, and insulting. Tardiness of more than 15 minutes is inexcusable. While legitimate factors like the traffic may keep them up to a half hour late for an appointment, *Madrileños* incur such delays not with cavalier abandon, but with deep contrition.

If you haven't been to Madrid before, your first surprise about the people will be that they *look* more northern European than *Mediterranean.*

Despite earlier centuries of demographic isolation, Castile has recently been somewhat of a melting pot within the realm, and is now enjoying its heyday as the great mixer of the Spanish provinces. Having read your history section carefully at the beginning of this book, you know that a period of Teutonic invasions extended from the third to the eighth centuries. This no doubt had much to do with the physical appearance of the people. The Germanic influence had less effect in the southern part of the peninsula, where Arab presence was always greater. To this day, there is probably as much difference culturally between a Castilian and an Andalusian as there is between a Spaniard and a Finn.

The next thing you'll notice is a real sense of decency among *Madrileños:* politeness seems inbred rather than enforced (automobile driving is the exception, as in most cities.) It's not unusual for people to come up to confused strangers in the street and offer their help, nor will the fish seller usually be too busy to explain cheerfully how to transform his impeccably fresh slab of fish into a culinary feast in your home. Given the limits on time and space in the capital, basic civility forms the backdrop of all direct human intercourse, with cheating or petty theft a rare exception between individuals openly dealing with one another. (Pickpockets are another matter.)

It's futile to describe the smile and the wish to be helpful — from top to bottom on the social scale as well as vice versa. You just have to experience it. The warmth of the people, as much as the supposed ideal climate (see above), has lured visitors for centuries. After hearing lengthy discussions about the economic factors in this century's Civil War, you'll be left with the impression that it just doesn't *jive*, the people seem so non-violent, even if loud at times or pushy in traffic.

These are generalizations of course, and all generalizations are false. Knowing the limits of such sketches, and aware that future generations may howl at our innocence when they take up this book from a dusty shelf in some second-hand bookstore, we offer the following checklist of cultural observations for ready conversion into daily life:

Honor

Spanish culture is one of the oldest on earth maintaining unbroken links to its own past. In the seventeenth century, official Spanish society revamped an earlier notion of honor based on heredity alone, and pegged the highest attainable human value to a matter of performance: was a *caballero* courteous, helpful to the defenseless, straight in his dealings with his peers? Only then could he be said to have *honra*, regardless of his social rank. Though rank continued to play a crucial role (and still does) in the way people treated one another, the individual could achieve *honra* like a state of grace, at whatever level he or she fit in the society.

Big deal, you say, looking back through a prism of Anglo-Saxon traditions now taken for granted, built by the old boys: Locke, Jefferson, Franklin. And yet in the centuries when our current assumptions were being contrived, birth was taken everywhere as the basis of a person's character, without much question. So it is today, if you consider the unsettled *nature-or-nurture* polemic, or the notion that some people have honor from the start while others never seem to obtain it.

The discussion in Spain in the seventeenth century was a true humanistic revolution, focusing Spaniards' attention on their own inner qualities — a value and process that cut entirely across social lines, while at the same time leaving those lines entirely intact.

Though the leaders of the discussion were the theorists and playwrights directed to the upper crust (Lope de Vega, Calderón de la Barca...), the ideas filtered to all sectors of Spanish society. Spanish society of the period was more stratified than even the Anglo-Saxon's, but its moral values filtered from top to bottom with much greater ease.

Lest you take the above as an academic digression, just try making your way around the Madrid of the 1990s — the seemingly modern forests and valleys of skyscrapers of the Paseo de la Castellana — without taking into account the backdrop that makes people flinch one way or the other! Failing to do so not only cuts you off from a fascinating social dynamic — half the fun of living in a foreign culture — it can even make it impossible to perform basic tasks like getting a plumber to fix the faucet in your house or getting a business firm to pay its bills for you. Swords won't come out because of your insensitivity, but the icy treatment and endless discussion will be high prices to pay.

One of the basic applications of the above is to avoid any discussion of truth and untruth. In the seventeenth century, when the day's values were more or less set in place, the ultimate insult to a nobleman was to pull his beard and say, "Liar!" — *¡Mentis!* Like it or not, the accused was obliged to challenge the offender to a duel or else give up every measure of self respect and social standing.

To this day, at all levels of Spanish society, calling a person *mentiroso* is an offense which has no equivalent in Anglo-Saxon culture. Disagree, yes, argue, fine — in fact Spaniards love the give-and-take of a good-natured argument. But never openly insinuate doubt for another person's word.

Spaniards' antennae pick up even the most oblique allusions. Terms to avoid:

"But you said last week..."

"That's true, but..."

"That's not what so-and-so says..."

To the Spaniard, these expressions are no different from saying, "You're a liar." Insults will get you nowhere fast, except into the quicksand of aimless and endless polemics.

Want to know the single most valuable piece of advice you'll get from this guide? Don't ever, ever use the word *problem* when dealing with a Spaniard (e.g., "There seems to be a problem here..."). Just don't. Whether it's dealing with the plumber and a broken toilet, an administrator and an illogical rule, or a printer and an annoying error, don't.

Corollary: having avoided using the word *problem*, leave no room for the other to believe that you might think something were his or her *fault*. When there is a problem, the only acceptable approach is to present a united front with the person who has the key to the solution: "It's you and me against *it* [or *them*]." Keep this attitude even with the person who was the cause of the *problem* in the first place. Remember:

• Americans solve problems (sometimes).

• The British outlive them (usually).

• The French debate them (always).

• Spaniards draw ranks against them, then coexist.

Social Stratification

One of the fascinating aspects of contemporary Spain is its continued acceptance of a social stratification that is considered primitive in Anglo-Saxon countries. Between the *señoritos* (the beautiful ones, the yuppies, the upper class, the *jet...*) and their subordinates (*jornaleros*) remains an abyss of social distance, while daily contact and shared values and perceptions somehow keep the system smoothly functioning. The modern refrain goes, *Conmigo comerás, pero cuello blanco no llevarás* — "You can eat at my table, but you won't be wearing a white collar."

If you read between the lines in your everyday dealings, you'll see this principle repeated over and over with your workmates, acquaintances such as your *portero*, and your teacher or employer. Don't fight it, don't judge it until you've observed it enough to know its strengths as well as its weaknesses.

Other Countries

While numerous charter flights exist from Madrid to the British Isles, there are none to Paris. Things German are treated as high chic in advertisements in the glossy magazines, while the romantic Portugal seldom figures. There are cultural reasons for these phenomena; you need to know some basics about how Spaniards view their European and overseas neighbors and why:

• Portugal: The poor cousin, the upstart that left the union in 1640 (as Catalonia would have, if it had had its way). Spaniards see Portugal the way Swedes see Norway: as the poor cousins. Among Spaniards who travel, few take the trouble to visit their western neighbor, though King Juan Carlos I did in 1990 as an expression of good will. Spaniards know or care as much about Portugal as they do about Kamchatka Province in the Arctic Circle.

Things are beginning to change in this regard, as the Spanish discover Portugal's potential for good value vacations and investments. With the restoration of Lisbon's historical Chiado section since its destruction by fire in 1988, much of the capital now buying up the area is Spanish.

• France: Because of the permeable membrane of the French-Spanish border during the Franco period, and the ability of enemies of the State to flee to the other side (ETA terrorists continue the practice), France was the only country known outside of Spain to most Spaniards. It became thus commonplace to an extent. The familiarity, along with the negative historical vibrations of Napoleonic atrocities, pushed France to the background in the 1970s and 1980s as a place to study or even visit. Spaniards understand and accept their cultural heroes (Picasso, Casals...) fleeing to the north. In the case of Picasso, however, they felt bypassed at best, insulted at worst, when a marriage of convenience turned into one of passion.

While there is some revival of interest in the cultural colossus to the north, many Spaniards see it as a large land mass with generally disagreeable people, standing between them and the English and Germans they so adore.

• England: Spaniards love England and the English. Glossy magazines filled with English interiors set the standard for decorative taste; the English (not American) language is the medium and expression of snobbery, with Spanish families of any means making every sacrifice to send their scions to the British Isles for polishing. After a thorough search, the editors have come up with no interesting historical or cultural explanations for this predilection. Well, it *was* the English who trounced Napoleon's troops in 1813, but even a Spaniard's memory doesn't usually go back that far.

• Germany: A 30-year-old Spanish journalist's comment sums it up— "They weren't *our* enemies in World War II." Germany is geographically distant enough from Spain to have been exonerated long ago for its behavior of the 1930s and 40s. Spaniards had enough tragedies of their own in this century; they're not interested in taking up those of other Europeans.

Spaniards admire German style, music and efficiency unabashedly; German reunification in 1990 aroused as much sympathy and enthusiasm in Spain as anywhere on the planet outside of Germany itself.

• USSR, Eastern Europe: Who? What? Spaniards are culturally and geographically as distant from Eastern Europe's promise and problems as from the moon. Yet a fascination prevails, to the extent that Spaniards delight in their new status and identity as Europeans. Gorbachev's and Havel's visits to Spain in 1990 yielded tremendous sympathy and considerable financial credits for their countries. A

Soviet orchestra conducted by *wunderkind* violionist Vladimir Spivakov is now based in Oviedo with a *Príncipe de Asturias* grant, much to the approval of Spaniards who keep track of such things.

• The United States: *El amigo americano*—an expression of the love-hate posture of Spaniards towards the American monolith, shared by many Europeans. Statistically, Spaniards are the most "anti-American" of Europeans, yet their attitude toward the U.S. is colored by the fact that few Spaniards have ever met an American. For many years, Spaniards blamed Americans for propping up the Franco dictatorship; with the death of Franco and the signing of a bilateral agreement in 1988 terminating American presence at the principal Air Bases in Spain, the political basis for animosity has largely disappeared. (U.S. pilots leave Torrejón Air Base on May 4, 1992.)

For the record: during the early period of the Cold War, President Eisenhower did barter for use of Spanish military bases as a stronghold against communism. In exchange, he pushed for the lifting of Spanish diplomatic isolation, resulting in Spanish entry in the U.N. in 1955. There has been close military cooperation ever since, both under the Franco regime and the current Socialist government.

Spain provided major assistance to the U.S. deployment in Saudi Arabia in 1990, with little protest from the public. The Spanish Socialists, elected originally on an anti-American and anti-NATO platform, now pay for the largest Fulbright exchange in the world, largely as a demonstration that the hatchet is buried, and U.S. as well as European links are greatly craved at all levels.

General Francisco Franco

Every Spaniard has strong feelings about Franco; few are willing to take up the matter with any but their closest friends. You may be surprised, however, at how few put Franco in either a purely angelic or diabolic category. While the dictator came to power with blood on his hands and imposed a stultifying austerity unparalleled by any Spanish leader since Philip II, no one doubts that Franco made Spain one of Europe's few self-reliant countries, or that in 1975 he left the country in a state of calm and potential, unknown in its modern history. One reason Spaniards live in haste these days is the belief that Franco's ghost will somehow come back to put an end to the binge they now enjoy.

Dictablanda, the play on words which reflects the Spanish ambivalence towards their longest reigning leader of recent times: *dictadura*, dictatorship; *dura*, hard; *blanda*, soft. One older man we know tells us he can't sleep at times, awakened in disgust by the thought that Franco was allowed to die unpunished in his own bed. Listen carefully, though, and you'll find others saying, "we didn't use to have these traffic problems..." — the code words all Spaniards know to mean "things were better under Franco."

At best, Franco and the horrendous Civil War (up to 1,000,000 victims) that brought him to power served as an example to all Spaniards of what they do not want to go through ever again. It taught them the virtues of consensus, or at least the need to tolerate one another's viewpoints. That tolerance is one of the aspects which allow the present system to work and to serve as a model for the Eastern European countries now emerging from their own dictatorships.

On the subject of Franco, never take silence as a lack of opinion: there's always something beneath the surface. To probe in that area is presumptuous and invasive of privacy; allow Spaniards their own space on the issue, let them bring it up of their own accord.

Racism

In a recent survey reported in *El País*, Spaniards came out the most racist of Europeans, the ones most likely to believe that "the presence of foreigners in the schools might decrease the quality of education." Two days later in a disclaimer, the paper ate crow, admitting it had read the figures upside down and that Spaniards were the *least* racist of Europeans.

The point is, both results were equally believable. On the one hand, as traditional exporters of labor, Spaniards are still unaccustomed to the social strains known in England, France, Germany and Scandinavia and brought about by immigration from Africa and the Middle East. On the other hand, xenophobia has never been one of Spain's *dadas*, at any rate not since the sixteenth century. You'll seldom hear a

Spaniard make a racist comment or xenophobic lunge. No one knows whether this is because Spaniards feel they are already ethnically mixed enough not to make a big deal out of such things, or whether they really haven't been confronted by any real challenges yet.

In December 1990, one of the hundreds of African immigrants huddled at the *Plaza de España* for lack of anywhere else to go and froze to death in a wretched underground dwelling. While on the one hand, it did happen, on the other, it created a major scandal, inspiring shame and pity among the majority of *Madrileños*.

Gypsies (Gitanos)

Every society seems to have a marginal population, with the dilemma of assimilation-versus-identity. Though Romantic operas such as *Carmen* put a good face on Spain's gypsies, the latter have it no easier than their relatives in Romania, Italy, or the other European countries where they are to be found.

It is probable that Gypsies originally came from the Indus River basin, moving first to Persia in the first century and then across Europe until the sixteenth century. They are now found on every continent. Of the five million in the world, some 750,000 live in Spain (half a million perished in Europe during World War II).

Though Spanish gypsies are Roman Catholic and speak Castilian, few of their neighbors take them for Spaniards. The society at large nurtures the image of them as stealing and cheating in order to make ends meet; as for their marginal distance from mainstream society, you'll find the usual chicken-versus-egg theories about whether they were forced to be apart, or preferred to be.

Spaniards will tell you to keep your distance from gypsies and to hold on to your wallet particularly when in Seville. Your editors are unqualified to have an opinion on this, but find that when Peter speaks about Paul, you learn as much about Peter as you do about Paul.

Arab, Christian, Jew

A few years before Franco's death, the playwright Fernando Arrabal wrote an open letter from his self-imposed exile in France, urging the *Generalísimo* to rescind five centuries of Spanish history by offering an embrace to the Arab and Jewish descendents of those who were shown the door in 1492. The past five centuries were but an aberration, he argued — the real Spain was that of the previous period, the harmonious co-existence of the three communities, each with its contributions to strengthen the whole. Three points to consider:

• In fact Franco did offer an embrace of sorts during World War II, refusing cooperation with Hitler in rounding up Jews the way Vichy France was doing, and even saving a few thousand trapped in the Middle East by directing Spanish embassies there to issue them phony Spanish passports.

• It's debatable just how harmoniously the three communities rubbed shoulders prior to 1492, but anyway, no one is working very hard on revising that history at the moment.

• The celebration of the Quincentennial of the Columbus voyage, coinciding with the date of the expulsion of Arabs and Jews from Spain, is turning real attention to the mending of historical fences. The Constitution of 1978 gave the three religions equal status, and sketched out the principle of separation of Church and State; in 1990 King Juan Carlos' son awarded the Prince of Asturias Prize to a representative of 500,000 Sefardic Jews, welcoming him "with all my heart." The Quincentennial Commission has established subcommissions, one to promote the appreciation of Jewish history *(Sefarad 92)*, the other, *(Al Andalus 92),* for the promotion of Muslim Spain.

Of Spain's 13,000 Jews, most arrived since 1945 from North Africa and Israel. Three thousand live in Madrid. A number of wealthy Arabs favor Spain's southern coast for vacations, whence the Kuwaiti community of several thousand who happened to be there on August 2, 1990. Spain has about 175,000 Arabs.

Spaniards will point out to you that as a nation they're an ethnic or racial mixture of the three groups; most are proud or at least intrigued by the fact and interested, if not knowledgeable, about their mongrel heritage. Your editors have found few hang-ups along these lines, and a greater degree of curiosity than prejudice — far more so, at least, than in much of northern Europe.

Immigration

With the economic successes of the past decade, population movements in Spain have clearly shifted to immigration over emigration. Though only 1.5 percent of the population of Spain are of foreign origin, xenophobia is expected to be on the rise in coming years.

Documented *aliens* living in Spain have grown in number from 181,000 in 1980 to 400,000 in 1990. In addition, the number of non-documented (illegal) aliens has jumped from 70,000 to 140,000, according to recent estimates. The Alien Residence Act of July, 1985, gave illegal residents ten months to apply for legal residence and work permits; only 38,000 did so.

While nationals of Morocco, Tunisia and Algeria traditionally have entered Spain without great difficulty, a new law requires visas, as is the case with all EC countries except Denmark.

The vast majority of non-documented aliens in Spain today are Africans. Protective measures to limit further, illegal immigration especially from Africa are currently intensifying.

Language

Though the Castilian Spaniards make no bones about it, they happen to possess one of the world's most sonorous and expressive languages. Granted, they have the *Real Academia* to standardize the thing and mark the inevitable changes. And yet even the most educated *Madrileños* eschew the whoopla their counterparts make about their languages in Paris, London, Leningrad, or for that matter, Mexico City.

There's no such thing as an inarticulate *Madrileño*: entirely across social lines they talk, argue, discuss, theorize.... They seldom talk *about* their language, but always manage to use it to full effect. Castilian Spanish is rich both in caressing sounds and jabbing irony. Its contact with Arabic left it laden with *refranes* and *dichos* — two-liners from the Arabic tradition with wisdom for every occasion. You'll never learn even a fraction of the standard repertoire of hundreds — even thousands — under the thumb of any Spaniard, but you'll find soon enough that the crafty mental leap you thought you were about to invent was worked out long ago in rhyming couplet, along with its contradicting version.

You either have mastered Castilian Spanish or are intending to spare no effort to do so. If not, we recommend you seek other horizons — as the great majority of Spaniards have mastered no foreign language any better than have the majority of Americans or Britons. They aspire to learn English and may do so by the third millenium. Of the few who claim to know English already, a small minority actually do. Remember, you're the visitor. Enough said.

If you come with Western Hemisphere Spanish in your back pocket, your job is nine-tenths done. *Madrileños* claim to have difficulty with *español* (as opposed to *castellano*); don't believe it. They will understand you, in fact they do so more every day as Latin Americans settle in Madrid. The accent of the Western Hemisphere, after all, is derived from that of Extremadura, where the Conquistadores came from. The lisp is the main difference (see below), and that presents no real phonemic impasse. As for the lexical differences, well — it's true that in Madrid a man might pass by in the car at 9:00 and *coger* (pick up) a lady and take her out to dinner, whereas in Buenos Aires you wouldn't want to do so without prior agreement, unless he were willing to stand charges for statutory rape. On the other hand, even proper Argentines talking to one another in Madrid will *coger* one another, blanching in horror at what they're saying but in the end realizing they both know what they *mean*.

International Spanish is exceedingly supple and ac-cepting of regional differences. Madrid is the European capital where the folk can and will understand best, even through errors, what the foreigner is trying to tell them. They're used to making the effort, and understand it's only fair for them to do so, as they work in only one language themselves.

Though you must make every effort to learn your *castellano*, don't worry too much about mangling verbs at the beginning, or mixing the sub-junctive rules with those you learned for French. Just spit it out as best you can; *Madrileños* make allowances for foreigners and children, whom they also tease for their errors, so be forewarned. As a child you had no choice; in this case, remember you put yourself into it, you have no one to blame but yourself.

Rules and Observations

Newcomers to Madrid who already have a good smattering of Spanish most often make the following points:

• *Vosotros* (the familiar plural): They really use it. You must learn it, especially with the imperative.

• Hyperbole *(Famosísimo):* That sort of thing. They use it at every opportunity. You're not required to use it yourself, but just be aware. Spaniards use understatement a lot, but they're more themselves with hyperbole. Making wild claims has never embarassed them.

• *Gracias:* You must answer *something* even if it's in English. The best answer to *gracias* is *de nada.* You can also say *a usted,* as in thank *you.*

• S plus a consonant at the beginning of a word is a no-no: Add E to compensate, thus: *estress, estupendo.*

• Accent: On the penultimate syllable, or else you have to use the accent mark to indicate the exception. Examples: *período, deposición, tránsito.* Exception to the exception: *ia* endings, which count as one syllable. Thus: *engracia* (enGRAcia), *Murcia* (MURcia). If you really want the stress on the *i,* you need to add an accent mark: *Andalucía.*

Final *z* always gets the emphasis, unless an accent mark indicates otherwise. Example: Martínez, Sánchez.

• The Lisp: This marvelous verbal characteristic — like the sound of the *r* with the crown on it in Czech — gives the spoken language an ornament to play with. The rule is simple: the lisp is always applied to *z,* and the soft *c* (preceding *i* or *e*). Never at any other time. You are allowed to drop the whole thing and speak like a Latin American — you *will* be understood. But if you want to be a member of the club, do it right. There are too many Anglo-Saxons running around Madrid saying *grathiath,* when the correct pronunciation is *grathias.* Saying *grathiath* is the linguistic equivalent of showing up to the big dance in a checkered jacket and striped pants. You'll stand out in a conspicuously negative way.

Now here are some words and idioms you'll hear a lot, ones you may not have gotten in your summer course in Cuernavaca. Some of them you may have learned without realizing how often they'd come up in Madrid. Unscientific research has shown the following to be the 117 most often used words in Madrid:

acto: ceremony *(en el acto:* while-u-wait)

agobiado: overwhelmed

apuro (s): predicament

apostar: place a bet

aprieto: a difficult situation, a jam

apuntar: write down

atasco: traffic jam

avería, en averías, averiado: damage, out of order, damaged

•

bicho: little critter, insect or animal

buena gente: good fellow, good gal

burro: stubborn, dumbass (often used affectionately)

•

caballero: Sir. Said among strangers without implying irony.

cabrearse: to get mad

cachondo: horny (not to be confused with *cachondeo!)*

cachondeo: joke, mess, trouble

caer muy gordo: to like something not at all

caña: a glass of beer at the bar (not to confuse *cana,* white hair)

¡que cara! what a nerve!

colgate: a child of the 60s who never advanced past that point

colocado: drunk *(borracho)*

compromiso: date, appointment

coñazo: a real pain *(dar el coñazo:* annoy)

coño: stupid ass (lit. "cunt")

cosa, chisme, also *trasto:* thinga-majig (the most important word in any language you're trying to learn!)

culebrón: TV series

cursi: affected, snobbish (see *hortera)*

chulo: nice, pretty

•

dar la cara: accept the blame

dedocracia: government appointments by favoritism (lit. "by finger")

(como) Dios manda: "comme il faut"; the way it's supposed to be

divertido: fun (not to confuse with *gracioso,* funny)

(un) duro: five pesetas

•

en lo que (a mí) respecta: as far as I'm concerned

enchufe: "pull" (influence)

enfadarse, enfadado: to get angry, pissed off

enhorabuena: congratulations

enterarse: to find out about, hear of*: no me entero:* "haven't got a clue"

eso es: that's right

estropear: to ruin, damage

estar sin blanca: to be broke (cf. *quedarse limpio)*

•

fatal: real bad

follar: to fuck

follón: noise, confusion

Fulano: What's-his-name

función: showing (film)

•

la grúa: the crane (the thing that's supposed to remove other people's illegally parked cars but gets only yours)

gilipollas: stupid, stupid ass (usu. a man)

gorrón: cheapskate (the one who slips out of paying the lunch bill.

grifo: faucet (for non-bottled water in a restaurant)

guapo (a): affectionate term of irony. Cf. *oye, guapo:* come off it, man!

•

hacer caso: to notice, pay attention
hacer la pelota: to suck up to
Holá, que hay: standard greeting for hello or howdy
¡hombre!: standard exclamation. (Said also among women)
hortera: tacky
¡hostia!: damn! (lit., the sacrament wafer)
(me) da igual: I don't care, it's all the same to me
si no (le) importa: if (you) don't mind
tener ilusión: to really want (feel like) something

•

jaleo: clatter, commotion
jersey: sweater
joder: to fuck (a mild curse in Castilian)
jo...: the contraction or euphemistic form of *joder*
juerga: party, spree

•

ligar: to cruise, pick up, get to know
lío, (mucho lío): a mess

•

majo (a): a fine person. Good in every aspect. The word used to mean "pretty," for people of the street, thus Goya's "Maja" series
mala leche: bad mood, irritable
marcharse: go off, scram (the slang for *irse)*
mariposa, maricón: homosexual; sissy

menos mal: it's just as well (French: *tant mieux*)
mono: cute
moro: (as in, "Moor"): can trust (him) as far as you can throw him (cf. *hay Moros en la costa:* the walls have ears.)
morro: nose, schnozzola
mote: nickname
mucho rato: a long time

•

nada (de): the best answer to *gracias,* you're welcome
nena, nene: girl, boy
ni idea: haven't got the faintest

•

ojo: watch out!

•

ni Pamplona: not a clue; zilch

paliza: a beating
pasota: hippie, dropout. A word of the 70s
pasta: dough, money
(te, le) parece? do you like it? would it suit you?
no pasa nada: no harm done
pelas: pesetas (used when counting: *cien pelas*)
(una) pena: a shame, pity
pesado: tiring; a bore
pico: plus a bit (e.g., *las ocho y pico,* a little after eight)
pincharse: to shoot up (heroin)
piropo: cat-call, wolf whistle
piso: apartment
pitar: honk (car)
polvo, polvete: a lay. *echar un polvo:* get laid
(hecho) polvo: exhausted (not to be confused with the above)

pontelo ponselo: "put it on him, put it on yourself," an anti-AIDS, pro-condom campaign of 1990

a la postre: all things considered; getting to the point

proporcionar: to provide

¡puta madre!: hot shit! (term of awe, most often for food or women)

•

quedarse, quedar con: to agree, have a date or appointment

•

ratero: pickpocket

recado: message; errand

SIDA: AIDS

soy yo: "speaking" (on the telehone). *(Soy Rafael..."*This is Rafael speaking")

suburbio: slum

susto: surprise, fright

•

(es) tonto del culo: (got his) head up his ass

tope: the mostest (lit. maximum)

tú mismo: it's up to you

a tu aire: as you wish

tu tranquilo: take it easy

•

vale: OK (the average *Madrileño's* every fifth word)

vete a la mierda: go to hell

Standard Adverbial Expressions

además: what's more...

cuanto antes: ASAP

cuanto más...más: the more...the more

desde luego: of course

en la medida que: to the extent that

de momento: for the moment

mientras tanto: meanwhile

a mi parecer: as I see it

para nada: "no way"

a saber: that is, namely

en seguida: right away

ni siquiera: not even

por supuesto: of course, needless to say

por lo tanto: thus, therefore

por lo visto: apparently

ya que: seeing as how; given that

A Word on Letter Writing

The formal greeting to the anonymous or little known recipient is *Muy señor mío*, or *Muy señores míos*.

Say *Querido* only to a very good friend (male or female). For acquaintances or unknowns, use *Estimado*.

Closings can be *atentamente* for the unknown or acquaintance, as well as *reciba un cordial saludo*. For good friendships, *un abrazo* (optional) for men and women; *beso* for lovers or from women to women (not normally men to men or between men and women).

In Madrid, forget anything you've learned about brevity in your college composition course. Brevity can be taken as an insult, e.g., getting right to the point — in letters as well as conversation.

According to the axiom, it is difficult or impossible to be lonely in Madrid. While this is true on the level of ephemeral social exchange in cafés and bars, you may find it tough going initially to develop the sorts of friendships that can make Madrid feel like your turf. *Madrileños* are cordial and friendly toward the outsider but construct their lives as do most Europeans, according to their own whims.

If you're a student from the U.S. or U.K., you will find there is no real campus or dormitory life (clubs, meetings, associations of the like-minded) as you have known back home. You're welcome in Madrid's many discos, bars and wherever else, but contact will remain at a relatively superficial level due often to the decibel level alone.

Lacking the ultimate answer to this challenge, we nevertheless present two suggestions:

One way of meeting Spaniards can be through *Segunda Mano*, the weekly publication at all newsstands that lists things for sale and services sought. For example, every issue includes personal ads by Spaniards seeking to exchange Spanish language lessons for English. There are other useful listings as well in this handy publication — not the answer to your every need, but a step in the right direction.

For students, the *Instituto Internacional* (Miguel Angel, 8) groups together a number of overseas study programs and holds events such as movies, Spanish performances and concerts. Most Friday nights, social gatherings are arranged where you can meet young people of your own and other nationalities.

Sexual Attitudes

As in other European cities these days, anything goes. *Madrileños* are so open-minded that even celibacy is accepted as a way of life, although the opposite is far more prevalent.

Like their fellows on the rest of the Iberian peninsula, *Madrileños* tend to be uninhibited. This will be clearly visible on the beaches, where toplessness extends to solid family mothers as well as swingers. One current polemic over whether the practice was first introduced by vacationing

Scandinavians seems a moot point. The point is, nudity is no longer a source of anguish to most Spaniards. Advertising uses the naked human form to benefit and profit, including on television.

The alarming number of AIDS (*SIDA*) cases in Spain is primarily due to the high incidence of drug use including heroin addiction. Outside of the drug-using community, AIDS is rarely mentioned or apparently feared. This nation of bull-fighters and car racers seems to require physical risk in order to get its adrenaline flowing. One sex shop on the Calle de Atocha offers itself immodestly as *El mayor centro erótico de Europa.*

Female and male homo-sexuality is generally accepted without a great deal of snicker-ing, and soft porn game shows are a staple in the television diet.

The 1990 government pro-condom campaign of *Póntelo, Pónselo,* ("Put it on yourself, put it on him") caused an uproar among church leaders, but the latter were roundly laughed off stage by Spanish youngsters.

In Spain, sex scandals such as the one that undid Gary Hart in the U.S. are virtually unknown. The former Vice President, Alfonso Guerra, was known by every Spaniard to share his attentions between his wife and son in Seville on the weekends, and his weekdays with the woman with whom he had a daughter and lived in Madrid.

Prostitution

The pricey and relatively safe massage parlors in Madrid are mostly around Doctor Fleming, Orense and the Eurobuilding and Santiago Bernabeu Stadium. Street-walkers in the Puerta del Sol, Gran Vía, Plaza de Bena-vente, Montera and Ballesta areas are available to clients willing to risk shortening their life spans.

Gay Madrid

For cruising by car—la Dehesa de la Villa is noted. The more dangerous areas are Retiro Park and the Avenida de América, by the Torresblancas building. Other meeting places are the Plaza de la Lealtad and the Templo de Debod, the latter for finding transvestites.

For civilized mixing, many try the Plaza Chueca district in the *Zona Gay*. The surrounding streets (Augusto Figueroa, Libertad…and the block between Prim, Conde de Xiquena and Almirante) have a number of gay bars, including Leather, Cross, LL, Falos and the Figueroa. One popular restaurant — not exclusively gay — is the Tienda de Vinos on Augusto Figueroa. The Calle Pelayo, also has gay establishments at numbers 2, 23, 30, 31 and 42. The verb to pick up is *ligar*.

The condition of women in Spain is now comparable to that found in other European countries. Following centuries of church repression — emphasized during the 40 years of Franco's dictatorship — Spanish women are quickly making up for lost time. Suddenly in the mid-1970s, women began to participate actively in politics, education, union movements and community life as never before. Their activities are evident from the many local *Asociaciones de Vecinos* to top official appointments such as ministries. In its 1988 annual meeting, the PSOE (ruling Socialist Party) established that 25% of its representation should consist of women.

Women go out freely without the traditional chaperones or *dueñas*. They travel, work, live their lives freely in what is now one of the most permissive societies in Europe. While vestiges of old-fashioned machismo exist in the minds of many, independent lives for women away from the bosom of the family are entirely accepted in current Spanish society.

Working Women

The difficulties and challenges for Spanish working women are as pronounced as for those of other nationalities — plus more. The lack of public kindergartens and day care centers adds hardship: when by stroke of luck a working mother finds a slot at a day care center, it might well require long trips to and fro, taking up a significant part of the mother's salary and working day. Local law permits 16 weeks of maternity leave, though that time is reduced by any sick leave during the period of pregnancy. Medical assistance and family planning are available at no charge (or for symbolic amounts) from Social Security. Spain has a zero population growth, comparable and even below those of northern European countries.

Unemployment (soaring in some regions to 15 percent)

affects women directly, as do low pay scales for those on the lower end of the company organigram. Despite these problems, working women are widely accepted socially in Spain, and many employers prefer hiring them. On the other hand, some employers, noting the total of 18 months lost by the average Spanish woman in caring for her 2.4 children, use the lost time as an argument not to hire women when there is a way around it. The *glass ceiling* in the workplace exists in Spain, though probably no more than in other Western societies.

Attitudes

As in many countries, women in Spain find the behavior of men to be condescending if not altogether insensitive and careless. In fact, given the new mobility of Spanish women, Spanish men have some difficulty adjusting to the disruption of traditional values. The days of deepest, darkest machismo disappeared in pace with women earning their own living. On the other hand, vestiges of machismo persist in conservative sectors of Spanish society, among women as well as men. The vestiges are subtle indeed, but present beneath the surface. If you present yourself at a restaurant or café with a man, you will probably be ignored at the beginning and end of the meal by the restaurant staff. If you go by yourself or with other women, you'll be tolerated but not exactly be given priority treatment.

More often than not, the 30-year-old working woman must endure a traditional ceremony to receive permission to marry. Catholic weddings include a ceremony in which the priest gives metal coins (the *arras*) to the bride, symbolizing the initial family wealth she has to administer cleverly. She passes them ceremoniously to the groom, who keeps them as the final and definite owner.

Though there are no automatic expectations of women in marriage as in more orthodox societies, generally both work and children are part of the bargain. Spanish men rarely accept their share of domestic chores, even when the woman is employed outside the home; child-rearing in particular remains a predominantly female function.

Piropos or cat-calls are still meted out by men in the street to women passing by (*Te hago un hijo* — "Let me be the father of your child"...) This may well seem offensive to a woman from an Anglo-Saxon background. Suffice it to say that the *piropo* is meant as flattery only, and that beyond the growing legal equality of the sexes, deeper changes in Spanish society will probably be slower in coming.

Women & the Law

A man in Spain can be convicted of rape only if there is clear evidence that the woman has resisted; the burden of proof is on the woman. Rape is only a misdemeanor in the eyes of the law, unless the victim can produce evidence of penetration.

After 45 years of antiquated divorce laws, a new set of statutes was introduced in August, 1981, largely based on those already existing in the rest of Europe. Sixty special judges, *juzgados de familia*, were appointed to administer the new law, which made distinctions between divorce, legal separation and annulment. Factors such as adultery, cruelty, desertion, alcoholism, drug addiction and mental disorder are now grounds for divorce initiated by women. Many Spanish couples now make pre-nuptial agreements *(separación de bienes),* to avoid nasty divorce situations which leave to the court the division of *bienes gananciales.* In many cases the Spanish husbands have a sixth sense which directs them to set aside certain properties and belongings which are not eligible for the estranged wife. Spanish men commonly *forget* to make alimony or child support payments, without fear of prosecution.

Abortion

In Spain, a woman may have a legal abortion in cases of rape, unwanted pregnancies of a mentally deficient woman, or cases of risk to the life of the mother or child. In addition, a number of clinics take a wide interpretation of the rules, bending them in favor of the woman who wants to end an unwanted pregnancy. These clinics tend to have a competent professional staff, working in technically very adequate conditions. Such clinics have largely supplanted the previous practice of flying to London for a discreet abortion abroad.

Walking Alone

The streets of Madrid are not yet as threatening as those in certain areas of New York or London. Nevertheless, life is somehow easier if you avoid certain districts or metro lines late at night. San Blas and Vallecas are two areas, for example, better left to themselves.

Clubs

A number of women's clubs offer meetings and activities. For information, contact the American Women's Club of Madrid, Plaza de la República del Ecuador, 6. Membership is open to all English speaking women, newcomers always welcome. Clubhouse open 10:00 a.m. to 6:00 p.m. Monday through Thursday, until 4:00 p.m. Fridays. City and historical/shopping tours; monthly book sale; weekly bridge; Spanish language lessons. Tel: 458-7840 / 259-1082.

Canadians run a similar organization, open to all English-speaking women: call Lola Hartman, Tel: 309-0507.

One fine organization run by Spanish women for women includes a support group for battered wives and a full program of activities:
Elena Valenciano
Asociación de Mujeres Jóvenes
Almagro, 28
Tel: 319-6846

Spaniards love heroes and stars. They emulate, loathe and feed on them all at once; what they do not do is ignore them. Nor must you, if you expect to make it through an average conversation without coming off as the indifferent foreigner. The following names are as essential to your vocabulary as *Buenos dias* and *gracias*, so you might as well learn them now:

• **Victoria Abril**: Female film star, considered Spain's sexiest by many. Chosen by Pedro Almodóvar for *Tie Me Up! Tie Me Down!* and recognized as Europe's best actress at the 1991 Berlin Film Festival.

• **Cristina Almeida**: Communist politician who traveled to Baghdad in late 1990 and got Spanish hostages released. Accused of falling prey to the Stockholm syndrome at the time, depicted unflatteringly in political cartoons carrying her hefty frame after Hussein, crying, "Saddam, I want your baby!"

• **Pedro Almodóvar**: Naughty young boy of Spanish cinema and the Homer of today's Madrid epic. The best known of Spanish film makers internationally. Made *Women on the Verge of a Nervous Breakdown* and *Tie Me Up! Tie Me Down!* (*¡Atame!*)

• **Emilio Aragón**: Host and comic of a popular show on *Telecinco*.

• **José María Aznar**: Young leader of the conservative *Partido Popular*, and outspoken critic of the Socialists.

• **Ana Belén**: Popular singer actress who combines charm and *weltschmertz*.

• **Felipe de Borbón**: Heir apparent to King Juan Carlos I, and one of Europe's more promising up-and-coming monarchs. Handsome, dignified, gracious, he is well liked even by non-monarchists.

• **Miguel Boyer**: Former Minister of Economy, now a private economist well known in Europe. Married to Isabel Preisler (see below.)

• **Montserrat Caballé**: Catalonia's great soprano; one of Spain's constellation of great opera singers.

• **José Carreras**: Operatic tenor whose career was interrupted in the mid 1980s by a lengthy illness. Returned 1989 to the delight of his audiences.

• **Luz Casal**: Spain's female popular singer most in demand.

• **Camilio J. Cela**: Controversial author and winner of the 1989 Nobel Prize for literature. Former censor for Franco.

• **Mario Conde**: Spain's answer to Donald Trump (pre-litigation), and formidable national entry to the Yuppy International. President of Banco Español de Crédito.

• **Plácido Domingo**: Spain's greatest operatic tenor; rival and occasional collaborator with Italy's Luciano Pavarotti.

• **Nacho Duato**: Ballet master who refashioned the *Ballet del Teatro Lírico Nacional* into a world class ensemble.

• **Miguel Durán**: Empire-builder for ONCE, the Spanish Society for the Blind. Paradoxically one of the greatest forces behind Spanish television.

• **Lola Flores**: Notable flamenco singer and dancer.

• **Manuel Fraga**: Aging backstage leader of the *Partido Popular*, formerly Minister of Tourism and Communication under Franco.

• **Baltasar Garzón**: Independent-minded judge who came down hard on Galician drug dealers *(Operación Nécora)* and on members of the GAL (a group of right-wing assassins who kill alleged ETA terrorists.)

• **Jesus Gil y Gil**: Construction tycoon and Mayor of Marbella. Wanted for corruption and manslaughter, but no constabulary dares serve a warrant. Star of a popular tv show on Telecinco, he is often pictured in and out of jacuzzis.

• **Alfonso Guerra**: Former Vice President under Felipe González, and his childhood friend from Andalucía. Considered the brains behind the PSOE until he was unseated by an influence-peddling scandal.

• **Juan Guerra**: Brother of Alfonso, a rags-to-riches real estate magnate. Accused by the media of influence-peddling, which he vehemently denies.

• **Jesús Hermida**: Spanish TV's evening news anchorman, whose didactic and somewhat affected presentation has improved ratings of the evening news. Former Washington correspondent.

• **Julio Iglesias**: Popular singer who presented the sun-tanned, melancholic image of suave middle age to the entire world.

• **Alicia Koplowitz:** With her sister Esther, probably the wealthiest women in Europe. Part owner of Madrid's tallest building, the Torre Picasso.

• **Rosa María Mateo**: Europe's most popular female TV news presenter.

• **Carmen Maura**: The star of Almodóvar's films until a personal falling-out with the director. Appears often on Spanish television.

• **Mercedes Milá**: Spain's Barbara Walters. To enormous national audiences, she interviewed major entertainment and political figures on Spanish National Television.

• **Pilar Miró**: Former Director of Spanish National Television, film director.

• **Andrés Pájares**: Notable actor, played the lead in *Ay, Carmela*, for which he received an award as best actor in Montreal, 1991.

• **Isabel Pantoja**: Prime singer of Spanish folk music.

• **Pedro Piqueras**: Spanish TV's afternoon news anchorman, one of Spain's most popular television personalities.

• **Jesús de Polanco**: Media mogul sometimes compared to the late Robert Maxwell and Rupert Murdoch. Owns significant shares of *El País*, the SER radio network, and Canal Plus television.

• **Isabel Preisler**: Julio Iglesias' ex-wife. Much in evidence in popular magazines.

• **Carlos Sainz**: Sports car racer; winner of the World Championship, 1990.

• **Marta Sánchez**: Singer whose main natural gifts lie between the neck and navel. Made major publicity points by visiting and performing for Spanish sailors in the Gulf in late 1990.

• **Carlos Saura**: Spain's second-best known film director internationally. Director of *Carmen*, *Blood Wedding* and others.

• **Jorge Semprún**: Former Minister of Culture. Ex-communist and unrepentent film scenario writer. Collaborated with Costa Gavras on *Z* and other political films of the 1960s and 70s.

• **Narcís Serra**: Vice President of Spain, following a stint as Minister of Defense. More managerial than military in his comportment and background.

• **Reina Sofía**: Spain's Greek-born queen, patroness of the arts and of social good works.

• **Carlos Solchaga**: González' Finance Minister, a potential rival of the President.

• **Antoni Tapies**: Catalan artist and designer, frequent winner of national and international prizes.

• **Gustavo Villapalos**: Rector of the Complutense University (the world's second largest).

HERE'S a comprehensive guide to services and institutions in Madrid as well as valuable information on how they function and what to expect.

Embassies and Consulates

What Your Embassy Is and Is Not

Embassies exist in order to represent one country's national interests in another. This generally means developing contacts on diplomatic, trade, political, military and cultural levels. While it is true that you as a taxpayer underwrite your embassy's existence, this does not mean that the embassy can tend to personal needs such as helping you get settled in Madrid, or advising you on local job prospects. The staff is simply not big enough. While an embassy may have a list of physicians and lawyers, it is often under legal constraint not to recommend one over the other.

The U.S. Embassy in Madrid, for example, has a fine cultural center, the Washington Irving Center (calle Villa Magna), whose purpose is to present American culture to the Spanish public. Americans as well as others are welcome in its library, but remember that its principal mission is to convey and explain U.S. culture, history, the arts, etc., to the Spanish.

Consular Services

The Consular Section of your embassy is generally the one you'll have contact with, for matters such as changes in civil status, legal documents and problems, and theft or injury. Your embassy cannot always solve all your individual problems, but generally people on the staff are willing to do their best to help. You're not expected to know exactly whom to address your question to, you should just ask for the Consular Section of your embassy to be directed to the appropriate Citizens Services department. Not all embassies function alike; the U.S. Embassy serves as basis for the information below, and more or less resembles others in its range of activities:

Passports

Your consulate can issue passports or replace lost or stolen ones. Americans returning home without time to wait a day or two for a proper passport can travel with a special letter issued by the consulate, but must pay a hefty fee if they choose this option.

Births

Local Spanish law requires registration of all children born, within 48 hours. Report births to your embassy to avoid legal complications and citizenship questions later.

Marriages

Consult your embassy for any legal requirements. Civil marriages in Madrid require an application form (pick one up at the Civil Registry at Pradillo, 66; a birth certificate with an official seal *(apostilla)*; proof that both parties are free to marry; a divorce or annulment or death certificate when necessary; a residence certificate (get this from the *Tenencia de Alcaldía*, in Madrid at Alcalá, 62. Normally, Spanish authorities require a posting of banns, but if you are an American or other citizen whose country does not require this, your embassy will issue you a document to that effect.

For a Catholic marriage, contact the closest Bishopric (in Madrid at Bailén, 8) with a birth certificate, baptismal certificate, and proof that both parties are free to marry. You have one week from the time of the marriage to present the certificate issued by the Church to the nearest civil registry.

Deaths

While this may not be a subject you're planning to think about in Spain, here's some important information concerning death. Report deaths immediately to your embassy. The U.S. embassy has after-hours and weekend services, just dial the main number (577-4000) and ask for the Protection and Welfare Unit of the Consular Section. A death certificate is required by Spanish law in all cases; it can be issued by the doctor in attendance or, in case of an accident, by the forensic doctor.

Funeral services *(Pompas funebres)* can be handled by E.M.S.F.M.S.A. at *Plaza de España*, 12, or *Servicios Funerarios,* Salvador de Madariaga, s/n (Tel: 405-0014). Shipping remains home — particularly to the U.S. — can be very costly, while local arrangements cost less, especially cremation.

Missing Persons

The Protection and Welfare Unit of the Consulate can check local sources and, in some cases, place items in the local media.

Consulates

Consulates are fully accredited diplomatic missions outside of the capital where the mission is an embassy. The U.S. has one Consulate-General outside of Madrid (Barcelona), and one Consulate (Bilbao):

U.S. Consulate-General
Vía Laietana 33
Barcelona
Tel: (93) 319-9550

U.S. Consulate
Avda. Lehendakari Agirre, 11-3
48014 Bilbao
Tel: (94) 475-8300

In addition, the U.S. has Consular Agents around the country, who are part-time representatives of the U.S. Government in cities too distant to be served directly by the Embassy or Consulate. There are six U.S. Consular Agencies in Spain, five under the supervision of the Consul General in Madrid, and one supervised by the Consul General in Barcelona:

U.S. Consular Agencies in Spain

• Malaga
Centro Comercial Las Rampas,
Fase 2, planta 1
Locales 12-G-7 y 12-G-8
29640 Fuengirola, Malaga
Tel: (952) 47-48-91
Fax: (952) 46-51-89

• Seville
Paseo de las Delicias, 7
41012 Sevilla
Tel: (954) 23-18-85
Fax: (954) 23-20-40

• Valencia
calle de la Paz, 6-5°, local 5
46003 Valencia
Tel: (96) 351-6973
Fax: (96) 352-9565

• Canary Islands
Franchy y Roca, 5-5-13
35007 Las Palmas
Tel: (981) 21-32-33
Fax: (981) 22-88-08

• Mallorca
Av. Jaime III, 26 entresuelo H-I
07012 Palma de Mallorca
Tel: (971) 72-50-51
Fax: (971) 71-87-55

• La Coruña
Canton Grande, 16-17
15003 La Coruña
Tel: (981) 21-32-33

The U.S. Embassy publishes the following statement on its Consular Agents: "Consular Agents have neither the same privileges and immunities nor the same training and experience as career Foreign Service employees. Because of their limited functions, resources and authority, Consular Agencies cannot provide the same support for Embassy offices that a constituent post would. They are not authorized and should not be expected to undertake political, economic or commercial functions. Consular Agencies are open only three hours a day, during which time the Agents are expected to be available to the public. (Although the Consular Agency in Seville is open to the public seven hours daily, the Agent is in the office only three hours.)"

British Embassy & Consulates

The British maintain three Consulates-General:
• Madrid
British Embassy & Consulate-General
Fernando el Santo 16
Madrid 4
Tel: (91) 419-0212 / 419-1528

• Barcelona
British Consulate-General
Edificio Torre de Barcelona
Avenida Diagonal 477-13°
Apartado 12111
Barcelona-36
Tel: (93) 322-2151

• Bilbao
British Consulate-General
Alameda de Urquijo 2-8°
Bilbao-8
Tel: (94) 415-7600, 415-7711

The British also maintain consular offices in eleven additional cities in Spain:

• Algeciras
British Consulate
Avenida de las Fuerzas
Armadas 11
Algeciras
Tel: (956) 66-1600 / 66-1604

• Alicante
British Consulate
Calvo Sotelo 1/2—1°
Apartado 564
Alicante
Tel: (965) 21-6022 / 21-6190

• Ibiza
British Consulate
Avenida Isidoro Macabich 45-1°
Apartado 307
Ibiza
Tel: (971) 30-1818

• Las Palmas/Las Canarias
British Consulate
Edificio Hocasa 6°
Calle Alfredo L. Jones 33
Puerto de la Luz-Apartado 2020
Las Palmas/Las Canarias
Tel: (928) 26-25-08

• Malaga
British Consulate
Edificio Duquesa de
Parcent 4-1°
Malaga
Tel: (952) 21-75-71 / 21-23-25

• Palma de Mallorca
British Consulate
Plaza Mayor 3D
Palma de Mallorca—12
Tel: (971) 21-24-45 / 21-20-85

• Santander
British Consulate
Paseo de Pereda 27
Santander
Tel: (942) 22-00-00

• Seville
British Consulate
Plaza Nueva 8
Seville
Tel: (954) 22-88-75

• Tarragona
British Consulate
Calle Santian 4
Tarragona
Tel: (977) 20-12-46 / 20-52-68

• Santa Cruz de Tenerife
British Consulate
Edificio Marichal 5°
Suarez Guerra 40
Santa Cruz de Tenerife
Tel: (922) 24-20-00

• Vigo
British Consulate
Plaza Compostela 23-6°
Apartado 49
Vigo
Tel: (986) 21-14-50 / 21-14-87

Other Embassies & Consulates in Madrid

• Australia
Paseo de la Castellana
53, Madrid
Tel: 279-8504

• Canada
Edificio Goya
Nuñez de Balboa, 35
Tel: 431-4300

• Cuba
Paseo de la Habana, 194
Tel: 458-2500

• Denmark
Claudio Coello, 91
Tel: 431-8445

• France
Salustiano Olózaga, 9
Tel: 435-5560

Consulate
Paseo de la Castellana, 79
Tel: 597-3267

• Germany
Fortuny, 8
Tel: 319-9100

• India
Avda. Pio XII, 30-32
Tel: 457-0209

• Ireland
Claudio Coello, 73
Tel: 576-3500

• Israel
Velazquez, 150
Tel: 411-6417

• Italy
Lagasca, 98
Tel: 577-6529

• Japan
Joaquín Costa, 29
Tel: 262-5546

• Netherlands
Paseo de la Castellana, 178
Tel: 458-2100

• Norway
Paseo de la Castellana, 31
Tel: 308-3394

• Portugal
Pinar, 1
Tel: 261-7800

• Sweden
Zurbano, 27
Tel: 308-1535

• Switzerland
Nuñez de Balboa, 35
Tel: 431-3400

Spanish Embassies & Consulates around the World

AUSTRALIA

• Yarralumla
Spanish Embassy
15 Arkana St.
Yarralumla, Act 2600
Tel: 73-35-55

• Sydney
Spanish Consulate-General
50 Park St., 7th floor
Sydney, NSW 2000
Tel: 261-24-33
Fax: 283-1695

• Melbourne
Spanish Consulate-General
766 Elisabeth St.
Melbourne W.I.C. 3000
Tel: (03) 347-19-66

GREAT BRITAIN

• London
Spanish Embassy
24 Belgrave Sq.
London SWIX 8QA
Tel: 235-5555
Fax: 235-9905

• Edinburgh
Spanish Consulate-General
63 North Castle St.
Edinburgh EH2 3LJ
Tel: 220-1843

• Manchester
Spanish Consulate-General
70 Brookhouse, Suite 1A
Spring Gardens
Manchester M2 2BQ
Tel: 236-1233

IRELAND
• Dublin
Spanish Embassy
17A Merlyn Park
Ballsbridge
Dublin 4
Tel: 69-1640

CANADA
• Ottawa
Spanish Embassy
350 Sparks St., Suite 802
Ottawa, Ontario KIR 7S8
Tel: 237-2193

• Montreal
Spanish Consulate-General
1 Westmount Sq., Suite 1456
Montreal, Quebec H3Z 2P9
Tel: 935-5235

• Toronto
Spanish Consulate-General
1200 Bay St. — Suite 400
Toronto, Ontario M5R 2A5
Tel: 967-4949

• Pacific Centre
Spanish Consulate-General
700 Georgia St. West
Suite 1100
POB 10025
Pacific Centre, B.C. V71 1A1
Tel: 688-9471

UNITED STATES
• Washington, D.C.
Spanish Embassy
2700 15th St.
Washington, D.C. NW 20009
Tel: (202) 265-0190

• Boston
Spanish Consulate
345 Boylston St. Suite 803
Boston, MA 02116
Tel: (617) 536-2506

• Chicago
Spanish Consulate
180 North Michigan Ave.
Suite 1500
Chicago, IL 60601
Tel: 782-4588

• Houston
Spanish Consulate
2411 Fountain View Suite 130
Houston, TX 77507
Tel: 783-6200

• Los Angeles
Spanish Consulate
6300 Wilshire Blvd., Suite 1530
Los Angeles, CA 90048
Tel: 658-6050

• Coral Gables
Spanish Consulate
151 Sevilla Ave.
Coral Gables, FL 33134
Tel: 446-5511

• New Orleans
Spanish Consulate
2102 World Trade Center
2 Canal Street
New Orleans, LA 70130
Tel: 523-4951

• New York
Spanish Consulate
150 East 58th St.
Floor 16
New York, NY 10155
Tel: 355-4080

• New York
Spanish Permanent Mission to
the United Nations
809 United Nations Plaza
New York , NY 10017
Tel: 661-1050

• San Francisco
Spanish Consulate
2080 Jefferson St.
San Francisco, CA 94123
Tel: 922-2995/96

Religion

Spain is over 90% Catholic with the remaining 10% divided among Protestant, Moslem, Jewish.... Madrid has many denominational churches, some of which offer services in English. Here is a list of the gamut of Catholic and Protestant churches, Mosques, and synagogues with emphasis on those which have services in English.

Catholic Services
Convent Chapel
Alfonso XIII, 165
Tel: 233-2032 am
234-5344 pm
(English services, confession before and during masses)

Parish of St. Francisco de Borja
Serrano, 104
Tel: 275-0973
(Spanish services, Sun. every hour on the hour, 8 am-noon)

St. Louis des Français
Lagasca, 89
Tel: 435-5160
(French services, Sun. at noon)

Protestant Services
Baptist
General Lacy, 18
Tel: 239-2537
(Spanish services, Sun. 11am &
6:30 pm)

Immanuel Baptist Church
Hernandez de Tejada, 4
Tel: 407-4347
(English services, Sun. 11am &
7 pm

Church of Jesus Christ of Latter
Day Saints
San Telmo, 26
Tel: 250-9001
(English services, Sun. Spanish
10-12 am& English 2-4 pm)

Episcopal Anglican Church of
St. George
Seventh Day Adventist
Nuñez de Balboa, 43
Tel: 276-5019
(English services Sun. 8:30, 10,
11;15 am)

Community Church of Madrid
Colegio Sagrados Corazones
Padre Damian, 34
Tel: 250-7100
(Interdenominational-Inter-
national English Services)

First Church of Christian
Scientists
Alonso Cano, 63—1-C
Tel: 259-2135

British Bible Society
Santa Engracia, 133
Tel: 254-5298

Lutheran Service
Paseo de la Castellana, 6
Tel: 435-4781
(German services, 11 am)

Jewish Synagogues
Balmes, 3
28010 Madrid
tel: 445-9835
(Friday night services, 7:30 pm)

Moslim Mosque
Mosque and Islamic Cultural
Center
Salvador de Madariaga
(at M-30)

The days of cheap hotels in Spain have been over for years. Prepare to pay plenty, unless you can live with rudimentary conditions (bath down the hall, dark or noisy quarters). The Spanish government gives ratings to the hotels with stars (not to be confused with Michelin stars, which come much more fully earned). The Spanish criteria for allocating stars are fair but do not have all that much to do with how comfortable your stay will be. The Spanish system pays more attention to the number of languages spoken by the hotel concierge, than to the bright and airy quality of the room you find yourself in. Therefore, you must shop around and bear in mind reasonable criteria.

Our list is by no means exhaustive, but does cover the thirty most tested and reputable hotels in the capital. The following may easily cost $250-300 US / £150-200 per night!

Apartamentos Centro Colon
Marques de la Ensenada, 16
Tel: 410-4600

Apartamentos Rueda
Martinez Campos, 20
Tel: 448-8200

Barajas
Avda. Logroño, 305
Tel: 747-7700

Castellana
Paseo de la Castellana, 49
Tel: 410-0200

Centro Norte
Muaricio Ravel, 10
Tel: 733-3400

Cuzco
Paseo de la Castellana, 131
Tel: 556-0600

Emperatriz
Lopez de Hoyos, 4
Tel: 563-8088

Escultor
Miguel Angel, 3
Tel: 410-4203

Eurobuilding
Juan Ramon Jimenez, 8
Tel: 457-1700

Eurobuilding II
Padre Damian, 23
Tel: 457-1700

Los Galgos
Claudio Coello, 139
Tel: 262-4227

Luz Palacio
Paseo de la Castellana, 57
Tel: 442-5100

Melia Castilla
Capitan Haya, 43
Tel: 571-2211

Melia Madrid
Princesa, 27
Tel: 241-8200

Miguel Angel
Miguel Angel, 31
Tel: 442-8144

Mindanao
San Francisco de Sales, 15
Tel: 549-5500

Palace
Plaza de las Cortes, 7
Tel: 429-7551

Pintor Goya
Goya, 79
Tel: 435-7545

Plaza
Princesa, 40
Tel: 247-1200

Residencia Aitana
Paseo de la Castellana, 152
Tel: 250-7107

Residencia Convencion
O'Donnell, 51
Tel: 574-6800

Ritz
Plaza de la Lealtad, 5
Tel: 521-2857

Serrano
Marques de Villamejor, 8
Tel: 435-5200

Trafalgar
Trafalgar, 35
Tel: 445-6200

Victoria
Plaza del Angel, 7
Tel: 231-4500

Wellington
Velazquez, 8
Tel: 575-4400

Zurbano
Zurbano, 79
Tel: 441-4500

In addition, a number of economical lodgings exist in Madrid, including youth hostels and *hostals* — establishments which do not quite rank as hotels, but which do provide reasonably clean living for reasonable rates (about $50 US / £30 per night). There are a number of these in Madrid; we can recommend the following:

Inexpensive Lodgings
Hostal Cantabrico
calle Cruz 5
Tel: 531-0130

Hostal Sud-America
calle Paseo del Prado 12
Tel: 429-2564

Hostal La Moderna
calle San Sebastian 2
Tel: 369-2031

Pension San Sebastian
calle San Sebastian 2
Tel: 369-1578

Hostal Residencia Benamar
calle San Mateo 20, 2-D
Tel: 419-0222

Hostal Leones
calle Nuñez de Arce 14, 2e piso
Tel: 531-0889

Youth Hostels
(Albergues Juveniles)
Casa de Campo
(in the park)
Tel: 463-5699
Metro: Lago

Albergues Juveniles
Santa Cruz de Marcenado 28
Tel: 247-4532
Metro: Arguelles

Health Services

Spanish doctors can be wonderfully humane and competent, but the health delivery system leaves much to be desired. Though a public health system exists in theory, every Spaniard making a decent wage seeks out private insurance schemes and private doctors. If your medical insurance covers you abroad you will first have to pay your doctors bills in Spain and then request reimbursement by mail.

Emergencies
Vital telephone numbers follow:

Urgent House Visits: 409-5530
Transfusions: 261-7505
Red Cross Burn Center:
                       544-5207
Red Cross Coronary Unit:
                       234-8866
Poison Center: 262-0420
Ambulances: 252-2792
Red Cross: 433-6966
Others: 415-0022
                       772-1912
                       259-1133
                       413-3448
                       245-1039

Each district of Madrid is equipped with first aid stations, called *Casas de socorro:*
Arganzuela   269-1463
Carabanchel   464-7632

Centro	521-1125
Chamberí	455-7048
General Ricardos	471-0751
Zona La Latina	265-0827
Moncloa-Aravaca	207-0026
Palacio	464-7632
Retiro-Moratalaz	420-0356
San Blas-Hortaleza	206-3306
San Cristóbal	797-2744
Salamanca	255-5218
Tetuán-Chamartín	279-1223
Universidad	466-2675
Usera	476-3366
Vallecas	203-1148
Vicálvaro	755-0202

Hospitals

As in the U.S., the hospital world in Madrid is a labyrinth of private and public establishments with uneven records of treatment. State hospitals are free to the public. They are not always the best in quality, but a few are very reliable. Two of the best are:
La Paz
Po. Castellana, 261
Tel: 734-2600

Clínica de Puerta de Hierro
San Martín de Porres, 4
Tel: 316-3367

(La Paz and Puerta de Hierro are intended for those covered by Spanish Social Security, but will treat anyone in a real emergency.)

Another option in choosing a hospital are the private clinics. They tend to be specialized; some belong entirely to certain insurance companies, others accept surgery cases only. In almost all cases, you need a doctor's referral to be admitted:
Clínica Ruber
Juan Bravo, 49
Tel: 402-6100

Clínica Zarzuela (Aravaca)
Crt. de Coruña, km 10
Tel: 207-9040

Clínica Boston
Hermano Garate, 4
Tel: 450-6300/6402

Clínica Cuzco
Po. Castellana, 170
Tel: 458-6063/6143

Ramón y Cajal
Crta. de Comenar Viejo, km 9
Tel: 729-0000

Cruz Roja Española
Avda. Reina Victoria, 28
Tel: 233-3900

Clínica de la Luz
General Rodrigo, 8
Tel: 253-0500

La Milagrosa
Modesto Lafuente, 14
Tel: 447-2100

San Francisco de Asís
Joaquín Costa, 28
Tel: 261-7100

ICE
San Bernardo, 68
Tel: 532-7820

Hospitals with known English-speaking staff:
British American Medical Unit
Conde de Aranda, 1
Tel: 435-1823
(Mainly outpatient. Medical specialties available: Cardiology, Gastroenterology, General Surgery, Gynecology, Hemotology, Internal Medicine, Neurology, Pediatric Cardiology; Rheumatology, Thoracic, Surgery, Urology, Vascular Surgery)

Interclinic Cincinnati
Claudio Coello, 117 Bajo
Tel: 576-9901/02

(Specialties available: Cardiology, Dermatology, Echography, General Medicine, General Surgery, Internal, Medicine, Laboratory, Obesity, Obstetrics/Gynecology, Pathology, Pediatrics/Neonatology, Plastic Surgery, Traumatology/Orthopedics, Ultrasound)

Massachusetts Institute de España
Macarena, 4
Tel: 259-8604/6621/3108

The Red Cross also has a network of services, available to all, regardless of nationality or insurance. The main Red Cross hospital is :
Hospital Central
Reina Victoria, 24 and 26.
Tel: 534-6604

Lexicon	
aspirina: aspirin	*hinchado:* swollen
ataque de corazón, infarcto: heart attack	*jeringa y aguja:* syringe and needle
ayunar: fast	*mareado:* nauseated
descansar: rest	*pastilla, comprimido:* pill
dolor de cabeza: headache	*preservativos/condones:* condoms
erupción: rash	*receta:* prescription
escalofríos: chills	*sed:* thirst
estreñido: constipated	*tamponés:* tampons
heces: stool	*termometró:* thermometres
hematoma: bruise	*tos:* cough

Innoculations

If you're traveling to a zone recognized for its health problems and need innoculations for smallpox, typhus, cholera or yellow fever, you can get them cheaply at the Ministerio de Sanidad, General Oraa, 39 from 10:00 am to 1:00 pm Monday to Friday. Take your passport and W.H.O. yellow health card.

Pap Smear Tests

Instituto Nacional de Oncología, Ciudad Universitaria gives free Pap Smear tests. Telephone 544-2456. The Centro Diagnóstico Precoz, Arga, 19, does Pap Smear tests and also mammography. Tel: 457-7179.

Pharmacies

On a rotating basis, different pharmacies are open on different nights. The daily press lists the ones open. You can also call 098 for this information.
Here are two U.S. pharmacies that are accustomed to doing business with Americans overseas and can fill prescriptions through the mail:

Morgan Pharmacy
3001 P Street, NW
Washington, D.C. 20007
Fax: (202) 337-4102

Columbia Plaza Pharmacy
516 23rd Street NW
Washington, DC 20037
Tel: (202) 331-5800
Fax: (202) 452-7820
(20% discount on orders coming by mail)

Medical Evacuation

God Forbid; but anyway, the following services do it:

Air Ambulance Network
Tel: (Miami) 305/387-1708

Air-Evac International
Tel: (Houston) 713/880-9767

SOS-International
Juan Hurtado Mendoza 11
28036 Madrid
Tel: 458-1657

World Access
(Blue Cross/Blue Shield)
Tel: (Paris) 44/1/42 96 10 77
(Washington) 202/479-8000

Alternative Healing

A variety of alternate healing methods are represented in Madrid. Homeopathic remedies, for example, are relatively easy to find in Europe in general, and coexist more peaceably across the continent than they do in, say, the U.S.

While alternate healing practitioners do not abound to

the extent they do in Paris or London, you can probably find one of the same type you're used to in Boston, Toronto or London. Here are a few:

• *Naturalist &*
Alternative Healers
Centro Medicina Naturista
Plaza del Carmen, 1°-5°
28013 Madrid

Andres Candido Herrer
Francisco Silvela, 21
28006 Madrid
Tel: 401-0891

Aurelio Palafox
Plaza Conde Valle Suchili, 7.
Apto. 701
28015 Madrid
Tel: 447-7404

• Homeopathic Healing
Sociedad Española
de Homeopatia
Francisco Silvela, 71
28028 Madrid
Tel: 262-0840

• *Natural Childbirth*
Génesis
Valverde, 28
28004 Madrid
Tel: 405-1689

• Herbal Therapy/Vegetarians
Centro Naturista de Madrid
Plaza Mostenses, 12
28015 Madrid
Tel: 248-6627

Asociacion
Vegetariana Naturista
Santa Cruz de Marcenado, 12
28008 Madrid

• *Acupuncture*
Instituto Español Medico de Acupuntura y Medicina Integral
Glorieta de San Bernardo, 7
28008 Madrid
Tel: 448-6009

Escuela de Terapias Orientales
Dulcia, 48
28020 Madrid
Tel: 279-1623

• *Chiromassage*
Gabinete de Quiromasaje
Paseo Castellana, 114-1°4°
28046 Madrid
Tel: 262-9123

Planet Art
Calle de las Fuentes, 8
28013 Madrid
Tel: 242-5597

• *Cognitive Therapy*
Ateco: Campanar, 10, Madrid.
Tel: 256-7998

- *Bioenergy*
Cipahr
Valverde, 8
28013 Madrid
Tel: 221-7831

Health Insurance

You may be covered by a policy from your country of origin, but you're better off getting insurance locally if you're intending to stay a long time. Spain has wonderful, humane doctors, but a dismal health delivery system entailing long waits and untended patients.

Spanish Policies Most Spanish private policies limit coverage to specified hospitals or doctors, which of course limits your options. On the other hand, they tend to be cheaper than other countries' policies. A good old Spanish tradition is the coupon system, whereby you pay into a plan and then settle your accounts with the doctor with coupons drawn from a book. One private Spanish company which draws respect is *Sanitas*, Francisco de Rojas, 8, Tel: 445-9016. Another is *La Estrella*, Gran Vía, 7, Tel: 532-7505. Another, which offers a greater degree of choice as to where you can be treated, and by whom, is *Unión Médica del Sur* (UMSSA). Tel: 441-5926.

If you're an EEC citizen, your national health insurance put together with the Spanish national plan may well cover you. The State-run system suffers from bureaucratic delays and entanglements, but may be your *simplest* solution if you're shopping around and are eligible. As in all things, see your nearest *gestor* to find out the right coverage for you and your situation.

British Policies Three companies have tailor-made policies for Britons living in Spain. One, the British United Provident Association (BUPA) offers a variety of plans depending on your age and the extent of coverage you wish. The Private Patients Plan (PPP) offers coverage a bit cheaper than the BUPA, with probably the most economical scheme if you want only hospital coverage, without outpatient treatment. The Exeter Hospital Aid Society is especially attractive to older people, as its premiums are not related to age. Study these options before leaving the UK, and be glad you're a Briton.

Danish Private Insurance One wild-card company that has gained rave reviews for foreigners living in Spain is Denmark A/S. They are known for quick settlements of claims and a variety of options, covering all illnesses. You can write to them (in English) to Denmark A/S, International Health Insurance, Sovereign Health Plan Dept., Palaegade 7, 1261 Copenhagen K, Denmark.

In general, you're better off working with the Spanish companies only if you're really full-time in Spain. If you come for the summer or a limited part of the year, stick with a company from home which can write you a special policy for overseas coverage.

If you live in Spain, you can get travel insurance from Royal Assistance, María de Molina, 1, Tel: 564-0202.

Urban Transport

Compensating for Madrid's horrible traffic congestion is one of the best urban transport systems in the world. Metros, buses and taxis are reasonably priced, with safe and frequent service.

Taxis

The taxi-to-population ratio in Madrid is one of the highest in the world, with 15,500 taxis for a population of four million (Paris has 10,000). Madrid's taxis are priced fairly and are easy to find in most sections of the city. Cabbies are the complaining, street-wise folk they are in most cities; where you encounter bark, you'll usually find it worse than the bite that comes with it: cabbies are generally competent, and stories of overcharging new-comers or taking them for a ride are rare. One peculiarity of Madrid taxi-hunting is that you must be facing the correct direction in the traffic flow; drivers will either react with irritation, or refuse to drive you to your destination if you've hailed them from the wrong side of the street.

Taxis are painted white with a horizontal red stripe on each side. A green cardboard *libre* sign on the dashboard indicates availability. A few bear names like *Aluche*, which means they are allowed to pick you up only if the place on the sign is your destination.

There are surcharges for luggage, and for rides on Sundays, holidays, and between midnight and 6:00 a.m. Tip moderately, don't over do it. Usually rounding up to the nearest 100 pesetas will suffice, with a minimum of 25 pesetas.

You can order a taxi by phone, though radio taxis are not the most reliable around. If you ask the dispatcher how many minutes wait they expect, they will give you a fair and honest estimate. They will ask for your name, telephone number, address and destination. Ordering from one day to the next (e.g., calling at 11:00 p.m. to get a cab for your 6:00 a.m. departure) is *not* recommended. Instead, call closer to the time you'll actually need the taxi.

You should have good luck with the following:

Teletaxi
Tel: 445-9008
Radio Taxi
Tel: 247-8200/8500/8600
Radio Taxi Independiente
Tel: 405-1213/5500

Buses

City buses (EMT — *Empresa Municipal de Transportes*) and microbuses follow a frequent schedule until midnight. They benefit from special lanes reserved for them and taxis, and can often beat the traffic in busy areas.

You must mount the bus from the front, and depart from the rear, as in most European cities. You can buy a single ticket only from the driver.

Estancos and kiosks sell *bonobús* cards which entitle you to ten rides at less than half price per single ride. If you're between 15 and 25 years old, you qualify for the *Carné Joven*, which gets you discounts on the bus, metro, RENFE (trains), museums, etc. To get one apply to:

Consejería de Juventud
Tel: 521-3960 / 522-6171

The Green Line, starting at the Plaza de Cibeles, can take you to twelve Madrid parks for the price of one ticket. The Blue Line, also starting at Cibeles, goes to twelve museums. Both lines operate every half hour.

EMT information: Tel: 401-3100.

IMPORTE
410 PTS.
E.M.T.

K 676683

EMPRESA MUNICIPAL
DE TRANSPORTES DE
MADRID, S. A.
DIEZ VIAJES EN AUTOBUS

| 1 |
| 2 |
| 3 |
| 4 |
| 5 |
| 6 |
| 7 |
| 8 |
| 9 |
| 10 |

instrucciones al dorso

Metro

As subway systems go, Madrid's is one of the more efficient and safe. Though you'll encounter crowding on some lines at some times, you will find the metro less daunting or dangerous than in London, Paris or New York. Incidents of agression or theft are very rare. If you're on a crowded car and concerned that others in front of you may not be getting off at your stop, you can ask ¿*Va a salir?* and they will either say *Sí* or step aside for you. They will do the same, so you should be ready for them to ask.

If you end up by the door on one of the newer cars, it is your responsibility to open it manually at each stop where someone wants to get off.

As in Paris and a number of other cities, the Madrid metro lines are identified by their two end points or destinations, thus, the *Canillejas-Aluche* line, or *Herrera Oria-Pavones.*

Note: Madrid metros run on the left. No one knows why for sure, but one person's theory is that it has something to do with adoration and emulation of the English (see above).

• Metro information
Tel: 435-2266.

With both the bus and metro, you can buy individual tickets, or purchase a *billete de 10 viajes* at considerable saving.

Interurban Bus

For trips to other destinations in Spain, the interurban bus can sometimes be quicker and cheaper than RENFE. The Estación del Sur is at calle Canarias 17, paradoxically near the train station *del Norte.* Telephone 468-4200. The major companies are Auto-Res serving the northern part of Spain (Fernández Shaw, 1, Tel: 551-7200) and Continental Auto serving the south (Alenza, 20, Tel: 533-0400).

Telephones

One of Spain's greatest modern aspirations is to bring its telecommunications service up to European and North American standards. To say that Madrid's telephone system is third-world is an exaggeration. It is true that conversations are often cut, long distance calls sometimes hang suspended in the ether, and installation of a private line can take up to a year (currently there are 400,000 on the waiting list for installation). On the other hand, more calls go through than don't, and international connections are direct. Beware, international rates are twice the normal European rates and four times the American. We repeat: four times the American rates. Long distance calls from hotel rooms are a form of charity you may not want to indulge in.

If you call the U.S. more than once a month, you'll want an AT&T, MCI, or other international calling card. For a long time *Telefónica* did not allow a direct dial to a U.S. operator, but now, finally AT&T has a Dial America Direct line from Spain to the U.S. The number is 900-99-00-11. The MCI Access number is: 900-99-00-14. Using one of these numbers for calls to the U.S. will cost one-quarter the cost of calling direct on the Spanish telephone service. If for some reason you cannot get through using this direct line to an AT&T or MCI operator in the U.S. follow the following procedure:

• Dial 005. A Madrid operator will answer.

• Give on request the international card number (beginning with 1M), followed by the number you're calling in the U.S., and then the number you're calling from in Madrid.

• The operator will either put you straight through or ask you to hang up *(cuelga)* and wait to be called back.

• You'll be billed from the U.S.,

Basic Numbers				
Direct dial for long distance	07	International information	008
International operator	005	Phone out of order *(averías)*	002
International operator		Time	093
for Europe	009	Weather	094
Person-to-person or special		Latest News	095
calls to U.S.	089	Sports information	097
Madrid information	003	Wake-up service	098

at one quarter the Spanish rate.

For direct dial to any number outside of Spain to be charged to your billing number in Madrid, dial 07 for an international line, wait for a second dial tone, then add the country and area code and number.

Phone booths work with coins of either 25 pesetas or 100 pesetas. Some, but not many, work with credit cards.

Billing for private lines comes every other month. Infuriating as it is, you must accept that *Telefónica* sends no itemized bills. They claim their equipment doesn't allow them to do so, and they are probably right. Bite the bullet, and arrange with your local bank to allow *Telefónica* to draw from your account directly for payment *(transferencia)*.

Directories *(guías)* are published in the American style — grey for alphabetical and yellow for businesses, by topic.

For long distance calls within Spain, precede the local number by the area code *(prefijo)*, always beginning with 9. Omit the 9 when calling from outside Spain.

Note: Madrid has changed *all* numbers in recent years. You may or may not get an intercept when you dial an obsolete number, so be sure to check with information 003 for the new number.

Telephone Prefixes
• To make international calls: (07) plus the country code
• To call the provinces from Madrid: (91) plus the number
• To call the provinces from Barcelona: (93) plus the number

Locutorios
Some PTT offices will allow you to call long distance from their premises, and pay on the spot. Their locations and times follow:

Locations	Work Day Hours	Sunday Hours
Pl. de Cibeles	8:00-24:00	8:00-22:00
Virgen Peligros, 10	9:00-22:00	9:00-22:00
Po. Recoletos, 41	9:00-22:00	10:00-21:00
Gran Vía, 30	Permanent	Permanent

Telegraph

You can send telegrams from some post offices or the *Entel* service: Plaza de España, 3; Alcalá, 44; and the Castellana Hotel.

Spelling

When spelling over the phone, use the standard identifiers for the letters:

A de (for) Antonio	J de José
B de Barcelona	K de kilo
C de Carmen	L de Lérida
Ch de chocolate	M de Madrid
D de Domingo	N de Navarra
E de España	N de nono
F de Francia	O de Oviedo
G de Gerona	P de Paris
H de historia	Q de queso
I de Italia	R de Roma
S de Salamanca	W de Washington
T de Tarragona	X de Xauen
U de Ursula	Y de yegua
V de Valencia	Z de Zaragoza

Lexicon

coger: answer the phone
colgar: hang up
diga (dígame): hello
está comunicando: he/she's busy
fax: fax
guía: phone book

le pongo/paso con: I'll connect you
marcar: dial
me pone con: connect me
número equivocado: wrong number
prefijo: area code
tarifa: charges

Postal System

The main Post Office is located at the Plaza de Cibeles, open Monday to Friday 9:00 a.m. to 10:00 p.m. and 9:00 a.m. to 2:00 p.m. Saturday. Local post offices in districts are usually open 9:00 a.m. to 2:00 p.m. Cibeles Post Office, Tel: 221-8195.

You can buy stamps at tobacco stores *(estancos)* and kiosks, which also sell parking tickets for specially designated zones. Postal rates seem to change at a brisk pace. Currently, a letter within Madrid requires 15 pesetas, Spain outside of Madrid 25 pesetas, EEC Europe 15 pesetas, non-EEC Europe 55 pesetas, and North America 75 pesetas.

Regulations require that packages not exceed 9cm x 14cm (3 ½ X 5 ½ inches). The sender's name and address should be written on the back of envelopes which must be white or light blue.

Red mailboxes guarantee 24-hour delivery for urgent mail. Otherwise, letters to the U.S. takes 7 to 10 days.

Messenger Services

For urgent messages that can't be delivered by fax in Madrid, efficient messenger services exist at reasonable prices. As they are based on the motorbike, they often are the fastest way to get a package through the Madrid traffic. Two reliable ones are:
• Gonaya Express
Tel: 326-5474 / 65
• Mundi Express
Tel: 533-2600

Lexicon

apartado: post box
certificado: registered mail
correo por avión: air mail

giro postal: money order
lista de correos: general delivery
seguro: insurance

Radio & Television

Unlike other western European nations, Spain is a nation of radio listeners. Though their habits are now changing with the recent explosion in the television market, Spaniards in recent years have been spending more time with the radio than they do with newspapers or even television. Spaniards get their news through the radio to a much larger extent than other countries of comparable economic development.

Spain's 40 million inhabitants have 35 million radio sets. Of the estimated average daily audience of 16 million listeners, the most by far listen to the private station SER. SER earned wide credibility during the attempted coup of February 23, 1981, by continuing their broadcasts throughout the incident without advertising. They enjoy state-of-the-art facilities and computerized operations, possibly the most modern in the world. SER radio personalities Concha García Campoy and Iñaki Gabilondo are known nationwide.

Radio Nacional, the government station, gives news every hour, with longer reviews at 2:00 p.m., 8:00 p.m. and midnight (Ernesto Sainz de Buruaga, who presents the 2:00 p.m. news, is well-known to all Spaniards). Radio 2, the government's second channel, is virtually the only one in the country to offer classical music around the clock. Radio 3, the "cultural channel," offers specialized musical programs and includes "Open University" classes every evening.

COPE, the Catholic station, popular among taxi drivers especially in the afternoon, broadcasts a wide variety of popular music, talk shows, and well-prepared news with national figures such as Luis del Olmo and Encarna Sánchez.

Onda Cero is the recently launched national network, belonging principally to ONCE, the well-financed National Society for the Blind.

According to *Estudio General de Medios* (EGM)'s latest poll, the national radio networks stack up as follows:

Station Audiencs

- Radio Nacional (RNE) (Government) 2,200,000
- SER (private) 6,800,000
- Antena 3 (private) 2,200,000
- COPE (Catholic Church) 1,700,000
- Onda Cero (Society for the blind) 1,000,000

Television

Until 1990, the government-owned station *Television Española* (TVE) was the only nation-wide network, operating in two channels: the first one was and still is dedicated to garnering the widest audience possible, the second has cultural and occasional sports programming. Together the two stations remain Spain's largest network, financed by government guarantees and advertising with which as recently as 1990 it was breaking even. Familiar news personalities Pedro Piqueras and Jesús Hermida give the national network a high profile, as well as Rosa María Mateo, Europe's most popular female television reporter.

With the passage of a law in 1988 permitting the creation of three private nationwide channels, the television situation changed radically, opening up to fierce competition and creating a much more popular pitch in the programming of all stations.

Antena 3 TV

The first of the privates to go on the air in January 1990, is controlled by the Godo family in Barcelona. Generally conservative in appearance, it has aimed for a popular and family audience.

Telecinco

The investment child of the Italian media magnate Silvio Berlusconi, has proclaimed itself Spain's entertainment channel, throwing to the winds any pretense of cultural or public service programming under the leadership of Valerio Lazarov. *Telecinco* is probably the favorite station of children.

Canal Plus

Modeled after the French station of the same name, it codes a good portion of its signal, selling decoders to subscribers for a yearly fee. Canal Plus aims for a smaller, élite audience, to which it brings films in the evening, soft porn at night.

None of the three private stations has done as well as expected, though all are gaining gradually on TVE's dominion. Serious budget losses have given vent to rumors that at least one of the private stations may go under in the near future. Despite the financial difficulties of the privates, Spain's booming market currently brings in over two billion dollars annually in television advertising revenue. TVE gets $77,000 for a 20-second spot in prime time.

In addition to the privates, Spain has eight autonomous stations which answer to regional governments and serve as regional adjuncts — competition, in some cases — to the national network. The one in Madrid, *Telemadrid*, was created in late 1989 and came on strong initially, but has sagged more recently under palace coups and internecine fighting within its management.

EGM puts the ranking of the various television stations as follows (figures total more than 100 because the percentages reflect the number of households which tune in to a station per day):

TVE 1	66.8%
TVE 2	22.3%
Telecinco	29.5%
Antena 3 TV	19.6%

Cable

The cable industry had no to-date real legal basis in Spain, though a number of pirate stations exist and legitimate cable associations have begun to sprout up around the country. By 1992 and the Olympic Games in Barcelona, a cable law will most likely be in place and we'll see a rapid takeoff in the industry.

Lexicon

(antena) parabólica: satellite dish
descodificador: decoder
diario hablado: news broadcast (radio)

emisión: broadcast
emisora: station
en directo: live (broadcast)
locutor: host; anchor
telediario: news broadcast (TV)

The Press

After decades of stifled public expression under Franco, Madrid's newspaper scene busted wide open after the dictator's death in 1975. Just a year later *El País* was founded, one of Europe's great dailies. Print journalism has since become the convoluted, competitive business it is in other European capitals, a heady affair with frequent personnel changes, constant moving about among the journalists themselves, an ever expanding array of journalism seminars and training programs and a certain amount of glamour.

Because the profession was so recently created, it has been marked by two drawbacks: young practitioners and somewhat sloppy work. You'll find among the by-line writers a high proportion of under-forties (rare among other Western newspapers) and a, shall we say, liberal approach to fact-checking and spelling.

Spaniards are not newspaper readers by and large, and Spain has one of Europe's lowest rates of readership. Nevertheless, the product is there, available, and the elite read and compare avidly.

Madrid has six major daily newspapers and two economic/financial dailies, all receiving news off the usual wire services, principally the government-owned one, EFE. In order of circulation, they stack up as follows:

El País (liberal-socialist)	376,000
ABC (conservative)	268,000
Diario 16 (centrist)	140,000
El Mundo (centrist)	100,000
Ya (Catholic, conservative)	69,000
El Independiente (leftist)	20,000
Expansión (economic)	23,000
Cinco Días (economic)	18,000

Newspapers in English include the *International Herald Tribune, The European*, as well as the imported London dailies such as *The Times* and *The Independent*. English-language periodicals include *Guidepost*, a useful aid to living in Madrid, and *Lookout*, a national magazine published in Fuengirola with good tourism pieces for the English-speaking community. Of the major U.S. and UK presses, most have bureaus in Madrid, though the *New York Times* recently closed its office here, and cost-cutting measures have begun to drive away others as well.

Among the disarming array of Spanish weeklies, many fill the basic function of *Newsweek* or *Time* while containing more gossip, horoscopes, television schedules, etc.

The addresses of the English-language periodicals are worth having, as they are useful for classified ads, or in the case of *Lookout*, can be used for book orders from their series:

Guidepost
Edificio España
Grupo 2 Planta 5
28013 Madrid
Tel: 248-0107
Fax. 542-6046

Lookout Magazine
Lookout Publications S.A.
Puebla Lucía
29640 Fuengirola
(Málaga)
Tel: (952) 460950
Fax. (952) 461022
Publisher/Editor: Ken Brown
Senior Editor: Mark Little

Iberian Daily Sun
Zurbano, 74
28010 Madrid
Tel: 442-7700

Spain: English Magazine
Doctor Esquerdo, 35, 1F
28028 Madrid
Tel: 256-1779

(Also has offices in the U.S. and U.K.):
Spain: English Magazine
Laurence J. Lehr
IVP Convention Services
2351 West Flagler Street
Miami, Florida 33135 USA
Tel: 305/649-5700

Spain: English Magazine
Clare M. Muñana
230 N. Michigan Ave.
Suite 1125
Chicago, Illinois 60601 USA
Tel: 312/248-3731

Spain: English Magazine
Robert Melville
25 Caxton Way
Wasford WD1 8UA
England
Tel: 923/32660

In addition to the standard weeklies and monthlies, the Madrid daily newspapers offer a wide variety of supplements, offered as gifts, with excellent weekly information on fashion, theater, concerts, film, nightlife and restaurants. Some come in the form of supplements to the Sunday edition of the paper.

Every Thursday *El País* gives a supplement in its daily edition, *Guía*, with a full listing of cultural events and enter-tainment. On Sundays it in-cludes *TelePaís*, a television guide for all channels.

Diario 16 distributes its own Friday magazine for free (with purchase of the newspaper), *Madrid*. Also on Fridays, the daily newspaper *El Mundo* gives out its own weekly entertainment guide, *Metropoli*.

You can also buy *Guía del Ocio* for 75 pesetas, containing much the same information as the weekly guides offered by the newspapers.

Should you need contact with English-language news services, their addresses follow:

U.S. Press in Spain

ABC News Television
Titulcia, 5
28007 Madrid
Tel: 501-6346
Correspondent: Marta Williams

Associated Press
Espronceda, 32 - 5°
28003 Madrid
Tel: 346-7100
Fax. 442-3612
Director: Susan Linnée

Business Week
Fernandez de la Hoz, 30 - 6°
28010 Madrid
Tel: 410-6998
Correspondent: Jack Patterson

Canal 47 WNJV Broadcasting
Juan Alvarez Mendizabal, 58
2800 Madrid
Tel: 247-1371
Correspondent: Hugo F. Arias

CBS News
General Días Portier, 45
28001 Madrid
Tel: 402-4810
Correspondent: John F. Byrne

Fairchild News Service
San Bernardino, 11
28015 Madrid
Tel: 541-4062
Correspondent: Barbara Baker

Financial Times
Florestan Aguilar, 7
28001 Madrid
Tel: 256-1924
Correspondent: Thomas Burns

The Hollywood Reporter
Ave María, 44
28012 Madrid
Tel: 227-6189
Correspondents: Carlos Hugo, Aztarain Aurelio

Newsweek International
Marbella, 66
28034 Madrid (Mirasierra)
Tel: 734-1795
Correspondent: Christopher Derek Ive

The New York Hotel Magazine
Serrano Anguita, 10
28004 Madrid
Tel: 446-7098
Correspondent: Elisabeth Coty

The New York Times
Marqués de Cubas, 12 - 2° C
28014 Madrid
Tel: 429-2517
Correspondents: Isabel Sato García
Robert Lee Royal

La Prensa Newspaper
Avda. Generalisimo, 3 - 9°
28922 Alcorcon(Madrid)
Tel: 641-5168
Correspondent: Alejandro Echegoyen

Time
Hermosilla 103
28009 Madrid
Tel: 435-3031
Correspondents: Jane Walker
Robert Lee Royal

United Press International
Espronceda, 32
28003 Madrid
Tel: 346-7100
Correspondents: Francisco Berzal Murillo, Sara Nicholson Montolio

The Wall Street Journal
Alfonso Rodríguez Santa María, 13
28002 Madrid
Tel: 563-1796
Correspondent: Nicholas Bray

The Washington Post
Florestan Aguilar, 7
28001 Madrid
Tel: 256-1924
Correspondent: Thomas Burns

U.K. Press in Spain
Daily Express
Francisco Lastres, 13
28028 Madrid
Tel: 255-3788
Correspondent: Edward Paul Owen

Daily Mail
Espronceda, 32
28003 Madrid
Tel: 346-7100
Correspondent: William Bond

Daily Mirror
Daily Telegraph
Espronceda, 32
28003 Madrid
Tel: 346-7100
Correspondent: Timothy Brown

Eurobusiness
Calle del Oso, 1 - 3°
28012 Madrid
Tel: 239-0909
Correspondent: Jane Monahan

The European
24, rue des Ecoles
75005 Paris, France
Tel: 43-29-5184
Fax. 43-29-0519
Contact for Spain: Pierre de
Boisguilbert

Financial Times
Dolores Romero, 44
28028 Madrid
Tel: 555-0326
Correspondent: Peter Bruce

The Guardian
P.° de Recoletos, 18 -7°
28001 Madrid
Tel: 575-3149
Correspondent: John Hooper

The Independent
Apolonio Morales, 31 - 1° A
28036 Madrid
Tel: 457-2616
Correspondent: Timothy S.
McGirk

Independent TV News
Marqués de Cubas, 12 - 5°
28014 Madrid
Tel: 637-2452
Correspondent: Henry Debellus

News Week
Marbella, 66 - 6° B
28034 Madrid
Tel: 734-1785
Correspondent: Tom Burn

Reader's Digest
Luchana, 19
28010 Madrid
Tel: 445-7927
Correspondent: Charles
Parmiter

Reuter's Limited
P° de la Castellana, 36 - 38°
28046 Madrid
Tel: 585-2100
Director: Robert Hart

The Times
Marqués de Cubas, 12 - 5°
28014 Madrid
Tel: 637-2452

TV Visnews
Ponzano, 37
28003 Madrid
Tel: 442-4093
Correspondent: Michael Gore

Like other European cities, Madrid is made up of distinctive neighborhoods each with its own character, often overlapping so that you'll sometimes lose the sense of exactly where you are in the city. The center is not vast by any means, and in the older sections particularly, you'll find that walking can be the best way of getting around.

The city hangs on a great spine called *Paseo de la Castellana*, or *Recoletos*, or *Prado*, depending on how far north or south you are. Sections to the east and west differ in character and share advantages and disadvantages as places to live, but there is no right or wrong side of the *Paseo*.

In general terms, the city can be divided like the face of a clock, with *Plaza de Cibeles* at the hub, where the hands of the clock are attached: at twelve noon you have *Plaza de Castilla* and *Chamartín*, areas toward which Madrid's energies are being directed, and the section of the future. The *Bernabeu* area (sports stadium) has delightful side streets and a lively night life. Further east you have the *Avenida de América* area, an often overlooked section with its own urban charm and some apartment deals still available.

At two and three o'clock you have *Barrio de Salamanca* and *Juan Bravo*, both nineteenth-century developments of great desirability to city dwellers and shoppers alike, somewhat comparable to New York's upper Lexington Avenue. At four and five o'clock you get to the older sections of the city, fronting on Retiro Park (one of Europe's most gracious) and the Prado area. This spectacular area, containing Madrid's Ritz Hotel, is off limits to most pocket-books, somewhat comparable to Fifth Avenue in New York, near the Metropolitan Museum.

As you round six o'clock you pass Atocha train station and cross the Paseo, known at this point as *Paseo del Prado*. Off to the west of the Paseo are Madrid's oldest sections, rich in history and lore, but problematic in everyday matters such as plumbing, parking and crime. Following the New York analogy, the areas such as *Lavapies* and *Huertas* might be comparable to Greenwich Village or Little Italy. Further off to the west (8:00 o'clock), you approach *Puerta del Sol*, *Plaza Mayor* and beyond, *Opera* and *Vistillas*. These are historically the very oldest sections of the city, both fascinating for city wandering and living, if you're willing to put up with some of the inner-city problems mentioned above, plus noise.

To the south, around *Atocha*, *Embajadores* and *Puerto de Toledo*, are more working-class areas, rich in lore such as the Rastro or flea market you should visit on Saturday or Sunday. They are not Madrid's most attractive areas, nor easy to reach by public transportation. You get what you pay for.

Moving up to nine and ten o'clock, *Gran Vía* and *Alcalá* come into view — Madrid's 42nd Street — then fronting on the Plaza de España, a bit of relief between the congested *Gran Via* and the packed student area off to *Argüelles*. The *Argüelles* congestion is nicely compensated by the *Parque del Oeste* it borders on, forming the real end of the city to the west, with the *Casa de Campo* across the river. Continuing to ten o'clock you arrive at upscale *Chamberí* and the University area beyond, with auxiliary sections *Chueca* and *Fuencarral* lying between the two, and the nightlife center of *Lavapiés* tucked between.

Moving north to eleven o'clock you arrive at *Azca* and *Capitán Haya*, also known as *Nuevos Ministerios*. This is one of Madrid's newest sections, the area of wide boulevards and massive department stores. If it's Old World charm you're after, look elsewhere. On the other hand, living and playing in this area solves some of the problems of living in a congested and overpriced city.

If suburban life is your preference, you'd do well to explore first the area west of the city, past the *Casa de Campo* in communities like *Somosaguas* and *Aravaca*. These areas have noticeably cleaner air and cooler weather than the central city, but necessitate serious commuting along overcharged feeder highways.

Everything is give-and-take; in selecting a neighborhood to live in, you need to be willing to put up with at least one of the following sources of stress:
• high prices,
• small quarters,
• Darkness at Noon (cf above),
• street noise,
• commuting,
• sharing with others.

You won't have to put up with *all* these hazards but you will have to decide which one or two of them you can live with. If you can, decide in advance, and limit the painful period of looking.

Although Madrid real estate prices fluctuate rampantly, here are a few rough estimates for renting an 80 square meter apartment in various neighborhoods in Madrid:

Chamberí	$1400 US/month
Chamartín	$1600 US/month
Salamanca	$1500 US/month
Atocha	$ 800 US/month

It can be discouraging arriving in the country of sunlight, only to end up in an apartment fronting an air shaft (patios, the *Madrileños* call them) with 90 precious square meters carved up into five claustrophobic rooms. The exercise of looking for apartments *(pisos)* has been dubbed by friends *Darkness at Noon* because so many a hopeful search has led to one of four major flaws:

• too dark if facing the rear;
• too noisy if facing front;
• too expensive if not dark or noisy;
• too far, if not expensive, dark or noisy.

In a housing market as tight as that of New York City and nearly as expensive, you'll have to sacrifice *something;* you might as well decide now which of the four flaws above you're willing to live with. If you're a student with pre-selected housing, rejoice and accept what you're given even if it doesn't look Spanish to you, or isn't your image of Ortega y Gasset's study.

Searching

If there's no one to find housing for you, you have three ways of going about it:
•Present yourself to one of the many real estate agencies and bite the bullet when they slap you with a bill equivalent to one month's rent.
• Follow closely the ads *(anuncios)* especially in *ABC* (also the Sunday *El País* and *Ya,* or the English-language weekly *Guidepost. Segunda Mano,* a printed marketplace for second-hand items and apartments, has three weekly editions. Be aware that many of the numbers listed are those of agencies who don't want to scare you off by advertising as what they really are. Happily, there is almost no jargon or abbreviated semiotics in Spanish housing ads.
• Beat the pavements in sections of the city you think you'd like, looking out for *Se alquila* signs in the windows or portals. Experience has shown this method the most exasperating but most successful in coming up with decent places to live in.

In addition, you can address yourself to a relocation company for a hefty fee, even before arriving on Spanish soil. One such is IRC Worldwide Ltd., International Relocation Company, Avda. Menéndez Pelayo, 15, 28009 Madrid. Tel: 574-8482, fax. 504-0677.

Whatever method you choose, it's a time-consuming, discouraging process. Others, preceding you, have met with success. You can as well.

The Portero

As you're looking for apartments, your principal *entrée* will be the *portero*. If you see a building you like in a section you can imagine living in, you can address your questions to the doorman even if there is no *alquilar* sign in the window of his building. If there is an apartment coming vacant within a few weeks or months, he will probably know about it and will generally share with you any information he has.

Once you zero in on a place you really like, the importance of your relations to the *portero* cannot be overemphasized. It wouldn't be overstating the case to say that your *portero* may be your most important human contact during your initial month or two in Madrid: in addition to putting you on to a find in his building after he's decided he likes you, after you've moved in he may be your only hope of getting a working toilet or an electrical socket that won't short out the whole neighborhood. Taking your *portero* out for a beer sometime during the initial period of your move may be your best investment of the year.

Porteros' hours vary, but generally they follow the hours of the shops, that is, 9:00 a.m. to 1:00 or 1:30, then again from 4:00 to 8:00 or so. Because they must sweep and otherwise service their buildings in the morning, the afternoon hours will be your optimal time for making initial contact during your apartment search. *Porteros* generally live in the buildings they oversee and are willing to work off hours on minor plumbing and electrical matters for extra pay. They serve as point of contact for workmen from the gas, telephone, etc. companies when you're out. It is customary to tip the portero 1000 pesetas a month, or more or less, depending on the area you live in.

Like the *concierge* in Paris, the *portero* is the omniscient being who knows the people and quirks of his building, as well as the *inquilinos'* (tenant's) comings and goings. There's no point in trying to have any personal secrets from your *portero*, you might as well just be his friend instead. He knows all, but usually guards his privileged information about your private life with utmost discretion.

Unlike the *Super* in New York, the *portero* is not expected to do all repairs or improvements, but only to lead you in the right direction for finding someone who can.

Renting

Once you've found an apartment, check the following before signing a lease:

• Heating: What sort is it? Is it adequate? How many months a year will it be turned on?

• Is there hot water? (never assume.)

• Does the plumbing work?

• Is there a phone? Will it be left for your use? (If not, expect a wait of up to a year for installation.)

• Are there enough electrical outlets, and is there enough power for your appliances?

• Are there closets and a storage area?

• Does the building have an elevator?

• Are previous gas, electric and water bills paid? (Recently there have been numerous reports of renters being stuck with their predecessors' bills. To avoid this, either get the landlord to agree to switch the accounts to your name, or at least stipulate in your lease that you won't be held responsible for the previous tenant's debts.)

Note that in Madrid the *empty shell* concept applies to housing: the owner *(dueño)* will give you walls and a key, nothing else. Paint jobs, appliance rental and installation are generally up to you.

Most rental contracts *(contrato de arrendamiento)* call for a one month security deposit and terminate at the end of one year. In addition, you'll be asked to pay a month's in advance, thus if your rent is 100,000 pesetas, you'll need 200,000 up front. Extremely important is the inclusion of two clauses — one allowing you to renew your rental at the end of a year, another holding the yearly increase to the *IPC*, the *Indice de Precios al Consumo* (Consumer Price Index) rather than leaving it to the whims of your landlord. At renewal time your landlord will inform you by letter (no lease amendment necessary) of the increase at the official IPC rate at the time (five to eight percent in recent years). Because the prices seem to spiral with no end in sight, landlords drool over the possibility of kicking you out so they can rent to the next person for much more than what you were charged.

When you sign a contract, make sure it includes:

• A description of the property, name and address of the owner and renter.

• Length of lease and amount to be paid each month.

• Mention of the intervals at which increases can be imposed.

• The amount of the security

deposit *(fianza),* with mention of whether it will be refunded at the end.

• Mention of whether utilities are included *(gastos comunitarios).*

• Stipulation of what services are provided.

• Inventory of any furnishings, utensils, etc.

• An understanding of who pays for what types of repairs.

Your search will generally take the same form as above. Once you get to the point of signing, check for the following in your contract:

• A full description of the property.

• A clear and unencumbered title.

• Services supplied by the seller (water, elevators, etc.)

• Total price, terms and dates of payment.

• A statement of which taxes, fees and costs will be paid by which party.

• Visit the *Registro de la Propiedad* to check for possible outstanding taxes and the full legal capability of the seller to sell. Príncipe de Vergara, 72, Tel: 411-1177 (central office — there also exist 37 district offices of the *Registro).*

• Visit also the *Gerencia de Urbanismo* of the *Ayuntamiento,* Paraguay, 11, Tel: 588-3300, to make sure the site of the property is not included in a city planning scheme that calls for major changes in the neighborhood.

• You will need also a *Cédula* (certificate) *de Habitabilidad,* issued by the Gerencia de Urbanismo of the Ayuntamiento, to assure the liveability of the dwelling.

Utilities

If you're renting, your landlord will probably ask you to put all utilities in your name (if not, don't press the issue, as the transfer can be a hassle and works to the advantage of the landlord, not yours.) Putting accounts in your name usually requires a trip to each utility concerned and a wait of several hours at each. Take all identification with you — passport, contract, previous bills on the same account if your landlord can supply you with them. Bring a book or some work to do, and decide in advance not to be exasperated by the long wait.

We strongly recommend that you arrange for monthly payments by direct transfer from your peseta account in Madrid *(transferencia).* Based on the written instruction you leave with your bank, the utility company will take money directly from your account and send you a record of what they've done, as will the bank. Paying utilities by check or cash in Madrid is complicated and time-consuming, so you have little choice but to trust the bank and utility company.

Remember that the working schedule for most utilities is Mon-Fri 9:00 to 2:00. Don't expect an answer in the afternoon, except from emergency numbers. For all utilities, find out from the central office which branch is nearest you.

Addresses
• Water
Canal de Isabel II
Joaquín García Morato, 127
Tel: 445-1000 (bills) / 446-2849 (repairs)

• Butane
Tel: 243-5600

• Propane
Tel: 268-0028

• Gas Madrid
Plaza de Olmos, 19
Tel: 589-6116
Tel: 589-6100 (bills)

• Repairs *(averías)*
Chamberí, 10
Tel: 447-3412
Barbieri, 20
Tel: 532-2800
Ronda de Toledo, 10
Tel: 265-1208
Emergency
Tel: 589-6555

• Electricity
Hidroelectrica Española
Hermosilla, 3
Tel: 266-3200 (repairs).

Union Electrica Fenosa, S.A.
Dr. Vallejo, 15
Tel: 270-5216

• Telephone
Compañía Telefónica Nacional de España
Gran Vía 28
Repairs: 002

Note: Depending on available space, students and visiting professors can live during the academic year at the *Residencia de Estudiantes*, Pinar, 21, 28006 Madrid, Tel: 261-3200.

Some Peculiarities of Madrid Buildings
Aticos: The classic Madrid apartment building consists of five to seven floors. The uppermost, the *ático*, has advantages and disadvantages: on the

positive side, *áticos* have the best views over the city and are the most removed from street noise. Often they have the largest *terrazas* of their buildings and can allow outdoors living in the spring and fall.

Madrileños shy away from them for practical as well as social reasons: they associate them with the *porteros* who used to live in them and still do to some extent, and therefore think of them as servants' quarters; more reasonably, they fear the heat that accumulates in them in the summer, rendering them nearly unbearable for a six-week period if air-conditioning is not included. If you can either be away in July, or are able to get air-conditioning, or don't mind heat, you should consider seriously any *ático* that comes along.

Locks: It is possible to be locked *in* when you're inside a Madrid apartment building. This may not seem to make sense, but it is so. If you're visiting someone and are on your way out, the etiquette is to call from the intercom to the apartment you've left, and your host will buzz you out. Certain lock systems require the owner's written permission in order to have copies made; where this permission is difficult to get, you can usually talk the locksmith into making you a copy if you can at least present a rental contract as proof that you are the tenant.

Water Pressure: Madrid named its main water supply, the Canal Isabel II, after Spain's nymphomaniac queen — perhaps in the hope that it would never run dry. Water does run low at times, especially in the summer months. The upper floors of apartment buildings can be affected; in some instances you'll find you can never get a forceful stream of water in your shower, or fill your tub in a reasonably short time. The problem can affect heating systems as well, leaving you chilly in the winter. Consider this aspect as you look at housing in the upper floors of Madrid buildings.

Left, Right: Each Madrid apartment is designated *izquierda* or *derecha*, according to how you face it when mounting the *stairs* of the building (not when exiting the elevator.) This anachronism can lead to confusion at times, unless you keep the principle in mind. The *primer piso* or *primera planta* refers to the floor above the ground floor, as in the French system.

Piso, Apartamento, Planta: Piso literally means an apartment occupying an entire floor of a building. The word is often used hyperbolically, to designate an apartment of suitable size — 100 square meters or so. Smaller units are called *apartamentos*, with one-room units called, as in the U.S., studios (*estudios*). The *planta* is the floor of a building, for counting purposes.

Patio: Don't be misled by this term and expect sun-filled sitting areas with potted tropical plants. The *patio* is often a simple air shaft, practical for hanging out clothes to dry (because of the dry climate, the electric clothes drier is seldom used in Madrid.) Outdoors living is reserved for the *terraza*. Incidentally, you can fill your *terraza* with plants by taking a trip out any of Madrid's main exit roads — Coruña, Burgos, or Zaragoza. You'll find *viveros* by the side of the road about 15 km out, where for about 10,000 pesetas you can select the plants you want and arrange to have them delivered directly to your terrace.

Toldos: Awnings are a must if you expect to use your *terraza* in the summer. By Madrid convention, your landlord will not add or fix these essential items without special arrange-ment.

Heating *(calefacción):* Avoid totally electrical apartments, the monthly bills will be astro-nomical. One of the mysteries of some Spanish dwellings is the hidden electrical switch for light, heat, etc.: look for it *outside* the door of the room where you want it. Check for the source of your hot water. If it comes from a central building source, you're OK — or if your apartment's water heater has at least a 75-liter capacity. If it has less, you're in for cold showers and other problems.

Washing Machines: The European system takes in cold water only, heating it inside the machine itself. This generally renders U.S.-standard washers unusable in Europe.

Furnished Apartments: Landlords have fixed ideas on the number of rooms each person can properly have, as well as furniture items. They can become suspicious if you want a double bed for yourself alone, or if you need a "practice" room to perfect your clarinet technique. These suspicions are based on practicality more than morality. Press for what you want, and you'll probably get it. As a foreigner, you're allowed to be eccentric.

Repairs

If your *portero* can neither fix it himself nor refer you to a good plumber, electrician, etc., try *Multi-Asistencia* at 431-3131 for all types of repairs and remodeling.

Bedding, Linen

Sheets, pillowcases, towels (and for that matter, underwear) are prohibitively expensive and of poor quality in Spain. We urge you to make these purchases almost anywhere else in the world before moving to Spain.

Domestic Help

There is no magic formula for coming by a good domestic. You can always put an ad in one of the weekly or monthly publications. Sometimes the *portero* can help.

Live-in maids get 36 hours off a week in Spain — usually Sunday plus two afternoons. In addition, they get a month's vacation, in one block of 15 days with the remainder taken as individual days. It is customary to tip a live-in half the monthly salary at Christmas, and half again in July.

After a 15-day trial period, the full-time domestic (*interna*) must be registered with Social Security, at the *Régimen Especial del Servicio Doméstico, Instituto Nacional de Previsión*, Sagasta, 6.

To drop a household employee, you must give the reason in writing and give seven days notice. The same applies to full-time cleaning women who do not live in *(externa)*.

None of the rules apply to *asistentas* who live out and work less than 40 hours a week for you.

Banking

Banking in Spain can be slow and frustrating if you are accustomed to speedy, North American drive-in service. Bank transfers of funds from your home country to your Spanish bank account can be painfully slow. But, the banking system does work reasonably well. Banks are open from 9:00 am to 2:00 pm Monday through Friday, Saturdays 9:00 am to 1:00 pm (noon, from June to September). Note: you won't get your cancelled checks back from a Spanish bank, though you can call in and get your balance at any time.

Undoubtedly, one of the first things you'll be interested in doing upon settling in Madrid is opening a bank account. Here are essentially the five kinds of accounts that exist in Spain.

Bank Accounts

• Tourist Accounts for Non-residents: You can deposit Spanish or foreign banknotes and travelers' checks, but you won't be able to change them back again. Withdrawals or checks in pesetas only.

• Convertible Peseta Accounts: Also for non-residents. You can deposit banknotes, foreign currency or travelers' checks; they are converted into pesetas at the rate of the day when you make the deposit, but you may convert the pesetas back to any foreign currency.

• Non-peseta Accounts for Non-residents: If you declare foreign currency on entering Spain, you are allowed to maintain an account for your foreign currency on which you can draw for payments overseas. You aren't subject to exchange control rules as long as you don't convert into pesetas at any point.

• Internal Peseta Accounts for Non-residents: A blocked account for later conversion into pesetas. Useful for property and investment purchases.

• Current Spanish Accounts *(cuenta corriente)* for Residents:

Or savings account *(cuenta de ahorro)*. An account as a Spanish citizen would have, allowing you to deposit, withdraw and write checks on pesetas, and to receive interest payments. Any form of money, and any currency, can be deposited. To make foreign payments in another currency or to export pesetas, you need to make a special application. While this is possible, it's trickier than it would be in the U.S. or UK.

Credit Cards

Credit Cards are widely used in Spain, with Visa, MasterCard, Diners, and American Express being the most readily accepted. Credit cards issued on Spanish banks are actually bank cards, not credit cards, in that they function in accord with your bank account, drawing the funds from the account directly. Here is a list of major banks in Madrid with their principal addresses and telephone numbers. There isn't a great difference in quality or cost of service among banks in Spain, so generally you're best off selecting a bank that is conveniently located to your home or work and that acts as a correspondent to your bank in your home country.

National Banks

- Banesto
Alcala, 14
Tel: 532-7200
- Bilbao BBV
Alcala, 16
Tel: 582-8000
- Central
Alcala, 49
Tel: 532-8810
- Citibank España
Plaza Independencia, 6
Tel: 431-5050
- España
Alcala, 50
Tel: 446-9055
- Exterior de España
Carrera de S. Jerónimo, 36
Tel: 429-4477
- Hispano Americano
Plaza de Canalejas, 1
Tel: 522-4660
- Natwest March
Miguel Angel, 23
Tel: 319-1112
- Santander
Alcala, 37
Tel: 581-4300
- Urquijo Union
Po. Castellana, 46
Tel: 435-1230
- Zaragozano
Po. Castellana, 89
Tel: 555-9013

International Banks

- Bank of America
Capitan Haya, 1
Tel: 555-5500
- Barclays Bank
Plaza de Colon, 2
Tel: 410-2800
- BNP
Génova, 27
Tel: 319-8049
- Citibank
José Ortega y Gasset, 29
Tel: 435-5190
- Credit Lyonnais
Po. Castellana, 35
Tel: 319-9514
- Lloyds Bank
Serrano, 90
Tel: 276-70-00
- National Westminster
Miguel Angel, 21
Tel: 419-39-56
- American Express
Plaza de la Cortes, 2
28015 Madrid
Tel: 429-5775

Currency Exchange

Of the many independent services in Madrid, *Exact Change* offers multi-lingual service, tourist information, extended hours and special rates for holders of *Madrid Inside Out.*
- Exact Change
Puerto del Sol, 12
Calle Carmen, 16
Calle Precidos, 23

adeudo: debit
cajero: teller
carta de crédito: letter of credit
carta: promissory note
cobrar: collect, receive payment
factura: bill

ingreso: credit
interés: interest
saldo: balance
saldo negativo: overdraftt
talonario: checkbook

Shopping

Madrid has over 50,000 stores, and an incredible array of merchandise, considering the limited offerings only a decade ago. Be advised that nothing is cheap, and that you'll wear yourself to the bone if you're looking for bargains that were available in the 1970s. Generally, stores are open Monday to Saturday from 9:30 a.m. to 1:30 p.m., then again from 5:00 p.m. to 8:00 p.m. This is the rule, but there is much deviation from one store to the other. Department stores *(grandes almacenes)* tend to be open 10:00 a.m. to 8:00 p.m., and some supermarkets *(hipermercados)* stay open to 10:00 p.m.

Drugstore chains such as VIPS and Bob's (books, records, videos, gourmet foods, gifts...) have more flexible hours, staying open generally from 9:00 a.m. to 3:00 a.m. Madrid also has a number of 7/11 stores with basic food stuff and magazines, staying open 24 hours.

Food Shopping

One of the charms of shopping in Madrid is getting to know your neighborhood fish salesman *(pescadero)* and baker *(panadero)*, as well as the neighbors you'll see regularly. Supermarkets are not as common as in some other European cities; you'll soon get used to making frequent trips to specialty stores for vegetables, fish, meat, etc. One tip: avoid doing large shopping runs on Monday, as the produce tends to be left over from the previous week, and are neither abundant nor fresh. Friday evenings and Saturday mornings are especially busy periods, when you might not want to venture into crowded markets.

The fish in Madrid is legendary, trucked in every night from coasts where, paradoxically, the catch can be hard to find because of the demand in the capital. Even during the early Franco period of scarcity in all areas, fish was always available in the capital, establishing a tradition which continues to this day. Madrid is still the best location in Spain for fish, in quality, variety and price.

If you're lucky enough to have a large covered market in your neighborhood, you're best off doing most of your food shopping there and developing a relationship with the merchants (tenderos) of the stalls you choose to frequent. The tendero will get a sense of your preferences and tastes and can help you buy the products best suited for you. Complaining about the item you bought the last time is proper and expected, plays fairly to the tendero's professionalism and assists him in serving you.

Covered food markets are open from 9:00 a.m. to 2:00 p.m., and from 5:30 to 7:30 p.m. They're closed Saturday afternoon and Sunday all day. If you buy in quantity, a good trick is to bring your own cart or bag with you, as the stores and stalls have bags big enough only for individual purchases. Supermarkets are beginning to be common in Madrid, differing from covered markets in their hours only in the afternoon, tending to stay open from 5:00 to 8:00 p.m.

For specialty and convenience shopping, the large department stores have food sections in their basements. *El Corte Inglés, Galerías Preciados, Sánchez Romero* stay open from 10:00 a.m. to 9:00 p.m., and have parking facilities. The larger stores make free deliveries of purchases of over 5,000 pesetas and will also take orders over the telephone.

Baby food can be purchased in pharmacies.

Note: in open food stands, when calculating in small amounts the *tendero* will often tell you the amount you owe in terms of *duros* or five-peseta pieces. Thus, *cinco duros* means five-times-five, or 25 pesetas.

Spaniards are respectful of lines, though you'd never guess it to look at one. What seems like an undifferentiated mass will usually be a well-defined pecking order in the minds of those waiting. While there may be no noisy protests for the violator, you can be sure you will be resented if you break in. With other customers waiting, you must ask *¿Quién tiene la vez?* or *¿Quién es el último?* before assuming you're next.

Bombonería: Candy stores carry special chocolates you can buy on your way to a friend's house or dinner invitation — including *trufas*, the aristocrat of chocolates to present. Get them fresh-made, or at least keep them in the refrigerator if you're not about to dive into them. One small chain of excellent *bombonerías* is Santa, at Serrano, 56 and Goya, 69.

Alimentación or *Ultramarino:* The medium-sized neighborhood grocery store, usually Mom-and-Pop, takes its name from the products, mostly spices, which used to come from abroad (*ultramar*). Here you can buy packed and canned foods, as well as dairy items. Sometimes you will find fresh produce and some meat or cold cuts, but the latter tend not to be of the best quality.

Bodega: Wine and liquor stores. Soft drinks are also available, as well as snacks or munchies. The *bodega* can also function as a bar at times.

Bollería: Bread and rolls. *Madrileños* almost never mix bread and pastry in the same store — a taboo of unknown origins.

Carnicería: Butcher shop. Meat is cut differently in Spain than in the U.S. or UK. Beef is not up to Anglo-Saxon standards, but the veal, pork, chicken and lamb are excellent. Meat is seldom pre-packed or cut, so you will have to state how you want it: *fino* (thin-sliced), *grueso* (thick), *deshuesado* (boneless), *sin grasa* or *magro* (with the fat removed).

Casquería: Sells animal organs, considered a delicacy by *Madrileños*. Here you can try your luck with *callos a la madrileña* (tripe), *sesos* (brains), or *riñones* (kidneys).

Churrería: These shops sell *churros* or *porras*, as well as fresh-fried potato chips. The former are pastries fried in oil and served with *chocolate*, a thick chocolate sauce (not a drink) served in a cup.

Fábrica de Pan or *Tahona:* Bakery. Usually the *fábrica* makes the bread and distributes it to the retailer, the *panadería*. The product comes out in thick bars called *pistolas*. They produce also *pan de rosco* (circular bread), *pan de hogaza* (round peasant bread), *gallegos* (round bread), and whole wheat bread (*integral*).

Panadería: Bakery. In addition to bread, they sell croissants, *caracolas, madalenas, napolitanas, ensaimadas* and *tartas de manzana*.

Pastelería or *confitería:* For pastries and candy. Don't expect to find bread here, or pastries in a *panadería*. Some of the common cakes are:

saras (butter pastries covered with almonds) *hojaldres* (*mille-feuilles*/(Napoleon) puffy paste with custard, fruit, etc.,)

tartaletas (small tarts filled with cream, fruits)

brazos de gitano (specially soft roll filled with custard, cream, chocolate)

cañas (long pastries filled with cream or chocolate).

Note: Madrid cakes and pastries are unworthy of the generally very high level of gastronomy in the capital. Don't expect the standards you've found in Paris, Rome or Vienna. Mallorcan and Catalan pastries are the best (*ensaimadas, cocas de San Juan, panellets...*). Be glad if you can find them.

Charcutería: Specialty store for cold cuts (*fiambres*). The specialties include Spanish Serrano ham (*jamón Serrano*) comparable to the Italian *proscuito*; *jamón de bellota, jamón de jabugo* (can cost 15,000 pesetas per kilo!) and *jamón York. Charcuterías* also sell smoked salmon and pâtés, sausages (*chorizos*). You can buy cold cuts either by weight (100 grams, 200, etc.) or by number of slices (*rodajas*), or by instructing the *vendedor* to slice more or less of a single piece. *Charcuterías* sell cheese as well as cold cuts, though you can also find a great variety of cheese at specialty stalls in the covered markets.

Frutería: For vegetables as well as fruit. The store will generally give you free parsely if you ask. Etiquette prohibits touching the fruit unless you're invited to do so by the *vendedor*.

Heladería: Ice cream stores become urgent necessities in the warm summer months. Many have tables to put out on the sidewalk, making themselves into *terrazas* as the situation and temperature calls for. Light, cold drinks include *horchata, granizados de café* or *granizados de limón. Heladerías* also serve soft drinks and beer.

Herbolario: Herb and spice shop.

Huevería: Egg shop.

Lechería: Dairy shop.

Mantequería: Dairy, delicatessen, wines and liquors.

Marisquería: Shellfish. You can either get seafood to go or, particularly in the late afternoon, linger and take *tapas.*

Pescadería: Fish shops. Fish is usually cleaned, cut and scaled by the fish seller at your request, for no extra charge. You can get *filete* (filet) or *rodajas* (slices). After acquiring some experience you'll learn to buy fish according to the season; the salesman/woman will be glad to give you cooking instructions. A sure winner is *dorada* (dorado), *lubina* (bass) or *besugo* (sea bream), cooked in the oven in a covered pan with salt for 20/30 minutes. Fresh *trucha* (trout) fried in a skillet with garlic and parsely is to die for. Important: clams and mussels which fail to open after cooking may contain botulism; don't take chances!

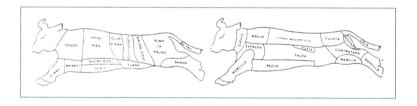

Lexicon

Meat and Poultry (Carne y Ave)

agujo: chuck
alete: brisket
añojo: beef (1-2 years old)
atado: tied
bacon, paucete: bacon
buey: beef

cadera: sirloin tip
carne para guisar: stew meat
carne picada: ground meat
casquería: tripe
cerdo: pork
chuletas: center cut chops
chuletitas, costillas: rib chops
cochinillo: suckling pig

conejo: rabbit
contra: bottom round
con hueso: with the bone
cordero: lamb
costillas: spareribs
enrollado: rolled
entrecot: steak
espaldilla: blade cut
filete: fillet
hígado: liver
jamón: ham
lechal: suckling lamb
lengua: tongue
lomo: loin
magro: tenderloin
mollejas: sweetbreads
morcillas: blood sausage
morcillo: soup bone, shank
muslos: legs
paleta: shoulder
pato: duck
pavo: turkey
pechuga: breast
perdiz: partridge
pierna: leg
pierna: pork leg
pies de cerdo: pig's foot
pollo: chicken
redondo: eye of round
riñones: kidneys
sesos: brains
sin grasa, magro: without fat
sin hueso: deboned
solomillo: tenderloin, filet mignon
ternera: veal
tocino: pork fat

Fish (Pescado)
almejas: clams
anchoas: anchovies
atún: tuna
bacalao: cod
besugo: sea bream
calamares: squid
centollo: king crab
esturión: sturgeon
gambas: shrimp
langosta: lobster
langostinos: sea crayfish
lenguado: sole
lubina: bass
marisco: shellfish
mejillones: mussels
merluza: hake
mero: grouper
ostra: oyster
pez espada: swordfish
rodaballo: turbot
salmón: salmon
trucha: trout

**Dairy
(Lechería, Vaquería)**
azucarado: sugared
blanco: plain
con frutas: with fruit
curado: cured, strong
de Burgos/fresco: fresh (cheese)
leche: milk
manchego: local cheese of La Mancha
leche entera: whole milk
    descremada: skim
    semi descremada: low-fat
    fresca: fresh
queso: cheese

rayado: grated
requesón: cottage cheese
sabor a..: flavored
yogur: yoghurt

Vegetables (Verduras)
aceituna: olive
aguacate: avocado
ajo: garlic
alcachofa: artichoke
apio: celery
berenjena: eggplant
calabarán: zucchine
calabaza: squash
cebolla: onion
champiñon: mushroom
col: cabbage
coliflor: cauliflower
endivia: endive
ensalada: salad
ensaladilla rusa: potato salad
espárragos: asparagus
espinacas: spinach
guisantes: peas
judía verde: green beans
lechuga: lettuce
lenteja: lentil
palmitos: palm hearts
patata: potato
pepino: cucumber
pimiento: green pepper
puerra: leak
seta: chanterelle mushroom
tomate: tomato
zanahoria: carrot

Fruit (Frutas)
albaricoque: apricot
cereza: cherry
ciruela: plum
frambuesa: raspberry
fresa: strawberry
grosella: black currant
limón: lemon
manzana: apple
melocotón: peach
melón: melon
naranja: orange
pera: pear
piña: pineapple
plátano: banana
sandía: watermelon
uvas: grapes

Special Shopping
Madrid has its flea markets, though it has been some years since there were any miraculous finds.

• *Rastro*, comparable to Portobello in London or Les Puces de St. Ouen or Montreuil in Paris, is festive for shoppers and pickpockets alike. It extends a few streets crossing Ribera de Curtidores, in the southwestern sector of the city in a triangle formed by the Cathedral of San Isidro, the Puerta de Toledo and the Glorieta (traffic circle) de Embajadores.

Most activity is concentrated on Sundays, but Saturday has as many offerings and is not as crowded. Among the antique and second-hand furniture shops you can also find some stalls carrying inexpensive new clothing. If you're good at restoration and have a good imagination, you can equip your house cheaply. If not, you'll find the *Rastro* expensive in the long run. You can bargain at the *Rastro*, but doing so will save a few thousand pesetas at most. Metro *Tirso de Molina* or *La Latina*.

• *El Rastrillo de Marqués de Viana*, along the street of that same name, is a smaller version of the *Rastro* and includes produce stands. Metro *Tetuán* or Bus 42, 49, 124, 125. Sundays and holiday mornings.

• The *Mercadillo Filatélico y Numismático*, under the portals of the *Plaza Mayor,* functions Sunday and holiday mornings. Stamps, coins, and other miscellaneous collectors' items can be found.

• The *Mercadillo Navideño*, also at the *Plaza Mayor,* opens in early December and continues until Reyes (January 6). Best for Christmas ornaments and party decorations.

• The *Mercadillo-Exposición de Pintura* at the *Plaza del Conde de Barajas* gives painters a market for their works on Sunday mornings.

• The *Rastrillo del Postigo de San Martín* stays open weekend afternoons during the Christmas season.

• The *Rastrillo de Ventas*, at the *Plaza de Toros*, provides much the same fare as the *Rastro*, only on Saturday mornings.

Department & Chain Stores

Madrid's large chains resemble those in the UK, U.S. and Canada. The standard one, *Corte Inglés*, carries the usual items, at the moderate-to-expensive range. *Corte Inglés* can be found all over Spain, with Madrid branches at:

Preciados, 3, Tel: 532-8100
Castellana, Tel: 556-2300
Goya, 76, Tel: 448-0111
Princesa, Tel: 542-4800

Recently added, the Madrid branches of Mark & Spencer cater to the more affluent shopper, specializing in clothes and items for the home: Mark & Spencer, Serrano, 52 and Castellana, 83.

Galerías Preciados is a cheaper version of *Corte Inglés*, with a greater number of locations:

• Arapiles, 10
Tel: 446-3200
• Magallanes, 28
Tel: 447-2569

- Goya, 87
Tel: 401-4300
- Plaza de Callao
Tel: 522-4771
- Serrano, 47
Tel: 431-4840
- Hermanos García Noblejas, 43
Tel: 267-4047
- Avda. Pedro Diez, 3
Tel: 471-2562
- María de Molina, 54
Tel: 411-0261
- La Vaguada
Tel: 730-3000

The huge shopping complex at *La Vaguada*, north of the city out the *Carretera de Burgos*, has some 300 specialized shops, including Alcampo supermarket and a number of movie theaters along the lines of the American mall. Metro Barrio del Pilar; Bus 42, 49, 83, M-3)

Late-night food shopping is concentrated in a single store, *Jumbo* on the Avda Pio XII (10:00 a.m. to midnight). *Jumbo* is open Sundays and holidays, but is extremely crowded during the hours when it's the only show in town. Tel: 259-0300.

The *Mercado de la Puerta de Toledo*, newly built on the site of the old fish market, is intended to give a lift to the depressed city area it's located in.

Value Added Tax (IVA)

The VAT (or IVA in Spanish) on manufactured items ranges from 6% to 33% for luxury items. Generally, prices listed in shop windows, restaurants, etc., include IVA of 12%, but on expensive items you should make sure this is the case before making a purchase.

Credit Cards

Merchandise in Madrid is bought with cash, local check or credit card, when presented in person. Credit card orders over the phone (for merchandise as well as theater and concert tickets) is an unknown practice.

Duty Free

If you are planning to buy an item for export as a tourist, you are eligible for a refund of the IVA on single purchases of over 47,400 pesetas. The discount will be 6, 12 or 33 percent of the original purchase price, depending on the item. The seller should provide a document detailing the value and nature of the purchase, for refund of the IVA on departure from the country. Citizens of non-EC countries (e.g., U.S. and Canada) must show the purchase, so don't pack it away until after you've left the country. Non-EC visitors will show their IVA documents, and receive their reimbursements later. For information, call the *Oficina Municipal de Información al Consumidor*, Tel: 464-9850 or 429-5353.

Specialty Stores

Nothing is cheap in Madrid as it once was. However, a number of specialty stores have plenty to offer, if you don't mind leaving a fair amount of money behind. (Note: beauty salons are called *salón de belleza*.)

Arts and Crafts, Antiques

• Artespaña. Gran Vía, 32
• Don Ramón de la Cruz, 33
• Hermosilla, 14
• Centro Comercial La Vaguada

Furniture and Spanish handicrafts

• Casa Diego. Puerta del Sol, 12
• Centro de Anticuarios Lagasca. Lagasca, 36 (eleven stores)
• Centro de Arte y Antiguedades. Serrano, 5. (Exhibition halls for paintings; 50 individual stores.)
• Galerías Kreisler Hermosilla, 8
• Mercado Puerta de Toledo. Ronda de Toledo, 1. (Art center, antiques, fashion, furniture, design, jewelry; 150 individual stores.)

• El Quijote. Capitán Haya, 48
• Real Fábrica de Tapices. Fuenterrabía, 2. (Carpets and tapestries made to order.)
• Rustika. San Bernardino, 3
• Tizona. Leganitos, 15-17

Ceramics

• Cantaro. Flor Baja, 8
• Caballo Cojo. Segovia, 7
• Sefarao 1 and 2. Gran Vía, 54 and 43
• Zuny. Plaza de Chamberi, 11

Gifts

• La Compañía de la China y del Oriente. Conde de Aranda, 14. (Large selection of decorative items and gifts.)
• La Continental. Príncipe de Vergara, 48. (Furniture and gift items.)
• Musgo. Hermosilla, 36; O'Donnell, 15; Santa Hortensia, 19; Paseo de la Habana, 34. (Design and gift items.)

Shoes

• Acosta. Hermosilla, 20 and 36; Padre Damián, 15; Claudio Coello, 95; Orense, 6; Multicentro; Profesor Waksman, 12. (Shoes, purses, belts, jewelry.)
• Camper. Ayala, 13; Paseo de la Habana, 50; Centro comercial La Vaguada
• Geltra. Alberto Aguilera, 70; Ayala 23; Bravo Murillo, 114 and 299; Goya, 65 and 89;

Gran Vía, 33; Orense, 7. (The best shoe store chain in Madrid.)
• Lurueña. Gran Vía, 60; Núñez de Balboa, 37; Serrano, 54; Velázquez, 28; Orense, 23; Centro comercial La Vaguada. (High quality shoes.)
• Paco Lobo. Serrano, 88; Princesa, 67; Lagasca, 67. (Sleek lines, children's and stylish shoes.)

Photo Stores
• Aquí. Plaza de Santa Ana, 1; Príncipe, 6; Cruz, 28; Cádiz, 7; Doctor Fleming, 30; Lagasca, 39; Espoz y Mina, 11, Príncipe de Vergara, 258; Barquillo, 11; General Díaz Porlier, 7.
• Carril. Raimundo Lulio, 1 and 2; Avenida de América, 2; Donoso Cortés, 1; Plaza de Olavide, 12.

Fashion
• Adolfo Domínguez. Ayala, 24; Serrano, 96; Ortega y Gasset, 4. (Men's and women's. Avant garde design.)
• Agatha Ruiz de la Prada. Marqués de Riscal, 8. (Women's. Daring fashion, according to one review.)
• Antinoos. Orense, 12; Padilla, 1. (Men's fashion. Modern elegance.)
• Coal. Valenzuela, 9. Women's. (One of Madrid's best stores.)

• Enrique P. Almirante, 6; Gaztambide, 24. (Latest men's and women's fashions.)
• Francis Montesinos. Argensola, 8. (Models by the young Valencian designer.)
• Giorgio Armani. Ortega y Gasset, 15. (Women's. Quiet, modern elegance.)
• Jesús del Pozo. Almirante, 28. (Men's fashion.)
• Loewe. Gran Vía, 8; Serrano, 26 and 34. (Men's and women's. Spanish classics at their best; one of Madrid's finest.)
• Massimo Dutti. Alberto Aguilera, 37; Velázquez, 41; Paseo de la Habana, 40. (Men's store; good buys on shirts.)
• Pedro Morago. Almirante, 20. (Men's latest design.)
• Royale. Ayalá, 13. (Classical and elegant.)

Children's Clothing
• Friki. Velázquez, 35.
• Maty. Maestro Victoria, 2
• Niños. Castelló, 35
• La Oca Loca. Lagasca, 61

Art
• Aguilar. Serrano, 24
• Tórcula. Claudio Coello, 17

Perfumes
• Alvarez Gómez. Serrano, 14; Paseo de la Castellana, 111; Sevilla, 2. (Perfume items for men and women.)

- Campos de Ibiza. Lagasca, 47. (Perfumes and cosmetics.)
- Hermes. José Ortega y Gasset, 26. (The Madrid branch of the Paris establishment from before the turn of the century.)

Boutiques
- Don Carlos. Serano, 94
- Fancy. Serrano, 98
- St. Laurent. Serrano, 100
- Ted Lapidus. Serrano, 53
- Lainez. Preciados, 2; Puerta del Sol, 11
- Gucci. Don Ramón de la Cruz, 2

Leather Goods & Suede
- Augusto González. Perciados, 21
- Bravo. Gran Vía, 31, Serrano, 42
- Fábrica de ante Jacinto Rodríguez. San Bernardo, 4
- Elena Benarroch. Monte Esquinza, 18
- Manuel Herrero. Serrano, 76
- Pekary. Goya, 83
- Parriego. Núñez de Balboa, 94
- Loewe. Serrano, 26; Gran Vía, 8
- Orlan. Serrano, 28
- Villagrag. Jorge Juan, 35

Brass and Silver
- José Villalba. Cabeza, 24
- Carpincho. Preciados, 33
- Ese. Juan Hurtado de Mendoza, 5

Pearls
- Perlas Majorica. Edificio España, Gran Vía, 84; Mesonero Romanos, 33
- Hotel Castellana (lobby). Paseo de la Castellana, 55
- Ysusi. Gran vía, 35
- El Quijote. Capitán Haya, 48
- Serafad 1 and 2. Gran Vía, 43 and 54.

Jewelry & Silver
- Aguayo. Serrano, 108
- Carrera y Carrera. Galería del Prado
- Joyería Pérez A. Fernández. Zaragoza, 3
- Montejo. Goya, 25

Music
- Luis Maravilla. León, 4
- Unión Musical Española. San Jerónimo, 26

Gourmet Foods & Sweets
- Bombonería Juncal. Recoletos, 15
- Bombonería Santa. Serrano, 56
- Casa Mira. San Jerónimo, 30
- Horno de Santa Teresa. Santa Teresa, 12
- La Gamella. Alfonso XII, 4
- Lhardy. San Jerónimo, 8
- Mallorca. Serrano, 6
- La Plaza. La Galería del Prado
- Sixto. José Ortega y Gasset, 83

• Casa Postal
Libertad, 37
• Postales-Objetos
Almirante, 23

English-language Bookstores

Turner English Books
Génova, 3
28004 Madrid
Tel: 410-2915 or 308-0709

Booksellers S.A.
José Abascal, 48
28003 Madrid
Tel: 442-7959

Madrid's largest and best bookstore, the *Casa del Libro*, also has an extensive section of books in English:
Casa del Libro
Gran Vía, 29
Tel: 521-6657

The *Aguilar* Bookshop has English sections in three of its outlets:
• Serrano, 24
Tel: 435-3642
• Goya, 18
Tel: 275-0604
• Paseo de la Castallana, 154
Tel: 250-3639

Don't overlook *VIPS* — a chain of seven bookstores cum gourmet foods sections, cum restaurants in some cases. Wide selection of foreign (including English-language) magazines and newspapers. Somewhat evocative of Kramer Books in Washington, in addition open almost around the clock. *VIPS* was founded by an entrepreneur who needed a loser as a tax write-off; to his dismay, the chain prospered and became one of Madrid's most successful businesses:
VIPS
• Julian Romea, 4
• Princesa, 5
• Orense, 79
• Velázquez, 136
• Paseo de la Castellana, 83
• Orense, 16
• Gran Vía, 43
(Open 9:00 a.m. to 3:00 a.m.)

Other bookstores

• Atheneum
General Moscardó, 29
• Librería Crisol
Juan Bravo, 38
• Estudio Dos
Serrano, 108
• Itaca
López de Hoyos, 141
• Librería Aviraneta
San Bernardo, 128
• Oxford Bookstore
Paseo de la Habana, 56

Another chain somewhat similar to *VIPS* is *Bob's*, which offers a video club as well as bookstore with magazines:
Bob's
Miguel Angel
Serrano, 41
Glorieta de Quevedo, 9

Travel Bookstores

Some of these shops have cult followings in Madrid and arrange special events such as readings, and slide lectures.
• La Librería
Señores de Luzón, 8
(Specializes in books about Madrid.)
• La Tienda Verde
Maudes, 38
• Le Tierra del Fuego
Pez, 21
• Años Luz
Francisco Ricci, 8

Driving

Every city complains about its traffic and parking; the case of Madrid must be as bad as anywhere outside of Lagos, Nigeria, and would tax the patience of a saint. Traffic cops in Madrid are well-meaning, but perform the way a tone deaf orchestra conductor would: following, not leading the flow. There is often no rhyme or reason for Madrid's traffic tie-ups; you can just about abandon logic such as "traffic going out of the city in the early morning must be lighter."

The truth is that automobile traffic in the city is bad and getting worse, with no real improvement in sight. If *Madrileños* could ever identify any single guilty party, they would probably lynch them.

One daily newspaper devotes a whole section every day to traffic problems, and openly blames the government when over a hundred people die nation-wide in a single holiday weekend.

As for deaths on the highway, Spain comes in fourth worst in Europe, at 6.1 deaths per 10,000 vehicles, after Yugoslavia, Portugal and Greece (source: British Consumers' Association, London.) If you figure the number of kilometers driven instead of the number of vehicles on the road, the results come out much worse, with Spain leading OECD countries by far, with the dubious distinction of 6.6 deaths per 100 million km driven (source: *U.S. News and World Report*).

Compare 2.5 in Italy or 1.6 in the U.S.

While Spanish death rates on the highways are too high by any reckoning, the creeping pace of traffic in Madrid probably saves a number of people from injury every day. By one recent poll, the average speed driven in the city (including sitting in traffic jams and at red lights) is eleven km per hour.

Moral: leave plenty of time whenever you attempt to drive somewhere within the city. When leaving for other destinations in a car, be aware that Madrid is Europe's only capital not to be connected by highway to any other large city. You can check road conditions by calling 742-1213. For long distances, train or plane is best.

Though reckless, Spanish drivers are at least not really hot-headed or hysterical, and they rarely argue acrimoniously over traffic. Fender-benders are a way of life in the city, and you'll often see strangers in a minor accident exchanging addresses and otherwise settling their differences with cool efficiency. *Madrileños* go through phases when in traffic jams: using their horns at first until realizing that the tie-up is like an Old Testament plague, bigger than anything mortals can do to correct; then they settle back for the duration, sometimes even laughing over the absurdity of their situation.

Peculiarities of Driving in Madrid

• When turning you may get a red light half way into your turn, which gives pedestrians the right-of-way. *Madrileños* in groups tend to obey such lights; individuals flout them. You may be honked forward in such a case, but you're breaking the law if you go. A blinking yellow light after a turn gives pedestrians the right-of-way.

• If you get a right-turn blinker from the car in front of you, it may be a rare instance of traffic courtesy, meaning "pass me." This will come up more on country roads than in the city, where truck and bus drivers tend to be much more polite and considerate than their Anglo-Saxon counterparts.

• Lanes are sometimes relative. Spaniards don't like straight lines, and the lines of the street sometimes bring out their anarchistic tendencies. While 90 percent of *Madrileños* actually are very good drivers, it's the ten percent you have to watch out for. Don't ever assume someone will stop for a red light.

• Triangles painted on the

pavement at intersections: they mean "yield right-of-way."

• Remember that in Europe, all other things being equal, the right-of-way is to the car on the right (not to the one coming from the larger stream of traffic).

Speed Limits

• Superhighways: 120 kph.
• Improved highways with hard shoulders: 100 kph.
• Other roads: 90 kph.
• City roads and streets: 60 kph.

Drivers' Licenses

You can drive in Spain with a Spanish driver's license (*carné de conducir*), an international license, or a third country license (U.S., UK) when accompanied by a certified translation. Translations must be renewed annually.

After nine months in Spain, you must have your own Spanish license. You may apply for one at the *Jefatura Provincial de Tráfico*, Arturo Soria, 143. If you do not have another driver's license from another country, you must take a Spanish written and driving test, which can be scheduled only through an accredited driving school (acamemia) at a cost of 80-100,000 pesetas. For simple conversion from another country's license, you need to present:

• The original driver's license.
• An official translation of it, which you can get at the *Real Automovil Club* (José Abascal, 10, Tel: 447-6198.)
• A medical certificate, made out at one of the official centers, showing your fitness to drive.
• A copy of your passport and residence permit.
• Three passport-size photos.

A *gestor* can help you with all of this.

As for purchasing a car, remember cars—both new and used—are very costly, on top of which a 30% excise tax is added.

Insurance

All drivers must purchase insurance, covering bodily injury costs of two million pesetas per person to a maximum of ten persons. The insurance company issuing the policy must be registered in the Spanish Special Registry of Insurance. You must carry the certificate as proof of being insured, should the Spanish police ask to see it in case of an accident. A basic liability policy not covering property will cost about 26,000 pesetas a year; for 100,000, you can get a policy covering property as well, without limits.

In an accident involving a death, sometimes the Spanish police will emprison the driver at fault. You can add a bail bond *(defensa civil)* clause to your policy to avoid this.

Accidents

Report to your insurance company by telephone or telegraph. Make a written report of any losses. If anyone was injured, you must report the accident to the Spanish police *(or Guardia Civil).* An injured person must be taken to the nearest hospital by anyone who even *passes* the scene of the accident. If the injured cannot be moved, you must stop passing cars and ask that they send for help, while you administer first aid. It's the law.

If you strike or are struck by another vehicle, get the following information: name, address, phone number, occupation, vehicle registration number, insurance company and policy number. You must get the other person's identification especially if he or she is not the owner of the car. You'll also have to show the same information about yourself.

R.A.C.E.

For about 5,000 pesetas a year, you can sign on with the *Real Automovil Club de España,* the equivalent of the American Automobile Association. Membership entitles you to a tow truck and repairs if you should have a breakdown. Headquarters are at General Sanjurjo 10, Madrid. R.A.C.E. can also give you information about reciprocal agreements with AAA, addresses of official centers in Madrid for getting your medical certificate for the Spanish license, driving schools, etc. The general office is at José Abascal, 10, Tel: 447-3200.

Pedestrians

Drivers show no quarter, so don't assume they'll stop for you. Pedestrian traffic lights are at times thus:

• Green: Walk and live.
• Blinking green: *Don't* start crossing. If you're caught in the middle of the street, run for all you're worth and you might make it to the other side.
• Red: If you leave the sidewalk, you're mad.

Bicyclists

Are you crazy?!

Motorcyclists

Get a helmet, get a muffler. Don't be like the others. If Madrid is officially the noisiest city in Europe, you don't want it to be *your* fault. *Madrileños* seldom protest the noise of the their city's motorcycles, but their unspoken rage will boil over one day.

All motorbikes must be registered with the *Jefatura Provincial de Tráfico*. If your vehicle is over 50 cc., you will need an application form, the manufacturer's certificate, industry certificate, appraisers certificate, and city hall registration. The *Jefatura* will collect a fee unless your bike is under 50 cc.

Parking

Look at any street of parked cars in Madrid, and you'll see a combination of despair and comical unconcern. On many streets, double parking is not even considered a real offense: *triple* parking, yes. The unwritten rule is the same as in New York City: double parking is socially permissible (not legally) as long as you can see and hear the street near where you've parked. When the car you've trapped begins honking, you have three minutes to appear and remove your car, or else you deserve to be punched out, and probably will be. Conversely, if you're the trapped one, it's not considered rude to wake up the neighborhood with

your own honking. In situations like the parking in Madrid, laws don't work, so social rules of comportment take over. The thing almost even works, as a result.

Remember when looking for a parking space: what once would have looked to you like a street with no spaces, will change with practice into a street ripe with possibilities, as soon as you modify your definition of what a parking space *is*.

Some sections of the city have parking for local residents only, subtly marked with discreet black bands you might not see at first, wrapped around telephone and electricity poles. If you are a resident of the zone in question, you must buy a parking card to prove it, displaying it in the windshield. You can buy one at the *Ayuntamiento de Madrid*, Alberto Aguilera, 20, Tel: 447-1709. If you aren't a resident, you can still park in the zone for an hour and a half.

If you park illegally and are towed away, your car will be at the *garage de Ayuntamiento*. If you find yourself with a Denver Boot *(cepo)*, call 092.

Conversely, if someone has parked so you can't exit, and if that person violates the rule of being within earshot, you can call for the tow truck (*grúa*) of the city police at 449-6161. With the amount of petty pilferage and double parking in Madrid, you're well advised to get a reserved parking spot at your residence, if at all possible.

In some areas parking is by a timed ticket left inside the windshield. You can buy one at the nearest kiosk or tobacco shop to the parking area.

Car Rentals

Most are open 8:00 a.m. to 7:00 p.m., 1:00 p.m. Sundays. Rates generally vary very little.
• Avis
Gran Vía, 60
Tel: 247-2048/248-4204
Hotel Luz Palacio, Tel: 441-0579
Airport
Tel: 205-4273
• Hertz
Gran Vía, 88
Tel: 242-1000

• Europcar
Orense, 29
Tel: 445-9930
• América
Cartagena, 23
Tel: 246-7919
• Atlas
Garcia Paredes, 12
Tel: 449-7580
• Budget
Estebanez Calderon, 5
Tel: 571-6660
Airport
Tel: 279-3400

24-hour Gas Stations
• Esmo S.A.
María de Molina, 21
Tel: 261-3631
• Campsa
Glorieta Puerta de Hierro
Tel: 216-2332
• Campja
Paseo de la Habana, 168
Tel: 259-0671

Lexicon

atasco: traffic jam
avería: breakdown
casco: helmet
ceda el paso: yield
cruce: intersection
dirección única: one way
gasolinera: gas station
hora punta: rush hour

límite de velocidad: speed limit
las marchas: gears
paso de peatones: pedestrian area
peaje: toll
peligro: danger
taller: repair garage; workshop
vado: no parking
zona azul: restricted zone

The Spanish System

Spanish education is divided into four phases: pre-school, primary, secondary and university. Primary education (E.G.B. — General Basic Education) extends from age six to fourteen. Secondary school (B.U.P.) includes university preparation (three years) or technical school training. There also exists a *Curso de Orientación Universitaria*, of one year. Universities grant three types of diplomas: a three-year program diploma, five-year diploma and doctorate. In Spain there are 30 state universities (including the Open University, UNED), and four private ones. More private universities are expected in the coming years.

Approximate figures of attendance

Pre-school	1,200,000
Elementary	5,700,000
Secondary	1,350,000
University	800,000
Vocational	850,000
Special Education	98,000
Adult Education	150,000

For general information on all matters related to education, address your questions to the Information Service of the Ministry of Education, Alcalá 34, 28014 Madrid. Tel: 521-2810.

Enrolling Your Child

You will have to choose whether you want your child in a Spanish, international or American/British school. There is no right decision to this dilemma, though in general the longer you foresee your stay in Spain, the more arguments there are for enrolling your child in a Spanish school. Should you decide to do so, you need to know the following about equivalencies:

(Note: These are generalizations, not fast rules. The more prepared a student is, the quicker he/she will advance through the system.)

• Spanish pupils in pre-school learn the rudiments of reading and writing, thus first grade continues, rather than starts, the educational cycle.

• Generally, the younger the pupil, the less dislocation within the system. The older he or she is, the more likely he/she will be set back a year or so to compensate for the difference in academic background and language.

• To enter a Spanish high school, the American-educated student generally must have had two years of U.S. high school training as a prerequisite.

• To enter a Spanish university, two years of U.S. university are required as a prerequisite.

• Spanish university education leads to the *licenciatura* within five years, about the equivalent of the American M.A.

English Language-oriented Schools in Madrid
(N=nursery, K=kindergarten, 13=first year of U.S. college)

School	Grades	Comments
The American School of Madrid Carretera de Humera km 2, Aravaca Tel: 357-2154	N-12	U.S. curriculum
British Council School Martínez Campos, 31 Tel: 308-3018	K-13	English & Spanish education for Spaniards
British Institute Almagro, 5 Tel: 319-1250	—	British
King's College Paseo de los Andes Soto de Viñuelas El Goloso Tel: 803-4800	K-13	British
Numont P.N.E.U. School Parma, 16 Tel: 200-2431	N-5	British
Runnymede College Arga, 9 (El Viso) Tel: 457-2327	6-13	British
St. Anne's School Tormes, 5 (El Viso) Tel: 259-1399	N-12	British and Spanish

School	Grades	Comments
Hastings School P. de la Habana, 204 Tel: 259-0621	N-6	British and Spanish
Kensington School Avda. de Bularas Pozuelo de Alarcón Tel: 715-4699	N-12	Spanish (bilingual)
Intern. Primary School Rosa Jardón, 3 Tel: 259-2121	N-6	British and Spanish
English Montessori School Eduardo Vela, 10 Aravaca, Madrid Tel: 357-2126	N-8	British and Spanish
International School Aravaca Avda. de la Salle Aravaca, Madrid Tel: 270-5106	N-13	Offers International Baccalaureat Diploma
L.A.E. (Liceo Anglo-Español) Serrano, 173 Tel: 563-9360	N-14	Anglo-Spanish high school
Saint Louis University Bravo Murillo, 38 Tel: 593-3723	—	Teaching School

Spanish Schools

Entrance in a Spanish school is not easy and requires interviews and, in some cases, exams. A partial list here indicates Spanish schools where English-speaking students have registered:

• Colegio Alemán de Madrid
Av. de Concha Espina, 32
Tel: 563-8177
• Colegio Alameda de Osuna
P.A. Osuna
Tel: 742-7246

• Colegio Estudio
Darío Aparicio 7 Aravaca
Tel: 307-0626
• Santa María de los Rosales
Ctra de Castilla, km 5,7
Tel: 307-0440

The *Lycée Français* is hard to get into but has taken English-speaking students on occasion: *Lycée Français*. Avda de los Madroños, Parque del Conde de Orgaz. Tel: 200-0940.

The Law

You can get a good background and reference to the Spanish legal system from David Searl's You and the Law in Spain, published by Lookout Publications, Fuengirola, Málaga. There you'll find a full guide, in English, to opening bank accounts, buying property, complying with tax laws, etc.

For the majority of visitors and residents who will never enter into the esoterica of local law, a few basics will suffice.

The maze of Spanish law can be impenetrable to the innocent foreigner. To deal with this known fact, the system provides the gestor, a Spanish agent who knows the procedures necessary for notarization of drivers' licences, tax returns, residence papers, etc., and can do the paperwork for you. Look in the Yellow Pages under Gestores Administrativos for the one nearest you.

The many changes in legislation following the death of

Franco appear in the Boletín Oficial del Estado, which is kept on hand by any gestor.

Notaries *(notarios)* play a more important role in the Spanish legal system than they do in the Anglo-Saxon, often stepping in for the making or probating of wills, sale of property, etc. Though you may need a lawyer for the preparation of a legal document, the notario will often be the one to do the official writing and filing. To make a will, for example *(Ultima voluntad),* the recommended path is to go to a lawyer first, who will then draft the document according to your wishes, then hand it on to a notary for signing and registration.

Arrests and Detentions

If you are arrested for some reason, you have the right to consult the Consular Officer of your Embassy. As in the U.S.

and UK, it is best not to make any written or oral statement until you have talked with your Consular Officer.

If you are detained, you will probably need a lawyer *(abogado)* and perhaps a procurador. The procurador serves as intermediary between the client, lawyer and judge *(juez)*. The lawyer will normally recommend the name of a procurador in civil cases involving more than 10,000 pesetas (as required by law), or in criminal cases.

A Note on Crime

Statistically, the greatest incidences of pickpocketing in Madrid occur in front of the Prado Museum, and at the Plaza Mayor (there the thieves know tourists are carrying cash). In Madrid, while pickpocketing and pilferage are on the rise and cars parked on the street overnight are fair game for mirror and radio collectors, violent crime is still a rarity. The Spanish roads are far more dangerous than criminals, in terms of dealing out injury.

Beware of the car rentals at Barajas: an average of one tourist a day is victimized by racketeers who follow rental cars from the airport, manage discreetly to puncture the tires, then offer to help and end up removing everything from the trunk and driving off. Should your car develop a flat tire, whatever you do, don't open your trunk to a well-intentioned stranger!

If you need to call the police while a crime is being committed, call 091 (yes, incredibly, you do need to put in 15 pesetas). If you want to report matters such as a theft at your home, a missing person, a crime you've witnessed, or a lost document, go in person to the nearest police station *(Comisaría)* and make a denuncia. Neighborhood comisarías and their phone numbers follow:
• Arganzuela
Tel: 227-1958
• Barajas
Tel: 205-5247
• Buenavista
Tel: 401-7013
• Carabanchel
Tel: 461-8933
• Centro
Tel: 521-0411
• Chamartín
Tel: 415-9612
• Chamberí
Tel: 419-8807
• Entrevías
Tel: 785-9014
• Estación de Atocha
Tel: 227-4627

- Estación de Chamartín
Tel: 315-9116
- Estación del Norte
Tel: 247-9335
- Estrella
Tel: 772-2971
- Fuencarral-Pilar
Tel: 730-2601
- La Latina
Tel: 247-9116
- Los Cármenes
Tel: 711-0015
- Mediodía
Tel: 227-0302
- Pozuelo
Tel: 715-4763
- Retiro
Tel: 429-0994
- San Blas
Tel: 206-5840
- Tetuán
Tel: 315-5406
- Universidad
Tel: 247-1529
- Usera
Tel: 217-2945
- Vallecas
Tel: 477-5496
- Ventas
Tel: 403-7162

Other Phone Numbers
- Municipal Police
Tel: 092 or 588-5000
- Municipal tow truck
Tel: 457-0666
- Guardia Civil
Tel: 233-1100

- Guardia Civil/Traffic
Tel: 457-7700

In rural areas the Guardia Civil polices roads, borders, bridges and coasts. The Guardia Civil also steps in for cases of road accidents.

Terrorism
While the terrorist threat has tended to be high in Spain, for better or worse incidents have been skillfully targeted and so far has scrupulously avoided tourists and foreigners. The victims are almost exclusively local constabulary (militia, army and police), done in by ETA and other separatist groups in the northern section of the country. While other groups may always be planning mischief stemming from tensions in the Middle East, the main perpetrator so far – the ETA – has been as intent on not harming foreigners (from whom they seek a good press) as they have been on causing disruption among the police.

During the 1991 Iraq-versus-World War, the Iraqi Ambassador to Madrid exhorted resident Arabs in Spain to spare the country of anti-Western terrorism – on the grounds that Spain was a friendly country to the Arab world. When seen in the light of eight centuries of continuous warfare and an Expulsion, this might seem a challenge to explain; and on the other hand, the proximity to North Africa, the Moorish cultural vestiges, and the racial mixture of the people may have something to do with it – as well as considerable Spanish financial contributions to the PLO and big Arab investments in most sectors of the Spanish economy.

Spanish Government Offices

Administracion Publica: Paseo de la Castellana, 3.	Tel:586-1000
Agricultura y Pesca: Paseo de la Infanta Isabel, 1.	Tel: 347-5000
Asuntos Exteriores: Plaza de la Provincia, 1.	Tel: 266-4800
Cultura: Pl. Rey, 3.	Tel: 532-5089
Defensa: Paseo de la Castellana, 109.	Tel: 555-5000
Economia y Hacienda: Alcala, 7-9.	Tel: 568-2000
Educacion y Ciencia: Alcala, 34-36.	Tel: 521-4806
Industria y Energia: Castellana, 160.	Tel: 458-8010
Interior: Amador de los Rios, 7.	Tel: 319-3900
Justicia: San Bernardo, 45-47.	Tel: 390-2000
Obras Publicas y Urbanismo: Castellana, 67.	Tel: 253-1600
Presidencia del Gobierno: Palacio de la Moncloa.	Tel: 244-0200
Trabajo y Seguridad Social: Bethencourt, 11.	Tel: 254-3400
Transportes/Turismo/Comunicaciones: S. Juan de la Cruz, 3.	Tel: 535-1375
Universidades e Investigacion: Serrano, 150.	Tel: 411-6047
Banco de Espana: Alcala, 50.	Tel: 446-9055
Jefatura Superior de Policia: Puerta del Sol.	Tel: 521-6516
Junta de Energia Nuclear: Avenida Complutense, 22.	Tel: 244-1200

Plaza Mayor Madrid
21-9-88

H

ERE is an orientation to academic, cultural and social life in the Spanish capital.

Studying in Madrid

When you have completed your secondary studies and want to enroll directly in a Spanish university, you must take an entrance examination offered in June and September of each year. Theoretically, students coming from countries with which Spain has signed a treaty of cultural exchange are entitled to five percent of the places available. Going on an organized exchange program facilitates the above.

If you are intending to enroll in the Complutense University, you should know that it is the second largest in the world (after Mexico City) and is not of uniform quality in all faculties and courses.

In addition to the various U.S. universities which hold their own courses in Madrid, consider also the possibility of a Fulbright post graduate scholarship, as Spain's is the largest Fulbright program in the world. For information for students, write to:

Institute of Int. Education
809 United Nations Plaza
New York, NY 10017
Tel: (212) 883-8200
For university teaching and advanced research abroad:
Council for International Exchange of Scholars
3400 International Drive NW
Washington, DC 20008
Tel: (202) 686-4000

North American University Programs in Spain
• Academic Year Abroad
Universidad Complutense
Facultad de Filosofía y Letras, Edif. A
28040 Madrid
Tel: 549-6089
(U.S. Contact: Dr. Degginger, AYA, 17 Rd. New Paltz, NY 12561.)

• American University Semester in Madrid
Camara de Comercio
Casa de Formación
Serrano, 208
Madrid
Tel: 431-9100
(U.S. Contact: Dr. Ismael, Study Abroad Program, Tenley Campus, American Univ., Washington, D.C. 20016)
Tel: (202) 895-4900.)

• Center for International Studies
Zurbano, 12
28010 Madrid
Tel: 319-0148
Director: Thomas Haigh
(U.S Contacts: In collaboration with College of William and Mary, Duke Univ. and Suffolk Univ. (Boston). Contact each for specific details.)

• Florida International University
Center for Inter. Studies
Juan de Mena, 10
28 Madrid
Tel: 231-7400

• Lake Forest College
Miguel Angel, 8
28010 Madrid
Tel: 308-2569
Director: Carmen B. Torralbo
(U.S. Contact: Dept. Foreign Language, Lake Forest, IL 60626. Tel: (708) 234-3100.)

• Marquette University
Facultad de Filosofía y Letras, Edif. A
Universidad Complutense
28040 Madrid
Tel: 549-6024
(U.S. Contact: Madrid Study Center, Dept. Foreign Languages, Marquette University, Milwaukee, WI 53233.)

• Middlebury College Program in Spain
Instituto Internacional
Miguel Angel, 8
28010 Madrid
Tel: 319-8188
(U.S. Contact: U.S. Spanish School, Middlebury College, Middlebury, VT 05753.)

• New York University
Instituto Internacional
Miguel Angel, 8
28010 Madrid
Tel: 308-2568
(U.S. Contact: Prof. Salvador Martinez, 19 University Place, Rm. 412, New York, NY 10003.)

• Schiller College
Rodriguez San Pedro, 10
28 Madrid
Tel: 466-2349

• St. Louis University
La Viña, 3
28 Madrid
Tel: 233-2032

• State University of New York—Albany-Buffalo
Instituto Internacional
Miguel Angel, 8
28010 Madrid
Tel: 308-1677
(U.S. Contact: Ms. Hannelore Passona, International Programs, UBL, 36, SUNY at Albany, 1400 Washington Ave. Albany, NY 12222.)

• Stetson University Study Abroad
Facultad de Filosofía y Letras
Universidad Complutense
28040 Madrid
(U.S. Contact: Dr. Elsie Minter, Dir., Office of International Programs, Box 8412 Stetson Station, DeLand, FL 32720.)

• Syracuse University in Spain
Instituto Internacional
Miguel Angel, 8
28010 Madrid
Tel: 319-9942
Director: W. Flint Smith
(U.S. Contact: DIPA, Syracuse Univ., Syracuse, NY 13210.)

Student Card

Any student from the age of 15 qualifies for an International Student Card, entitling the bearer to special rates in theaters, museums, buses, trains, and on special charter flights. Bring a photo and documents proving student status to:
Oficina de Viajes
Dirección General de la Juventud
Fernando el Católico, 77
Tel: 544-2290
or
José Ortega y Gasset, 71
Tel: 401-9500

Studying Spanish

There are a multitude of institutes and private schools that offer Spanish language instruction. Many offer courses, in addition, in Spanish history and culture. Some but not all of the institutes in Madrid are:

• ACHNA (Asociación Cultural Hispano-Norteamericana)
San Bernardo 107
28015 Madrid
Tel: 447-1900

• Berlitz
Gran Via, 80
Tel: 541-6104

• Centro Cultural Hispano Europeo
Dr. Castala, 32
28009 Madrid
Tel: 574-3713

• ALCE (Aula de Lengua y Cultura Española)
Bolivia 38 1.D
28016 Madrid
Tel: 250-9859

• Residencia EASO
Gran Vía, 64 - 7,8
28013 Madrid
Tel: 542-3183
(Summer courses)

• Facultad de Filosofía y Letras, Edificio A
Universidad Complutense
Ciudad Universitaria
28040 Madrid
Tel: 549-6500

• Dirección General de Relaciones Culturales
Dirección de Intercambios y Becas
Ministerio de Asuntos Exteriores
José Abascal, 41
28003 Madrid

• Estudio Internacional Sampere
Castelló, 50
28001 Madrid
Tel: 275-40-25

• Centro de Idiomas
Sagasta 27 - 3. Izq.
28004 Madrid
Tel: 446-6979

• ELS International
Cuatro Amigos, 1 y 3
28029 Madrid
Tel: 314-7430

For general information contact:
• Instituto de Cooperación Ibero-americana
Sección de América del Norte
Av. de los Reyes Católicos, 4
Madrid
Tel: 583-8100, ext. 236 and 237

For further information in the U.S. (lists of institutes in whatever city you're interested in) write to:
• Spanish Education Office
150 Fifth Ave., Suite 600
New York, NY 10011
Tel: (212) 741-5144

You can also call Berlitz for a package deal including lodging with a family:
• Berlitz Study Abroad Division
293 Wall Street
Princeton, NJ 08540
Tel: (800) 257-9449
    (609) 497-9938

To study Spanish on your own at home, at work, or while travelling, the Paris-based language method publisher, Assimil, has an excellent book and cassette program designed for English speakers called *Spanish with ease*. Available in European bookshops or the US from: A-L Books (45 Newbury Street, Suite 305 , Boston, MA 02116, Tel: (617) 536-0060). Price: $11.95 for the book, $59.95 for the cassettes).

Libraries in Madrid

• Biblioteca Pública Municipal
Torrelaguna, 33
Tel: 881-8351
Open Mon.-Fri. 3:20-9:00 p.m.

• Biblioteca Pública Municipal Estaban Azaña
Plaza Juan XXIII, entrance Garcilaso de la Vega
Tel: 881-8346
Open 3:20-9:00 p.m.

• Biblioteca Iberoamericana
Casa de la Entrevista
San Juan
Tel: 888-0175
Open Mon.-Fri. 4:00-8:00 p.m.

• Centro Municipal
de Documentación
Zuloaga, 1.
Tel: 881-7049
Open Mon.-Fri. 4:00-9:00 p.m.

Clubs and Organizations

Madrid has a number of clubs for English speakers. Below follows a list of the ones which have advertised, at one time or another, in *Guidepost*:
American Club of Madrid
Gran Via, 86
Edificio España, Grupo 5, Planta 9.
Tel: 247-7802
Founded in 1952, non-political, non-profit organization that is focal point for American business-men, professionals, diplomats, and their Spanish friends. Monthly meetings featuring top person-alities. Seminars, social events, etc.

American Women's Club
Plaza del Ecuador, 6
Tel: 259-1082, 458-7840
Clubhouse open Mon-Fri. 10 a.m.-6 p.m. and until 9 p.m. on Mon. Lunch available. City and historical tours, thrift shop, library, bridge, etc. New members always welcome.

American Legion Post 292
Apartado 50, 533
28080 Madrid
Tel: 763-7663
Meets on the third Thurs. of the month at the Hotel Aitana on the Castellana. The first and only

American Legion Post in Spain, it is always interested in having U.S. War Vets join.

American Organization of Opera & Classical Music
Apartado 14615
Tel: 241-5576
Call if you are interested in attending concerts at the Teatro Real.

British Hispanic Cultural Foundation
Paseo de los Andes s/n
Soto de Vinuelas, El Goloso
28790 Madrid
Tel: 403-3410
Founded in 1980, the Foundation is associated with King's College. The main objectives are promotion of British Hispanic cultural relations and exchanges, and the award of scholarships for studies.

Democrats Abroad
Apartado 47067
28033 Madrid
Open to U.S. citizens of voting age residing in Spain who subscribe to the principles of the Democratic Party of the U.S.

Fundacion Ponce de León
Lagasca, 16
28001 Madrid
Tel: 435-6500
Spanish classes. Lecture series on Art History.

International Newcomer's Club of Madrid
Tel: 207-7213
Welcomes all English speaking women. Where newcomers and old timers meet to join in activities of mutual interest. Neighborhood coffees, knitting, Crochet, Spanish and French lessons and review of community events. Meetings second Fri. of each month.

Madrid Players
Tel: 410-6810
English speaking amateur theater group. New members welcome.

Network
Tel: 650-0256 / 216-1482
Non-profit organization, mutual support group for career or professional women.

St. George's Guild
Nuñez de Balboa, 43
28001 Madrid
International and interdenominational group which meets on the first Tues. morning of each month from Oct. to June for coffee and talk.

Ten years ago, no one could have imagined the expansion that's taken place in the Madrid gallery scene. Madrid has zoomed forward in this area and is now a world center. Local artists sell on the world market, and local galleries and museums enjoy unsurpassed prestige. The beginning of this movement can be dated at about the time Picasso's *Guernica* was returned to Spain (1981).

For students and undiscovered practitioners, the *Círculo de Bellas Artes* functions as a school, meeting center and prestigious gallery. Modeling sessions include the male and female figure. Frequent lectures, courses and exhibitions. Marqués de Casa Riera, 2. 28014 Madrid. Tel: 531-7700; fax 531-0552. Box office tel: 521-1834.

Exhibitions, lectures and other events take place at the Fundación Juan March, though without the didactic intent of the *Círculo de Bellas Artes*. Castelló, 77. Tel: 431-0382.

An important commercial exchange for paintings and sculpture is ARCO (*Arte Contemporáneo*), organized every February by IFEMA (*Institución Ferial de Madrid*). Casa de Campo. Tel: 470-1014. ARCO attracts artists from all over the world in February and commands good prices for the pieces sold.

The main exhibition halls for contemporary art include:

• Centro de Arte Reina Sofía. Santa Isabel, 52
• Centro Cultural Conde Duque. Conde Duque, 11
• Centro Cultural de la Villa. Plaza del Descubrimiento
• Museo de Arte Contemporáneo. Avenida Juan de Herrera, 2
• Sala de Exposiciones Canal Isabel II. Santa Engracia, 125

Galleries

Of the hundreds of galleries of contemporary art, here are some of the better known ones:
• Aele
Claudio Coello, 28
• Ansorena
Alcalá, 54
• Arte-Madrid
Independencia, 2
• Biosca
Génova, 11
• Celini
Bárbara de Braganza, 35
• Columela
Lagasca, 3
• Durán Exposiciones
Serrano, 30
• Jorge Kreisler
Prim, 13
• Juan Gris
Villanueva, 22

• Juana de Aizpuru
Barquillo, 44
• Juana Mordó
Villanueva, 7
• Moriarty
Almirante, 5
• Sotomayor
Espalter, 8-10
• Theo
Marqués de la Ensenada, 2
• Zenhid
Marqués de Urquijo, 18

Teatros Bellas Artes Madrid

The following cultural centers host numerous cultural events and exhibitions. Ask to be added to their mailing lists so as to be informed regularly of such events. Artists, musicians and writers moving to Madrid or planning to visit Madrid might wish to contact these centers to inquire about the possibilities of scheduling exhibitions, readings, or concerts.

• Washington Irving Center (U.S.)
Marqués de Villamagna, 8
Tel: 435-7095/435-6922
• British Council
Almagro, 5
Tel: 319-1250
• Institute Français
Marqués de la Ensenada, 12
Tel: 319-6401
• Canadian Embassy
Nuñez de Balboa, 35
Tel: 431-4300
• Australian Embassy
Paseo de la Castellana, 143
Tel: 571-4299
• German Institute
Zurbaran, 21
Tel: 319-3235
• Italian Cultural Institute
Plaza Mayor, 86
Tel: 247-5205

Madrid is one of the richest museum cities in the world. Many tomes have been written about the relative merits of each of the many visits; we offer here only a profile of the major ones, with our recommendation of the top five — Prado, Palacio Real, Galdiano, Army (*Ejército*), Railway.

Madrid's Museums

• Army Museum
Mendez Nuñez, 1
Tel: 251-4264
10 a.m.-2 p.m. Closed Mon.
Highlight: Cervantes' pen and sword.

• Bull Fight Museum
Alcala, 237
Tel: 255-1857
10:30 a.m.-1 p.m., 3:30-6 p.m.
Closed Sat. & Sun.

• Cason del Buen Retiro
(Extension of Prado Museum)
Felipe IV, 13
Tel: 468-0481
9 a.m.-7 p.m. Tues-Fri., Sun. closes at 2 p.m.
Highlights: Picasso's Guernica, works by Juan Gris.

• Contemporary Art Museum
Avn. Juan Herrera, 2
Tel: 449-7150
10 a.m.-6 p.m., Sun. closes at 2 p.m. Closed Mon.

• Goya Pantheon Museum
Glorieta del Paseo San Antonio
de la Florida
Tel: 247-7921
11 a.m.-1:30 p.m., 3-5 p.m.
Closed Wed. & Sun. afternoons.
Highlights: Frescos by Goya and
tomb of artist.

• Lazaro Galdiano Museum
Serrano, 122
Tel: 261-6084
10 a.m.-2 p.m. Closed Mon. &
holidays
Highlights: Important European
paintings, decorative arts.

• Palacio Real
Bailen 8
Tel: 248-7404
9:30 a.m.-1:45 p.m.,3:30-5:15
p.m., Sun. till 1:30 p.m.
Highlights: Official rooms of
the palace.

• Prado
Paseo del Prado
Tel: 468-0950
9 a.m.-7 p.m., Sun. closes at
2 p.m. Closed Mon.
Free with student ID
Highlights: Spanish, Italian,
Flemish, Dutch, French, Ger-
man, English paintings.
Note: The best guide to the
Prado is *Guide to the Prado*
(Silex, Madrid) available from
A-L Books, 45 Newbury St.,
Suite 305, Boston, MA 02116
USA for $14.95.

• Railway Museum
Paseo de las Delicias, 61
Tel: 227-3121
10 a.m.- 5:30 p.m., Tues.-Sat.
Sun. closes at 2 p.m. Closed
Mon.

Excursions

You may or not care for long car drives. Happily, in order to get to lovely rural areas and towns outside of Madrid, you can reach a half dozen within less than two hours of driving. You can return to Madrid wonderfully refreshed after a day or two in the hills of Navacerrada to the north, or the spritely fountains and unkempt charm of Aranjuez to the south. We offer below a selection only of our favorite excursions; for the complete story, we refer you to Fodor's or Frommer's, both of which are exhaustive.

Beginning with the city itself, city bus tours are run by three operators:
• Pullmantur, Plaza de Oriente, 8 (Tel: 241-1807)

• Trapsatur, San Bernardo, 23 (Tel: 266-9900)
• Juliá Tours, Gran Vía, 68 (Tel: 270-4600)

The three are nearly identical. You can join them at their own points of origin, or show up at American Express (Plaza de las Cortes, Tel: 429-5775) a half hour before. American Express will sell you the ticket for the same price and get you to the bus on time for departure. Bus tours go on half-day and full-day excursions of Madrid itself, as well as Toledo, Aranjuez, El Escorial, Valley of the Fallen, Avila, Segovia and La Granja. These are all magnificent visits; if you're working or studying in Madrid and have visiting friends or family members, it's perfectly honorable to put even your favorite person on one of these buses while you're at work or class, thus sparing yourself a trip you've taken already a dozen times.

Walking Tours

For Spanish speakers only. For information, contact the Municipal Tourist Office, Plaza Mayor, 3, or the Tourist Office, Señores de Luzón, 10 (Tel: 248-7426). Open mornings only.

RENFE and Bus

The Spanish national rail system offers weekend package tours to places as near as Aranjuez, or as far as Cuenca and beyond. For a round trip on the same day, prices vary around 1500 pesetas; for two days with hotel included, a little over 10,000 pesetas. For details, call RENFE, 228-3835 or 227-7058. Inter-city buses service some of the destinations below from the Estación del Norte. For information, call 248-4891.

By Car

Avoid Friday afternoons, and if you're going for the weekend, try to return to Madrid by mid to late afternoon Sunday to beat the maddening traffic. *Puentes* (holiday weekends) are dicey, and if you can possibly go counter to the traffic flow, you'll be better off.

Madrid is the only European capital not connected to any other major city by highway (see *Driving*). This is *not* a reason to avoid the delightful central Spain countryside, but it is a reason for caution when on the road and any attempt you can make to go against the flow wherever possible. A major highway, however, will soon link Madrid to Barcelona, making it possible to drive between the two cities in about six hours. Only a couple of links remain to be built. Still, Spain has only 2,200 kms of limited access highway. Compare this with Italy, which has three times more in length of highway, with one half the surface area to cover. In September 1991, the EC scolded Spain for this situation.

Visits Within a Two-hour Drive of Madrid

South

Toledo: Cathedral/city walls/El Greco's studio/sword factory/Hospital de Tavera/two synagogues built by Moors and later transformed into churches. Remember, Toledo was for many centuries politically, socially and religiously more important than Madrid. Today, Toledo seems more like a museum than a living city.

Aranjuez: The other city to the south, less than an hour's drive from Madrid. Royal Palace/Jardín del Príncipe/Casa del Labrador/strawberries and asparagus when in season. Immense, lush gardens and sensuous palaces in one of central Spain's few river valleys. A gem, often overlooked by tourists in a hurry. Pause for a meal or *merienda* at the Rana Verde by the river's edge, and forget the stresses of modern living. Don't bother staying overnight; you're so close to Madrid, and there are no charming hotels here anyway. *Chinchón:* A pleasant little village with a rustic Plaza Mayor and a fine Parador.

Northwest

Avila: Probably Europe's most perfect walled city, and the highest city in Europe's second highest nation. Cathedral (rough-hewn, rugged Gothic-fortress, enormously appealing)/Convent of Saint Theresa/Palace of Los Deanes/Palacio Valderrábanos (now a hotel). Saint Theresa and her friend San Juan de la Cruz were gutsy, lively characters whose spirits reign solidly over this delightful, living city. A beautiful spirituality pervails; don't take our word for it, go and see it for yourself.

San Lorenzo de El Escorial and Valley of the Fallen: Monuments by Spain's most somber dictators — Felipe II and Francisco Franco, respectively. El Escorial, the severe, geometrical religious retreat concocted by Felipe II with its 16 patios, 88 fountains, 1500 doors, 2600 windows and 300 rooms. Apart from the convent, the city attracts *Madrileños* in the summer months because of its slightly higher elevation and cooler temperatures. Many *Madrileños* have summer and weekend houses there. As for the Valley of the Fallen (*Valle de los Caídos*), erected by Franco to honor his own dead in the Civil War of 1936-39, perhaps it's good enough just to know that it's there. Visiting it doesn't gladden the heart in the least.

Segovia and La Granja: Just over the pass through the impressive Navacerrada hills of Segovia province (skiable in winter). Segovia: the Alcázar, scene of some of the filming of *Camelot*/Cathedral, its sun-brightened outer walls/2000-year-old Roman aqueduct. La Granja, seven kilometers away: former summer residence of the Spanish kings/gardens patterned after those of Versailles but much more beautiful, tucked in a mountainside. Notably cooler than the plains below (the Spanish kings may have had their flaws, but they knew how to choose palace sites). La Granja has one hotel only, a cheap one: Hostal Roma (Tel: 47-07-52).

La Barranca: A hotel in the hills with mountain trails to explore, a romantic hideaway. Tel: 856-0000; full and half pension only. An escape from culture and history, should you need one.

North

El Paular: (2 kilometers from Rascafría). Thirteenth-century Carthusian convent (later given to the Order of Saint Benedict); sun-bleached outer walls, a spreading valley with its mantle of green. This place is so beautiful it hurts. The convent is now partly a hotel (Tel: 869-3200). Males can stay with the monks at the monastery for a minimum of three days, reservations necessary (Tel: 869-1425). We tell you about El Paular because you were kind enough to buy this book. But please, please, don't spread the word.

Pedraza de la Sierra: A medieval town in the hills, with an exquisite castle. A favorite of *Madrileños* for weekend meals. Fine antique shops. There are only eleven hotel rooms in this village; we're not going to tell you where.

Riaza: Lovely highlands village with a communal-feeling Plaza Mayor. Sixteenth-century church, Nuestra Señora del Manto. Local restaurants especially for lamb. One hotel, La Trucha, Tel: 911/55.00.61).

Buitrago: A pleasant way-station on the road leading north, with a medieval fortress abutting a reservoir and a lovely Gothic church. Don't bother looking for any decent restaurants or hotels, just stop there on your way to or from the northern destinations.

East

Alcalá de Henares: A sad, tumbledown town east of Madrid — but, anyway, the birthplace of Miguel de Cervantes Saavedra and the site of a striving new university with a strong American Studies department.

Park of the Palau Reial de Pedralbes 13-9-86

Madrid is as sports-mad as any modern city, with an impressive variety of offerings both for the spectator and participant. For those who aim merely to stay in shape with swimming, jogging, etc., there are a number of possibilities, however, none are both cheap and easy, due to the dense population and modest number of parks and open fields in the downtown area.

Jogging

Other guidebooks will tell you that Madrid has the largest proportion of parks to urban area of any European city. While this is legally true, most of the square footage is found in the immense Casa de Campo, the park to the west of the city, beyond easy access for the majority of *Madrileños*. The only park of any size in the center of the city is the Retiro — a wonderful area for jogging, people-watching and taking an *horchata* on a warm summer's evening, but the only open area of any size within the city center.

If, like most *Madrileños*, you don't live near enough to these two parks to get yourself there easily or often, you're relegated either to anteing up and joining a health club to run on a treadmill, or finding a clever city circuit to jog through. The optimal times for the latter are Saturday and Sunday mornings before 10:00 a.m., when the city sleeps in and cars aren't choking the roads.

Jogging in public is perfectly socially acceptable in Madrid despite the paucity of public areas set aside for it. Standard-setters like Jimmy Carter and Madonna have indulged; so can you.

Swimming

A number of public swimming pools accommodate the public on a pay-as-you-go basis, from 500 to 1000 pesetas. The five principal outdoor pools are:

Centro Natación Mundial 86
Juan Esplaniú, 1
Tel: 409-5351
(10:00 a.m. to 8:45 p.m., 400 ptas.)

Complejo Deportivo Somontes
Carretera del Pardo, km. 34
Tel: 216-1034
(9:00 a.m. to 9:00 p.m., 500 ptas.)

Motel Avión
Avenida de Aragón, 345
Tel: 747-2355
(11:00 a.m. to 8:00 p.m., 600 ptas.)

Club Stellar
Arturo Soria, 231
Tel: 259-1632

Piscina Marbella
Vía Lusitana, 13
Tel: 216-9040

Madrid's Best Indoor Pool
Polideportivo Chamartín
Plaza del Perú
Tel: 250-1223
(10:00 a.m. to 8:00 p.m.,
250 ptas.)

Health Clubs
(Gimnasios)

While expensive, the indoor health clubs around the city solve some of the problems of getting a good workout, providing equipment, lockers, steam baths and massage. Most require a hefty membership fee in addition to a monthly charge; others work on a pay-as-you-go basis. Caution: joining and paying does not always guarantee availability of the fitness equipment you're interested in, or even the steam bath. You often need to call and reserve in advance to assure the workout you had in mind. A selected list follows:

Club Financiero Génova
Centro Colón
Marqués de la Ensanada, 14
Tel: 410-4900
11:00 a.m. to 10:00 p.m.
(Squash, mini golf, gym, sauna, massage.)

Squash
José Abascal, 46
Tel: 441-5642
8:00 a.m. to 12:00 midnight
(Squash, gym, sauna, massage, steam bath, jacuzzi.)

Hotel Miguel Angel
Miguel Angel, 29
Tel: 442-0022
(Covered pool, sauna, massage, gym, jacuzzi.)

Hotel Mindanao
San Francisco de Sales, 15
Tel: 449-9500
11:00 a.m. to 8:00 p.m.
(Indoors and outdoors pools, sauna, massage.)

Gimnasio Muvia
Alcalde López Casero, 13
Tel: 404-1061
(Weight room, aerobics, sauna)

Gimnasio Fitness Gym
General Perón, 25
Tel: 555-5150
8:00 a.m. to 10:00 p.m.
(Aerobics, stretching, sauna, dietetic bar)

Gimnasio Euronautilus
Infanta Mercedes, 58
Tel: 279-1191
9:00 a.m. to 11:00 p.m.
(Martial arts, aerobics, nautilus)

Gimnasio Mr. Gym
Comandante Zorita, 48
Tel: 234-5096
8:00 a.m. to 11:00 p.m.
(Kung Fu, karate, aerobics, sauna, sun room, jacuzzi)

Other specialized sports centers
• Skating
Ciudad Deportiva del Real Madrid
Castellana, 259
Tel: 315-0046
(11:00 a.m. to 1:30; 5:00 p.m. to 11:30)

• Golf
Real Club de la Puerta de Hierro
Puerta de Hierro
Tel 216-1745
(Has also tennis)

Golf la Moraleja
Carretera de Burgos, km. 8
Tel: 650-0700

Miniature Golf
Complejo Deportivo Somontes
Carretera de El Pardo, km. 3,5
Tel: 216-9040

• Tennis
Club de Tenis Chamartín
Federico Salmón, 4
Tel: 457-2500

RACE (Real Automovil Club de España)
Carretera de Burgos, km. 25
Tel: 652-2600
(Has also golf, table tennis, swimming)

• Bowling (bolera americana)
AMF Bowling Center
Castellana, 77

• Horseback Riding
Escuela Española de Equitación de Somosaguas
Avenida de la Iglesia
Pozuelo
Tel: 352-1086; 352-1247

Professional Sports Events
The main spectator sports in Madrid are soccer, horse and dog racing. Depending on the season, the followings can be massive, noisy and festive, as in any European city. You can go to a Spanish sports event without fearing violence from the fans, or apocalyptic events such as those experienced in recent years in some of the northern European countries.

The main soccer (*fútbol*) stadiums are Bernabeu on the Paseo de la Castellana, and Vicente Calerón on the Manzanares River.

The horse track, Hipódromo de la Zarzuela, is out of town on the Coruña road to the west.

The greyhound race track, Canódromo, is on Vía Carpetana, 57. There is also car racing at Jarama track near Madrid.

All events are advertised in the daily press and in the weekly supplements offered by most daily newspapers

Leisure Sports

Private federations take it upon themselves to provide information to the general public on fishing, sailing and the like. A partial list follows:
• Sailing
Federación Española de Vela
Juan Vigón, 23
Tel: 533-5305
• Fishing
Spanish Fishing Federation
Navas de Tolosa,3
Tel: 232-8353
• Skiing
Spanish Skiing Federation
Claudio Coello, 32
Tel: 575-0576
• Spanish Winter Sports Fed.
Claudio Coello, 32
Tel: 435-4964

• Golf
Spanish Golf Federation
Capitán Haya, 9
Tel: 555-2682
• Other sports
Consejo Superior de Deportes
Martín Fierro
Tel: 449-7200

The Bullfight (Corrida)

Bullfighting is listed here as a sport, though many consider it art, theater, ballet, what have you. Many find the *corrida* (bullfight) not only difficult to digest, but — worse — boring. A growing number of Spaniards now agree with this. The sport/art nonetheless remains popular.

If you've never been, and you do choose to have a look, read first the excellent, now classic essay in the *Fodor's Guide to Madrid*, quite likely the best on the subject. And get *sombra*, not *sol* seats, shade, not sun.

The two main venues in Madrid are *Las Ventas* (calle Alcala) and *Vista Alegre* in Carabanchel. The season goes from April to October (Sundays and Thursdays), with a peak period during the three weeks of the Feria de San Isidro in May.

Tickets are on sale 10:00 to 3:30 the day of the event, or at the official *taquilla* (ticket office) at Victoria, 9. Other outlets charge a 20% commission.

Spaniards love the cinema and regularly fill over 6000 movie theaters nationally. Spain also has 1300 cinema clubs. Eleven percent of all adults go out to the movies at least once a week. With 140 films to choose from a week on television, many stay home to watch; 3.5 million Spaniards have VCRs, compared to 14 million television sets. The home video market has fallen on desperate times, mainly due to the many pirated copies of films Spaniards make on their own VCRs. Spain captures seven percent of the export market for American cinema, ranking above Italy and Australia.

Spain's best-known film directors internationally are Pedro Almodovar *(Women on the Verge of a Nervous Breakdown* and *Tie Me Up! Tie Me Down!)* and Carlos Saura *(Carmen, Blood Wedding*, and *Ay, Carmela).*

Though the 1980's were creative years for Spanish cinema, the industry lost out commercially to the expansion of television. Only 47 films were produced in 1989, the lowest number in Spain's recent history. As a result, many films were produced in cooperation with television stations, e.g., Carlos Saura's *Ay, Carmela.* Of the fifteen top-selling films in Madrid in 1990, all but three were foreign imports — the majority of those American.

Spain has 40 film festivals a year, many of them regional and specialized. The notable ones are in San Sebastian (late September); Valladolid (late October); Madrid (April; sci-fi); Barcelona (November); and Gijon (July).

Spaniards are slowly getting used to subtitles, but generally prefer their foreign films dubbed. Their dubbing industry is among the best in the world, but there's always a jagged edge to hearing Woody Allen whine in Castellano. Below, a list of movie houses in Madrid which show original version films with subtitles (an excellent way to improve your Spanish is to see an American movie in *v.o.* — original version — and pay attention to the subtitles):

Albatros Príncipe Pío
Cuesta de San Vicente, 16
Tel: 247-8427

Alexandra
San Bernardo, 29
Tel: 542-2912

Alphaville
Martín de los Heros, 14
Tel: 247-8233

Bellas Artes
Marqués de Casa Riera, 2
Tel: 522-5092

Bogart
Cedaceros, 7
Tel: 429-8042

California
Andrés Mellado, 47
Tel: 244-0058

Duplex
General Oraa, 67
Tel: 262-0002

Infantas
Infantas, 21
Tel: 522-5678

Lumière
Princesa, 5
Tel: 542-1172

Renoir
Martín de los Heros, 12
Tel: 248-5760

Rosales
Quintana, 22
Tel: 541-5800

Gambling

Spaniards are enamored with gambling and indulge in it at all levels. At one end of the spectrum, one of the world's most plush casinos has recently been remodeled in Madrid; at the other end are the ubiquitous slot machines in nearly every bar and café in Madrid, where for *cinco duros* (a 25-peseta coin) you can set off the computerized lights and jangling noise of the inexorable machines.

Lotteries are legal and numerous, each of them flourishing on its own. Nearly all *Madrileños* and a majority of Spaniards tend to lead secret lives, devoting much more attention to the various lotteries than they pretend to. A common sight is that of the *Madrileño* going into his billfold for peseta notes and finding it so packed with lottery tickets that it opens up with them like a Japanese underwater flower.

Four principal lotteries dominate national betting. Whether you *plan* to indulge in it or not, you'll probably be swept along at one point or another. At the very least, you'll need to know which is which, or else risk being a marginal *Madrileño* when the "Gordo" pops and all your Spanish associates are talking of nothing else.

• ONCE: The well-endowed

Society for the Blind sells a daily lottery from their own designated kiosks (there are 15,000) and also by the legally blind who are allowed to sell tickets individually in the street. Tickets cost 100 pesetas. The Friday drawing yields the biggest prize of the week, up to 2,500,000 pesetas, plus an extra 100,000,000 peseta prize on special occasions.

• Lotería Nacional: Tickets cost 500 or 1000 pesetas, sold at specially designated kiosks. The *Gordo* (The Big One) costs 2500 pesetas to enter, and is drawn on December 22 for truly astronomical prize money. The *Niño* (The Kid) goes on January 5, with the winner rating front-page news coverage the following day.

• Primitiva: Tickets cost 100 pesetas minimum, with drawings *(sorteos)* Thursdays and Saturdays. A lottery with daily drawings. Tickets are sold at specially licensed *estancos.*

• Bono Loto: The free ticket looks like a Bingo sheet. You choose six numbers in the cross hatching; you can register your bet at specially licensed *estancos;* each bet is valid for four days, with daily drawings. Another major lottery with daily drawings, also at 100 pesetas.

The *Nacional, Primitiva* and *Bono Loto* are State-owned enterprises, whose profits revert to *Hacienda,* the tax ministry.

In addition, there exist the *Quiniela hípica* and *Quieniela deportiva* which depend on horse races and soccer matches. Small street-front concessions marked with signs "1 X 2" sell horse race tickets *(carrera)* and soccer matches *(partidos)* in series of 14.

As a Spaniard of adoption, you may try to remain immune to the lottery madness in the capital, but you probably won't hold out for long.

Other forms of gambling include racing (horse and dog), bingo and the casino. Horse racing is held at the Zarzuela track out the Coruña highway from spring until fall; the greyhound race track is at the Canódromo, Vía Carpetana, 57. Bingo parlors are all over the city (you need an ID to enter). The Casino *Gran Madrid* is in Torrelodones, 28 kilometers out the Coruña highway.

There are so many restaurants and bars in Madrid, you could almost say that each *Madrileño* has his or her own. Soon enough, you'll find the one you prefer for different times of the day, or different seasons. Wherever you end up living, your neighborhood will provide you with your own bar or *tasca*; if it's not to your liking (noisy, smoke-filled, smelly...) you need only look about a block further, before finding something more suitable.

Bars and restaurants — the one blends into the other — each has its own rhythms, extending from breakfast for your *café con leche y un bollo* to the pre-lunch drink where you can *tomar algo* (drink a beer or soft drink) or to the afternoon *tapas*, *pinchos*, *banderillas* and other appetizers, or else to the honest dinner hour which begins sometime around 10:30 for most *Madrileños*. You can start as early as 9:30, however, without fear of being taken for a Martian.

The meal times go as follows:

• Breakfast *(desayuno)* (not a major meal in Spain): 7:00 a.m.to 9:30

• Lunch *(almuerzo)*: 1:30 p.m. to 4:00

• Dinner *(cena):* 9:30 p.m. to midnight

• Snacks *(merienda):* a miscellaneous eating hour preceding dinner (5:30-8:00 p.m.)

Ethnic Foods

To the *Madrileño*, foreign food means dishes from Valencia, Galicia or the Basque country. Indeed, they would reason rightly, with such wide and rich offerings, why search elsewhere? Though there are more international restaurants than ever before in Madrid, the concept is a relatively new one and has never really caught on as in Amsterdam, Paris, London or New York. Most Chinese restaurants are execrable, Italian for the most part tend to be mediocre (except for a few). The few Japanese restaurants are good but prohibitively expensive. The glory of international food in Madrid is the handful of Indian restaurants, some of which are as fine as any, anywhere.

Tipping & Service

As in other western European countries, the service charge is almost always added to the bill (you needn't ask, just assume that it is). In addition a tip *(propina)* is optional. Waiters appreciate even a symbolic amount left in the obligatory little dish on which the bill is presented. In these days of credit cards, leave a little cash on the dish as *propina*, not on the credit card slip. The amount can be a couple of hundred pesetas for the average lunch, or a percentage of five to ten in the better dinner venues.

Coffee

A category of its own. The standard breakfast in a public eating establishment is *café con leche y un bollo* (or *tostada*), which *Madrileños* take on their way to work, standing at the bar. *Café* is always expresso, unless you ask for *café americano* or *café descafeinado*. The waiter will wonder how any human being could stomach such stuff, but will serve it cheerfully without making moral judgments. As far as taking milk in your coffee, *solo* is black expresso coffee; *cortado* is one step up, with a small amount of milk only; *con leche* is a mix of coffee and milk more or less akin to *café au lait*, with the milk heated. Many *Madrileños* take *café con leche* in the morning (it comes in a big cup), *solo* or *cortado* at lunch or dinner. The size of the cup shrinks toward the end of the day, so if you want a large cup in the afternoon or evening, ask for *café con leche de desayuno*.

Beer (Cerveza)

If you want draught beer (very popular in Madrid even as an apéritif), ask for *una caña*. On hot days if you want the refreshment of a beer without the heavy effect you get walking out into the hot street, try *una clara*, a mixture of beer with lemon soda.

Other Beverages

If you've out-coffeed yourself and want an alternative to tea from a tea bag, you can order *infusiones* — herb teas of *poleo* (linden blossom), *menta* (mint), or *manzanilla* (camomille). When ordering a glass of wine, if you want something a little better than the house offering, order *una copa de Rioja*. Most *Madrileños* don't consume soft drinks, but you can find them when you want them. Ordering *chocolate caliente* gets you something other than what you'd expect — a thick mass of melted chocolate in a cup, not really in liquid form. Something a Spaniard would order only in the morning to dip his *churro* into. To get the hot chocolate known in other countries, try ordering a *batido de chocolate caliente*, or a *cacaolat* (a brand name). More realistically, just give up the idea and make your own at home.

Water

Tap water is definitely potable in Madrid, though in the hottest summer months, bottled water may be tastier and even safer. Water never comes automatically in a Madrid restaurant, and the notion of ice cubes is alien (in fact, ice cubes are considered unhealthy, lowering the body temperature at a time when it needs to be higher, for digestion). If you want a carafe of tap water with your meal, order *una jarra de agua*. Bottled mineral water comes with or without gas *(agua con gas, agua sin gas.)* The *agua sin gas* tends to be better in Spain, and it, too, is healthier than *agua con gas*, which has additives to give the artificial bubbles. The term *Vichy* means *agua con gas*.

Non-smokers

Just forget it, you'll never find such a thing as a non-smoking section in a Spanish restaurant. Yes, Spaniards are well aware that they're killing themselves with active and passive smoke, and yes, they're aware that increasing numbers of establishments in the U.S. and elsewhere do not allow smoking. But this is one custom they're not about to imitate. You'll find soon enough which are the places that offend least.

Rating System

Restaurants are classified by the Spanish government from five forks (the highest) to one. Most *cafeterías* and restaurants display their rating on the front door. The official rating reflects the food quality to some extent, but more so the décor, number of dishes in the repertory, and number of languages used in the menu and by the head waiter.

Types of Eating Places

• *Paradores, hosterías* and *refugios:* These are government-run operations in special areas of scenic or touristic interest. They are reliably pleasant, with good quality of standard fare, and generally do not require reservations.

• *Cafeterías* and Bars: Without being full-fledged restaurants, these establishments generally serve a more varied menu than the American equivalent. Usually you're seated and served at table, though many have bars where you can stand and have *tapas* or sandwiches or other light fare. *Cafeterías* with reliable fare are the chains "California," "Nebraska" and "Bob's." There are also large numbers of individual establishments. *Madrileños* use *cafeterías* when they're on their way to the theater or movie house and have a half hour to spare. In addition to *tapas*, *cafeterías* serve *bocadillos* (bread rolls with a slice of ham or cheese); *pulguitas* (small rolls with cold cuts); *mixtos* (grilled bread with ham and cheese) and *pincho de tortilla* (omelettes with as much potato as egg, and usually some onion).

• *Cafés* and *terrazas:* Cafés which serve mainly just drinks and serve as the traditional venue for *tertulia*, or other forms of intellectual ferment, are sadly disappearing from Spain. A few in Madrid have survived with dignity for over a century and deserve special comment. They have served as meeting-places for the *Generación de 98* and the *Generación de 27* and offered the public places where ideas were spawned and transmitted. In some cases, they were the scenes even of the *writing* of literary works. *Gijón*, *el Espejo* and others still go strong, now serving more of a selection of food than before. If you can get a window seat at any of these, you'll be glad to be able to see life walk by in front. You're free to spend as long as you like without re-ordering or vacating. The standard order is coffee, beer or *Cuba Libre* (gin or rum and Coca-Cola).

• *Terrazas*, or sidewalk cafés, function only in the warmer weather. Most *cafeterías*, *cafés* and *heladerías* extend to the sidewalk as soon as the weather permits, usually in late March or April, continuing until October. *Madrileños'* favorite sport is to sit at them in the warmer months, spending hour after hour chatting, eating, meeting friends, or just reading the paper. There seems to be no social division at these wonderful establishments, and children enjoy them with their parents. At the peak of the summer heat (July-August), the *terrazas* give sanctuary to human beings who can't sleep or even stay comfortably in their sweltering apartments. They congregate at their neighborhood *terrazas* until 2:00 or 3:00 a.m. *Madrileños* are exceedingly open not only to their own conversations with their friends, but show friendliness and even curiosity toward the foreigner. The curiosity is usually genuine; you needn't defend yourself against it.

Note: the waiter *(camarero)* at the outdoors café has a special code of conduct you'll want to get used to, so as to keep the experience as relaxed as possible. The *camarero* may seem to ignore you or react slowly; he won't take offense if you call out *rotundamente*. Often he'll forget or mix up your order. You can either make a fuss about this and sidetrack your evening, or you can just take what's given and pay more attention to the conversation you're having, or the people-watching you're engaged in. Even at their worst, *camareros* don't mean to slight you, and they're generally a lot friendlier than they first appear. There are many ways to get their attention; one correct one is to raise your hand and call *camarero* discreetly.

Other Eating Places

• *Bodegas, cantinas:* Originally, wine cellars where people bought bottles or jugs of wine. Currently, they function more like cafés, serving *pinchos* or other food with their drinks. Some restaurants call themselves *bodegas* in reference to their underground location which are decorated to resemble the *bodega* where wine used to be aged in casks.

• *Cervecerías:* Literally, "beer halls." The same sort of establishments as cafés or *tascas*. They serve beer and other drinks, with light food. Some are old and elegant.

• *Marisquerías:* Like the above, specializing in shellfish as their light food. Often you can either stand at the bar or have a seat at one of the few tables. *Marisquerías* also sell shellfish to go.

• *Churrerías:* Serve hot chocolate and *churros* (fritters). Generally open in the late afternoon and early morning, where late-night revelers make one last stop before heading home at 5:00 or 6:00 a.m. for bed.

Note: the quality of rest rooms *(aseos or servicios)* varies greatly from place to place, with the lowest common denominator descending rather low indeed. To avoid unpleasant surprises, you may want to carry tissues or toilet paper with you. Enough said.

Selecting a Restaurant

Spaniards live to eat. Meals are a highly social activity in addition. A dilemma comes with the demographic pressures now weighing on Madrid, in the sense that the traditional bargains — excellent food and service at low prices — are becoming rare. Still, there are numerous wonderful restaurants, and many holes-in-the-wall which produce fantastic variety and quality in a friendly ambiance.

You're better off making a reservation for lunch or dinner in most restaurants, as they fill up completely if they're any good. You can always arrive a half hour early (1:30 for lunch or 9:00 for dinner), but the empty seats may well be reserved and unavailable. Often you'll find that while a restaurant may not have available seats at its first evening sitting (9:30 or so), the later seating at 11:00 or 11:30 will be available. The rush hours are 3:00 for lunch and 10:30 for dinner.

Meals at restaurants consist of a first course *(primer plato)* of soup, stew, vegetables *(pisto or menestra),* followed by a second course *(segundo plato)* of fish or meat, with dessert of fresh fruit, yoghurt, flan, ice cream, etc. Desserts are the least imaginative of the courses. Most restaurants have a *menú* or fixed meal, at 1000 to 1500 pesetas. You can also order à la carte as you would at most Continental restaurants. Restaurant personnel vary in their attitudes about sharing dishes, skipping first courses, etc. Many are highly tolerant and really don't mind if you depart from the rules. Others are less flexible.

Meat & Cooking Degrees

The expressions are *hecho* (medium), *poco hecho* (rare) and *muy hecho* (well done). Spanish restaurants overcook their meat, so if you really want yours rare, insist on it *vuelta y vuelta.*

Paella

In Madrid, this internationally known saffron rice, chicken and/or seafood dish, is considered foreign, as its origin is Valencian. *Madrileños* eat it only at lunchtime, not dinner — often as a *primer plato*, as prelude to meat or fish. Copious.

Vegetarians

There's always something on every menu. If fish is part of your repertory, rejoice, as you're in one of the best fish cities in the world. Spanish cooking calls for little bits of ham in nearly everything, but sometimes you can get the waiter to hold the ham from your artichoke dish or *menestre.* It depends, of course, on how much of the menu is pre-cooked by the chef. There are a few vegetarian restaurants in out-of-the-way places in Madrid, considered looney bins for eccentrics. You don't really need them, with the wide selection in Spanish and ethnic restaurants already available.

Typical Spanish Foods (Source: *The Bear Facts*)

Bacalao a la vizcaina: cod, thyme, red pepper, bayleaf, onion, garlic and fried croutons

Callos a la madrileña: tripe Madrid style

Chipirones: young squid cooked in their own ink *(en su tinta)*

Chorizos: strong tasting, peppery sausages

Cocido: stew made of beef, bacon, blood pudding, *chorizos*, chicken and chick peas

Cochinillo asado: suckling pig

Cordero asado: roast lamb

Flan: caramel custard

Gazpacho: cold, raw vegetable soup, made with garlic, onion, bread, tomatoes, salt, pepper, cucumber, green peppers, oil and vinegar

Jamón serrano: cured prosciutto-like ham

Sangría: punch made with red wine and fruit

Sopa de ajo: soup made with bread and garlic and an egg

Tapas: small snacks, attractively displayed often on the bar or counter, eaten as informal appetizers. May include variety of meat, fish, or seafood, small sandwiches, sausages, wedges of omelettes, olives, marinated vegetables, etc. Consumed with wine, sherry or beer

Tortilla española: omelette made with potatoes and onions

agua mineral: mineral water
ajo: garlic
al horno: baked in oven
azucar: sugar
caja: cash register
caliente: hot
camarera: waitress
camarero: waiter
cenicero: ashtray
con gas (sparkling)
cuchara: spoon
cuchillo: knife
entremeses: appetizers
fruta: fruit

helado: ice cream
hielo: ice
la cuenta: bill, check
mantequilla: butter
pan: bread
pimienta: black pepper
plato: plate
postre: dessert
régimen: diet
sal: salt
servilleta: napkin
sin gas: (without carbonation)
tenedor: fork

Restaurants by Category

We have not intended to gather an exhaustive list here: the tour guide books and weekend leisure supplements do that with great competence. Below we offer only a few restaurant suggestions by category, some we know and are fond of:

Deluxe

Lhardy
Carrera de San Jerónimo, 8
Fine international cuisine in a nineteenth-century décor

Fortuny
Fortuny, 34
Tel: 410-7707
Cuisine based on the freshest offerings of the market

Jockey
Amador de los Ríos, 6
Tel: 419-1003
Spanish

El Bodegón
Pinar, 15
Spanish

Zalacaín
Alvarez de Baena, 4
Tel: 261-1079
Basque. The uncontested best restaurant in Spain

Expensive

El Amparo
Callejón de Puigcerdá, 8
Tel: 431-6465

Balzac
Moreto, 7
Tel: 248-0177
Basque, with one of the most charming décors in Madrid

Casa Botín
Cuchilleros, 17
Tel: 266-4217
As traditional as they come : Madrid's oldest restaurant, in fact. Some nights visited by tunas, *traveling minstrels in Renaissance garb*

Horno de Santa Teresa
Santa Teresa, 12
Tel: 419-1061
Traditional Spanish

José Luis
Rafael Salgado, 11
Tel: 457-5036
International

Príncipe de Viana
Manuel de Falla, 5
Tel: 457-5952
Basque

Sacha
Juan Hurtado de Mendoza, 11
Tel: 457-5932
Catalan-French

Taberna del Alabardero
Felipe V, 6
Tel: 247-2577
Traditional Spanish : part of a chain with representation in Washington, D.C., though much cheaper than the one in Washington

Fine dining (moderate to a-bit-pricey)

Alkalde
Jorge Juan, 10
Tel: 276-3359
Basque

Jai Alai
Balbina Valverde, 2
Tel: 261-2742
International

Brasseri de Lista
Ortega y Gasset, 6
Tel: 435-2818

Casa Ciriaco
Mayor, 84
Tel: 248-0620
Old-time atmosphere

La Dorada
Orense, 64-66
Tel: 270-2000
Andalusian, seafood

La Giralda
Maldonado, 4
Tel: 577-7762
Andalusian

Odeon
Rafael Calvo, 40
Tel: 410-0074
Spanish modern

O'Pazo
Reina Mercedes, 20
Tel: 234-3748
Galician, seafood

Restaurante Paulino
Alonso Cano, 34
Tel: 441-8737
Spanish : good, simple, well-priced

Solchaga
Plaza de Alonso Martínez, 2
Tel: 447-1496
Old-fashioned dining rooms, more like a private house than restaurant

La Trainera
Lagasca, 60
Tel: 576-8035
Seafood

St. James
Juan Bravo, 3
Tel: 221-1638
Spanish, seafood

International

• Russian
El Cosaco
Plaza de la Paja, 2
Tel: 265-3548

Rasputín
Yeseros, 2
Tel: 266-3962

• Indian
Annapurna
Zurbano, 59
Tel: 419-2553

Tagore
Padre Damián, 37
Tel: 250-1641

Baisakhi
Agastio, 75
Tel: 413-1534

Ramayana
Fundadores, 20
Tel: 355-5880

• Italian
Ciao
Apocada, 20
Tel: 447-0036

Spago
Don Ramón de la Cruz, 12
Tel: 276-5427

• Japanese
Don Zoco
Echegaray, 3
Tel: 429-5720

• American
Armstrongs
Jovellanos, 5
Tel: 522-4230

Cactus Charly
Caballero de Gracia, 10
Tel: 532-1976

• Vegetarian
Jugolandia
San Bernardo, 88
Orense, 6

La Biotika
Amor de Dios, 3
Tel: 227-6061

La Galette
Conde de Aranda, 11

El Restaurante Vegetariano
Marqués de Santa Ana, 34
Tel: 532-0927

Cafeterías (chains)
• California
Goya, 47; Gran Vía, 49
Salud, 21

• Manila
Montera, 25; Gran Vía, 47

• Nebraska
Gran Vía, 55 and 32; Alcalá, 18
Mayor, 1

One favorite hole-in-the-wall is a Valencian *(paella)* restaurant, La Panocha. Alonso Heredia, 4. 245-1032.

Tasca — Tapas
The games begin at 8:00 p.m., or thereabouts. *Tasca*-hopping is a sport and art. You're supposed to know what to order, where, when. We leave the exact technique and arcana to the guidebooks which devote themselves to this topic (Frommer's does pretty well). Personally, we're agnostics and improvisers. Nearly any bar or *cervecería* does well with the standard fare. The following places are known for doing a bit better:
• Las Bravas. Alvarez Gato, 3
• Los Motivos. Ventura de la Vega, 10.
• Taberna Toscana. Ventura de la Vega, 22.
• La Trucha. M. Fernández González, 3.
• Casa Labra. Tetuán, 12.
• Casa Sierra. Gravina, 1.
• Cervecería Alemana. Plaza Santa Ana, 6.
• Café Bar Los Galayos. Plaza Mayor, 1.
• Cervecería Santa Bárbara. Plaza de Santa Bárbara, 8.
• El Anciano Rey de los Vinos. Bailén, 19.
• Antonio Sánchez. Mesón de Paredes, 13.

Wines

Though Spanish wines generally aren't as snooty as some of the classics from the colossus to the north (Château d'Yquem, Baron de Rothschild, etc.), they have nothing to apologize for. Often the Spanish wines can surprise the visitor favorably. The strongest offerings are the Rioja reds, the Catalan whites, and the sherries from Jerez in the south.

• Sherry: Is it a wine? Is it a liqueur? It's actually a cross between the two. The Jerez region in the south produces a particularly sweet grape, though "sweet" is not the word you'd use to describe the fine, dry texture of these wonderful products.

• Montilla: The Amontillado you know from Edgar Allan Poe has its origin in this region near Córdoba. It comes in *fino*, medium dry and cream.

• Rioja: Perhaps the most famous of Spanish wines, the Riojas are strongest in their reds from this region in northeastern Spain in the Ebro valley. The Riojas are perhaps the most varied of the Spanish wines and include rosados (rosés) as well.

• Málaga: Spain's imperfect answer to the sweet Sauternes that can come at the end of a meal. Most Málaga wines are on the sweet side and have been supplanted by finer categories from other regions.

• Penedés, Catalonia: One of the world's great wine regions, especially for whites and

sparkling whites ("cavas"). You can visit the fine vineyards and bodegas of Catalonia in Penedés, Priorato, Alella and Tarragona.
• Navarra: Comes in a close second to Catalonia, with a number of unjustly ignored wines — equally fine in the white, red and rosado categories — such as Señorío de Sarria and Chivite.
• Galicia: As this region borders on Portugal, the semi-sparkling white wines characteristic of Portugal can be found here as well. Some of the better names are Valdeorras, Albariño, Monterrey, and Ribeiro.
• Duero: The Duero valley in the area of Valladolid produces a fine array of red wines — Vega Sicilia is the aristrocrat of these. Others have their provenance in the Ribera del Duero region.
• Others: Spain's lesser wines — from the central region, the north (Rueda, Roro, León), the Levante and the Balearic Islands— are good additions for the mixing that goes on in modern wine production; sometimes these wines will find their way anonymously into another, more respected mark as the needed missing element, thereby quietly backing the nobility of wines of higher pedigree.

Visiting Wineries

Most of the visiting of wineries in Spain goes on in the sherry region of Andalusia, certain areas of the Rioja valley and in Penedés in Catalonia. A number of organized tours exist (ask your hotel if you're in the region in question), though these generally are not offered during the vintage time of September and October. Tours usually follow conventional business hours, i.e., 9:00 to 1:00, and 4:00 to 7:00.

Lexicon

vino corriente: ordinary wine
copa: glass (tumbler)
copita: long stem wine glass
tinto: red
blanco: white
rosado: rosé
clarete: light-bodied red wine
seco: dry
dulce: sweet
brut: extra-dry
abocado: medium-sweet
vino de mesa (vino de pasta): table wine
espumosa: sparkling
cava: sparkling white wine
champán: champagne (a generic, not brand name)
rancio: wine aged in a cask
cosecha (vendimia): grape harvest (vintage)
bodega: wine shop; winery
sangría: wine and fruit juice

On a scale of 1 to 5 (5 is best), major groupings of wine are ranked as follows:

	Rioja	Penedes	Ribera del Duero	Valdepeñas	Rueda
1964	5	5	5	—	—
1970	5	4	5	5	3
1972	1	5	2	2	1
1973	3	4	4	4	1
1974	2	1	3	2	3
1975	3	4	3	3	3
1976	3	5	4	1	2
1978	3	5	2	1	4
1979	3	2	3	1	3
1980	3	4	3	4	2
1981	4	4	5	5	4
1982	5	4	4	3	4
1983	3	3	4	4	3
1984	2	4	2	5	3
1985	3	4	4	2	3
1986	3	2	4	4	2
1987	4	2	3	3	3
1988	3	3	4	4	3
1989	3	3	5	5	3

It goes without saying that Madrid nightlife has become one of the city's liveliest and latest, and culturally diverse, attractions. With the exception of bars and restaurants, which appear elsewhere in *Madrid Inside Out*, here's a simple tour through some of the nocturnal haunts.

Flamenco

You should see it, of course. Once, twice... If you tire of it, don't be alarmed, it doesn't mean you hate Spain, but only that you've gotten beyond the tourist stage and have become a real resident.

Flamenco shows begin around midnight. Call in each case to find out.

Flamenco Shows

Arco de Cuchilleros
Cuchilleros 7
Tel: 266-5867
Metro: Sol. • 10:30 p.m.

Café de Chinitas
Torrija 7
Metro: Santo Domingo
Tel: 248-5135 • 9:30 p.m.-3 a.m.

Corral de la Moreria
Moreria 17
Metro: Opera
Tel: 265-8446 • 9:30 p.m.-2 a.m.

Pena Flamenca la Carcelera
Montelon, 10
Tel: 200-9469 • Saturdays from 10 p.m.

A note on night life: complete listings appear in every newspaper's weekend supplements, and in the *Guía del Ocio*. A minimum is mentioned here to get you started; other sources are available especially if one of the categories below catches your fancy.

Tablaos (restaurants with floor shows)

Here's where you find the Bertolucci scenes you thought had passed out of being with the Sixties. We save them for out-of-town guests and find them fun on occasion.

Florida Park
Menéndez Pelayo
Tel: 573-7805 • 9:30 p.m. to early morning, with show at 10:30 p.m.

Lola
Costanilla de San Pedro, 11
Tel: 265-8801 • 9:30 p.m. to 4:00 a.m.

Noches del Cuplé
Palma, 51
Tel: 416-5683 • 10:00 p.m. to 2:30 a.m.

Scala Meliá Castilla
Capitán Haya, 43
Tel: 571-4411 • 10:30 p.m. to
4:00 a.m.

Discos

Madrid's disco scene is lively, to say the least. Of the hundreds of establishments, many cater to a younger crowd, but admit all. All compete to be the yuppiest and most chi-chi. Many young *Madrileños* put all their energies into looking good at a disco. To see them at their best, you have to catch them at their quasi-religious rituals.

Discos generally charge an entrance fee of about 1000 pesetas, which pays for your first drink. They open at 8:00 p.m. but really get started at around midnight.

• Archy. Marqués de Riscal, 11.
• Boccacio. Marqués de la Ensañada, 16.
• Four Roses. Osa Mayor, Aravaca.
• Joy Eslava. Arenal 11.
• Keeper. Juan Bravo, 39.
• Mau Mau. Padre Damián, 23.
• Pachá. Barceló, 11.
• Piña's. Alberto Alcocer, 33.

Cinema

See section on *Cinema*. Remember to look for "*v.o.*" in the listing *(versión original)* if you want to avoid Spanish dubbing. Madrid's wonderful Filmoteca shows oldies, foreign films and otherwise rare and exotic memorabilia. Santa Isabel, 3. Tel: 227-3866. It's the cheapest show in town, at 150 pesetas.

Theater

See the *Guía del Ocio* or newspaper listings. The basics follow:
Zarzuela
Jovellanos, 4
Tel: 429-8225
That precursor of musical comedy, Spain's most Spanish theater

Teatro Español
Príncipe 20 (Plaza Santa Ana)
Tel: 429-6297
For the Spanish classics of the Siglo de Oro.

Centro Cultural de la Villa de Madrid
Plaza Colón
Tel: 575-6080
Good offerings in the world's most claustrophobic and piti-fully designed space.

Albéniz
la Paz, 11
Tel: 522-0200
Wonderful, imported theater from all over Europe, perfected experimental plays from Catalunya, etc. Our favorite theater, off the Puerta del Sol.

Bingo

Yes, Bingo. *Madrileños* have a good time at it, and so can you.

• Canoe. Paseo de la Castellana, 93
• Hogar de Avila. Villanueva, 2
• Hotel Conde Duque. Plaza del Conde de Valle Suchil, 5
• Hotel Meliá Castilla. Capitán Haya, 43

Parks

The main ones are Retiro, the Parque del Oeste and the Casa de Campo. All are wonderful, though different in character. It doesn't matter, just go to the one you're closest to on a nice weekend day, and take in the sun and spectacle. Many people miss the wonderful Botanical Gardens, next to the Prado at Plaza Murillo, 2 (8:00 a.m. to 6:00 p.m. daily). When the lines at the Prado become excessive, just duck next door and have the Gardens almost to yourself.

Classical Music

Of the many faces of its Rip Van Winkle act these days, Madrid astonishes perhaps most in its classical music scene. The city is currently bursting with fine performances, new ensembles, triumphal returns, and an array of halls with clean sound in lovely surroundings. With supply exceeding demand, you can get tickets easily enough for most events, usually for under 2000 pesetas.

The National Orchestra of Spain plays in their new hall inaugurated in 1988, the Auditorio Nacional. Of the halls built in the past ten years, The National Auditorium is one of the finest-sounding and best-feeling anywhere.

Tickets for the O.N.E. cost 500 to 2500 pesetas and can almost always be found up to an hour before performance time. For opera you go to the *Teatro de la Zarzuela*, built in 1856 from a model based on La Scala in Milan. Opera productions are offered there from January to July, with Zarzuela from October to December, and ballet during December and January.

The Orchestra of the RTVE, now celebrating its 25th anniversary, performs in the *Teatro Monumental* in the middle of the city, former home of the O.N.E.

Currently, closed for renovation, the Royal or "Opera" Theater is an 1817 building opposite the Royal Palace at the Plaza de Oriente, the site of opera and symphony concerts in the nineteenth century, and used by Verdi in 1963 for a performance of *La Forza del*

Destino. When it reopens it will be the scene of opera, symphony, Zarzuela and ballet and will be official headquarters to 13 of Madrid's 90 local ensembles.

Many of Madrid's best concerts are held at The National Auditorium which often has to schedule them tightly at 7:30 and 10:30 for the same evening.

Note: Madrid's halls generally accept neither credit cards nor reservations over the phone. However, they'll send brochures and calendars on request.

Festival de Otoño (late September to mid November)
Comunidad de Madrid,
Consejería de Cultura,
Talavera, 11
Tel: 457-9882

Festival Italia España (December-January)
Ortega y Gasset, 29
Tel: 578-3344

Música Barroca y Rococo de San Lorenzo de El Escorial.
(Summer Festival)
Associación de Música Barroca.
Francisco de Rojas, 9
Tel: 448-3115

Orquesta Sinfónica y Coro de RTVE
Sor Angela de la Cruz, 2
Tel: 570-7003

Orquesta y Coro Nacionales de España
Auditorio Nacional de Música.
Príncipe de Vergara, 136
Tel: 337-0212
The *taquilla* (box office) is open Monday 5:00 p.m. to 7:00; Tuesday-Friday 10:00 a.m. to 5:00 p.m.; Saturday 11:00 a.m. to 1:00 p.m.

Fundación Juan March
Castelló, 77
Tel: 435-4240
Free chamber concerts, Wednesday noon and various evenings.

Teatro de la Zarzuela
Teatro Lirico Nacional
Jovellanos, 4
Tel: 429-8216

Radio Nacional de España (RNE)
Radio 2. RNE Prado del Rey
Tel: 711-8000

Out All Night
Last but not least, we offer the reprint of a now-famous itinerary, originally published in the July, 1989, *Vogue.* It shows you how to get through a 24-hour binge in Madrid, taking in the best at the proper times.

Publishing a book on Madrid without Alan Jolis' master opus would be like showing up to a wedding in slippers.

The New Madrid—Right Times/Places

(Reprinted from *Vogue*)

1:00 p.m. *Grand Café Gijon*, 21 Paseo de Recoletos. Literati hangout—for drinks and gossip before lunch.

2:00-4:00 p.m. *L'Hardy*, 8 Carrera de San Jerónimo; Tel: 521-3385. For consommé and sandwiches (paid for on the honor system) in circa 1839 restaurant.

4:00-6:00 p.m. *Circulo de Bellas Artes*, 42 Calle Alcala; Tel: 531-8507. Art Deco bar/meeting place.

6:00-7:30 p.m. Nap—to prepare for the long night ahead.

7:30-10:00 p.m. Tapas bar-hopping in Old Madrid.

10:00 p.m. Dinner at *Viridiana*, 23 Calle Fundadores; Tel: 246-9040. Named for the 1961 Bunuel film prohibited by Franco, this in spot has one Michelin star. Or: *El Mentidero* Japanese cuisine...*El Cenador del Prado*, 4, Calle Prado; Tel: 429-1549—elegant, high-profile dining.

Midnight. *El Museo Chicote*, 12 Calle Gran Via.

1:30-4:00 a.m. Discos/nightclubs: *Archy*, 11 Marques de Riscal...Pacha, 11 Barcelo ...*Rick's*, 26 Calle Infantas ...*Imposible*, 3 Travesia del Conde Duque.

4:00-6:00 a.m. After-hours clubs: *Voltereta*, 3 Calle Princesa ...*Kitsch*, 26 Calle Galileo...*Aire*, 8 Calle Bermudez... *El Sol*, 3 Calle Jardines.

6:00-7:00 a.m. Breakfast at any bar open for workers and taxi drivers. Have hot chocolate and churros (Spanish *beignets*).

7:00 a.m.-1:00 p.m. Stroll *Retiro Park*...or sleep.

THE following pages have been specifically included in this edition of *Madrid Inside Out* to facilitate visits in 1992 centered around the extraordinary Quincentennial festivities in Spain. General tourist and travel information along with the special events information has also been included to serve both general travelers at all times as well as visitors partaking in these Quincentennial events in this historic year.

Introduction

The Quincentennial celebration of Columbus' momentous voyage in 1492 undoubtedly merits the historic events Spain has planned to commemorate this international red-letter date. In contemporary terms, this orchestration represents the final push in a long process for Spain's entry — psychologically as well as politically and economically — into Greater Europe.

As historic events are sharing top billing in Madrid, Seville and Barcelona, cultural links with Western Hemisphere countries are being forged by the State-sponsored Quincentennial Commission, which has in the U.S. a Washington, D.C. office and is working with a large number of local organizations around the world on cultural and civic exchange within the 1992 celebrations. The supervisory organization for all activities is the *Commissión*

Nacional Para el V Centenario. The organization responsible for the creation and execution of many of the projects is the *Sociedad Estatal para la Ejecución de Programas del Quinto Centenario,* headed by Director Angel Serrano.

The Commission is also sponsoring *Al-Andalus 92,* a series of events honoring the Muslim presence in Spain prior to the 1492 expulsion, and *Sefarad 92,* with a parallel series of events devoted to Spain's Jewish past. The programs call for the improvement of Moorish buildings in *Nueva Granada* and buildings such as the Samuel Levi house in Toledo. Spain currently has 175,000 Muslims and 13,000 Jews.

Most states in the United States have a commission for administering Quincentenary events—usually in care of the Governor's Office. The national commission in the U.S. is

headed by Mr. Frank J. Donatelli:
Christopher Columbus Quincentenary Jubilee Commission
1801 F St. NW
Washington, DC 20006

In addition, The Spain 92 Foundation has offices in New York, Washington and Los Angeles:
•New York
150 East 58 St. 16th Floor
New York, NY 10155
Tel. (212) 758-1492
Fax (212) 832-1992
• Washington D.C.
1821 Jefferson Place, NW
Washington, DC 10036
Tel: (202) 775-1992
Fax: (202) 775-3719
• Los Angeles
P.O. Box 50450
Pasadena, CA 91115
Tel: (818) 564-1992
Fax: (818) 564-1492

A large number of bilateral projects are being conducted between Spain and the U.S., including literary prizes, the creation of a ballet, numerous television series to be shown in both countries, high school exchanges, sister cities exchanges, awards to Spanish teachers in the U.S., library projects, and the visit of replicas of Columbus' three caravelles to 12 U.S. ports.

As if the Quincentennial, with Expo 92 and the Olympic Games weren't enough for one nation in the same year, Madrid is also celebrating its role as Europe's Cultural Capital. The city's infrastructure is constantly improving to accomodate the multiplicity of cultural events. In preparation, the Centro Reina Sofía has been remodeled to house contemporary art; the municipal library in the Retiro district has been spruced up; and the new Opera House (formerly the Teatro Real) is to be unveiled, with the most extensive stage apparatus in Europe.

Slightly outside the limelight, but essential to the 1992 events, are five shakers and financiers behind it all, names that are reaching prominence as the events get under way: José Miguel Abad - the Olympic Games; Jacinto Pellón - Expo 92; Angel Serrano Martínez-Estellez - the State Commission for the Quincentennial; Angel Luis Ruiz de Gopegui - Extremadura Enclave 92; and Pablo López de Osaba - Madrid: 1992 Cultural Capital of Europe.

And finally, once the whoopla is over, the most

important event of all will be set in place — the invisible one after the fanfares have exhausted themselves, but the one which will have by far the greatest effect on Spain's future: the entry into the European Inner Market, with a common European currency with Spanish participation.

Important Dates
• Madrid: Cultural Capital of Europe: January 1-December 1992
• Seville: Expo '92: April 20, 1992- October 20, 1992
• Barcelona: Olympics: July 25-August 9, 1992

Madrid: European Capital of Culture 1992

Madrid has been named the eighth European city to hold this distinction following Athens (1985), Florence (1986), Amsterdam(1987), Berlin (1988), Paris (1989), Glasgow (1990), and Dublin (1991). After Madrid, Antwerp, Lisbon, Luxembourg, and Copenhagen will follow consecutively.

The Consortium for Madrid 1992 (COM 92) has created a general program of more than 1800 separate events spread throughout the city. The program follows three basic lines:

• **Madrid, Madrid, Madrid**: A shop window of the living culture of Madrid today with the participation of the captial's artists and intellectuals, exhibitions, recordings, films, theater, dance, historic presentations, etc.

• **Madrid, European Capital of Culture**: Activities underlining what Madrid has to offer—new theaters, important groups and theatrical companies from Europe and the rest of the world, including the latest innovations in the arts.

• **Programs in Collaboration**: In the spirit of coordination, the Corsortium has arranged with a wide variety of cultural institutions an impressive collection of joint activities in dance, theater, literature, music, audiovisuals, and plastic arts, with the idea of reenforcing its already strong commitment to cultural achievements.

Additionally, hundreds of special projects have been developed as part of the larger impact of the Consortium of Madrid '92. These include the publishing of a magazine called

Madrid 92, a book of cultural capitals, commemorative medals, a series of ecological posters in all the European Community languages, debates, the Gastromonical Olympics, European film awards, and sports events.

Although all programs and schedule dates should be confirmed in advance, here is an indication of what has been planned.

Madrid, Madrid, Madrid

• Painted Madrid	
Museo Minicipal	Nov.-Dec. 1992
• Exposition on Spanish Television	
Parque del Retiro	May 2, June 28 1992
• Exhibition on Madrid's Press	
C.C. de la Villa	May-June 1992
• Madrid at Arms	
Museo del ejército	until May 2, 1992
• Tribute to Dance	
(site to be confirmed)	Sept- Dec. 1992
• Tribute to Jazz	
Sala Galileo Galilei	*(to be announced)*
• Tribute to Flamenco	
Teatro Alfil	*(to be announced)*
• Four Centuries of Madrid Theater	
(at six major theaters)	May 15-July 31 1992
• *El gran mercado del mundo* (Calderon)	
Plaza Mayor y aledaños	June 12-20, 1992

Madrid, European Capital of Culture

• Edge 92 *(International Biennal of new arts)*	
(various sites)	April-May 1992
• Repeticion/Transformacion	
(Contemporary Painters Series)	
• Centro de Arte Reina Sofia	Sept-Oct. 1992
92 Video Clips for 92	
(12 hours of presentations)	Sept. 15-20, 1992
• Panorama of European Video Art	Oct. 1-15, 1992
• Tribute to Poetry	
(various sites)	*(to be announced)*

• Photographs of Flamenco
Elke Stolzenberg
Instituto Aleman   Nov. 15-Dec. 18, 1992

Fuera de Serie
• Auditorio Nactional, Sala A
Royal Philharmonic
V. Askhenazy   Jan. 19, 1992
• Berliner Philharmoniker
D. Barenboim   March 3, 4, 1992
• Chicago Sympony Orchestra
D. Barenboim   April 7, 8, 1992
• Orquesta de Paris
S. Bychkov   May 7, 8, 1992
• Philadelphia Orchestra
R. Muti   May 17, 18, 1992
• Montreal Symphony
C. Dutoit   June 2, 3, 1992
• Scala de Milan
R. Muti   July 10, 1992
• Wiener Philharmoniker
C. Abbado   Sept. 16, 1992
• Royal Concertgeboun
G. Solti   Dec. 9, 10, 1992
• *Teatro español de ultima hora*
"Madrid, Capital of Glory" (Manuel Gutiérrez Aragon)
"The Myth of Don Juan" (Bob Wilson)   May-Nov. 1992
• Comédie Française
El Barbero de Sevilla   Sept. 21, 27, 1992
• El Berliner
Don Juan (Bertol Bretch)   late June 1992
• Lauren Bacall & Anthony Quinn
Cartas de amor   May-June 1992
• Vanessa Redgrave
El Jardin de los Cerezos (Chekov)   May-June 1992
• Peter Brook
El Hombre que confunio a su mujer con un sombrero
(Oliver Sacks)   Sept. 1992

Programs in Collaboration

- *Ultimos descubrimientos*

Festival de Otoño

"Repons" (Pierre Boulez)

"Einstein on the Beach" (Philip Glass)   Oct. 2-10 1992

- *Castillos en el aire*

Adventures of Don Quixote

Sala San Pol   Oct. 1-15, 1992

Expo 92

The cornerstone of the 1992 celebrations is by far Expo 92, hosted by the Andalusian city of Seville. No mere World's Fair, Expo 92 carries the status of a Universal Exposition, along the lines of Brussels (1958), Montreal (1967) and Osaka (1970). Seville's Expo 92 has the distinction of being the last of the Twentieth Century, and the largest in history. The event will be held from April to October 1992, for a 176-day period. Over 225,000 visitors a day are expected to arrive at Expo 92.

Expo 92, carrying the theme "The Age of Discoveries/Fiesta," is intended by Spanish authorities to perform not only as a showcase for Spain, but also as a magnet for development for Andalusia, one of the country's poorest regions.

Along with Expo President Emilio Cassanello, Commissioner General Manuel Olivencia has arranged participation from over 100 nations, involving $7 billion in public works in preparation, and bringing in $3 billion in public and private monies for site construction. The present schedule calls for the construction of a high-speed (2 1/2 hours) train between Madrid and Seville. The Seville terminal includes parking for 40,000 cars and 1,100 buses. Expo's identifying landmark, a 90-meter-high "lookout" tower, already looms 90 meters over La Cartuja island in the Guadalquivir River. After Expo 92 is gone, the main building is to be converted into Spain's first World Trade Center, based on an additional $50 million deal.

The Exposition itself includes 55,000 cultural and entertainment performances— including concerts by Plácido Domingo, Zubin Mehta and the Vienna Opera, and a host of others. Some 100 Chiefs of State are visiting the site, where they will be received by King Juan Carlos. In addition, there are 96 restaurants, 350,000 trees and plants, 51 shops and a monorail crammed into the 215 hectares of the Expo site. Attending Expo costs 4,000 pesetas (almost $40 US) per person, per day. Discounts are available for season tickets, multiple entries, and children.

According to Expo 92 officials the following cultural activities are definitively scheduled although for precise ticket information and availability it is best to inquire directly with Expo 92 information at Tel: (34) (1) 448-1992. Note that the area code for Seville from outside Spain is (34) (5) or (95) from inside Spain.

Information Concerning the U.S. Pavillion Expo 92

Pabellon de los Estados Unidos
Apartado de Correos 92/001
Expo 92 Sevilla
Tel: 423-7859
Fax: 423-7877

Information Concerning the U.K. Pavillion Expo 92

Department of Trade and Commerce
Expo 92
10-18 Victoria Street
London SW1 HONN
Tel: (44) (71) 215-3233

Information Concerning the Australia Pavillion Expo 92

Pabellon Australia
Hotel Melia Sevilla
Apartado 4F
Avda de Borbolla s/n
41004 Sevilla
Tel: 442-5501
Fax: 442-1511

Information Concerning the Canada Pavillion Expo 92

Pabellon Canada
Isla de la Cartuja
41010 Sevilla
Tel: 446-0624

Expo 92 Data

• Seville's Universal Exposition is the largest in history and the last in the twentieth century.

• The Expo 92 site consists of 215 *hectares*. (See enclosed illustrated map entitled "La Isla de la Caruja" from *El Pais*.)

• 110 countries are participating. (28 European, 33 from the Americas, 19 Asian, 20 African, and 10 from Oceania).

• 23 international organizations are involved and actively present as well as 17 autonomous communities and 47 corporations.

• The latest additions to the Exposition include the former Soviet republic Estonia. Also to note: Yugoslavia, despite its Civil War, is prominently present with its prefab pavillion designed by Koni Company. Kuwait has contributed a pavillion, and South Africa, entering a phase of new international acceptance, has constructed a pavillion.

Listing of Activities at Expo 92

• Ten Pop-Rock Concerts	May 24, June 10, 17, July 21, August 5, 12, Sept. 7, 23, 27, Oct. 6, 1992
• Robert Joffrey Dance Co.	Sept. 14, 15, 1992
• Alvin Ailey Dance Co.	Sept. 21-22, 1992
• Mozart's *Don Giovanni,* staged by Peter Sellars	April 22, 24, 26, 1992
• Verdi's *Masked Ball,* Placído Domingo singing the lead role, Metropolitan Opera of New York	May 30, June 2, 5, 1992
• Liza Minelli Show	July 4, 1992
• Jazz Tribute to John Coltrane	July 1992
• *West Side Story* production	Sept. 1992
• Motown Gala	Oct. 1992
• Robert Wilson production of Burroughs novel	*(to be announced)*

Auditorio de la Cartuja

(One of the largest stages in the world, auditorium seating up to 10,000 people)

• Lausanne Ballet, choreographed by Maurice Bejart	April, May 1992
• *The Price of the Pagodas* Benjamin Britten	May 1992
• Nederlands Dans Theatre, choreographed by Jiri Kylian	May 1992
• *El Sombrero de Tres Picos,* Grands Ballets Canadiens	July 1992
• *Napoli, La Sylphide,* and *La Ventana,* Royal Ballet of Denmark	Sept. 1992
• Luciano Pavarotti	Sept. 2, 1992

Teatro de la Expo — Teatro Central

Avant-garde theater hosting works in new tendencies, holds up to 1300 spectators.

• *Don Giovanni*	April 23, 1992

- *Brace Up* (Wooster Group)   May 1992
- *Kaspar* (Danat Danza)   May 1992
- Frankfurt Ballet (William Forsythe)   June 1992
- *The Legend of Don Juan*   July 1992
- *Lapin Chasseur*   July 1992
- *The Black Rider*
(Bob Wilson, music by Tom Waits)   July 1992
- Laurie Anderson   July 1992
- *Asdrubila* (Carlos Santos)   July 1992

Open Cinema
Cinema holding 1500 people features
giant 20 meter wide outdoor screen.
- Six cinematic "cycles" showing throughout the Exposition

El Palenque
Site for Opening Ceremony, holds up to 1500 people.
Daytime venue for folklore and Spanish traditional music.
- A Taste of Dance, 120 big dance bands   June-Sept. 1992

Teatro de la Maestranz
Opera and symphony theater holding 1800 people.
Hosting the largest stage in Spain (18 x 9.5 m).
- *Rigoletto, Tosca*   May 1992
- *Carmen* (Bizet),
performed by Placido Domingo   April 24, 27, 30,
                                                          May 3, 1992

- *La Favorita* (Donizetti),
stage director Luciano Pavarotti   May 1992
- *Un Ballo in Mashera*
(Metropolitan Opera House of New York)
stage director Piero Faggioni   May, June 1992
- *La Forza del Destino, Las Bodas de
Figaro,* conducted by Zubin Mehta   June, July 1992
- *Requim,* Scala Milano,
conducted by Ricardo Muti   July 1992
- *La Traviata,* Scala Milano,
conducted by Ricardo Muti   July, Aug. 1992
- *Don Giovanni,* conducted by Bruno Weil Sept. 1992
- *El Barbero de Sevilla,* Rossini Opera   Sept. 1992

- *The Flying Dutchman* (Wagner)
Dresden Semporeper   Sept.-Oct. 1992

Teatro Lope de Vega

This theater offers a program of Spanish works staged by well-known directors, linking the Iberoamerican Exposition of 1929 and Expo 92.

- *Don Quijote*
(Cervantes directed by Mauricio Scaparro)   April 21-26, 1992
- *La Zapatera Prodigiosa*
(Lorca directed by Nuria Espert)   May 5-10,1992
- *La Niña de Plata* (Lope de Vega
directed by Adolfo Marsillach)   May 19-24, 1992
- *(To be announced)*
Directed by Peter Brook   May 26-31, 1992
- *Peer Gynt*
(Ibsen directed by Ingmar Bergman)   June 16-21, 1992
- *La Vida es Sueño*
(Calderon directed by Jose Luis Gomez)   June 1992
- *El Alcalde de Zalamea*
(directed by Robert Sturua)   June 30-July 5, 1992
- *Don Juan* (directed by Rafael Alberti
with monologue by Vittorio Gassman)   Aug. 1992
- *Fuenteovejune* (Lope de Vega
directed by Declan Domellan)   Sept. 8-13, 1992
- *El Barbero de Sevilla*
(Beaumarchais directed by Olivier Giel)   Sept. 22-26, 1992
- *Ulises y la Ballena Blanca*
(directed by Vittorio Gassman)   *(to be announced)*
- *Sililoquies*
(Dario Fo and Dustin Hoffman)   *(to be announced)*

Miscellaneous Events

- Stevie Wonder's musical tribute to
90-year old Spanish composer Manuel Rodrigo
- Dustin Hoffman and Laurie Anderson in various performances
- Martha Graham Dance Company premiere of its late founder's last ballet

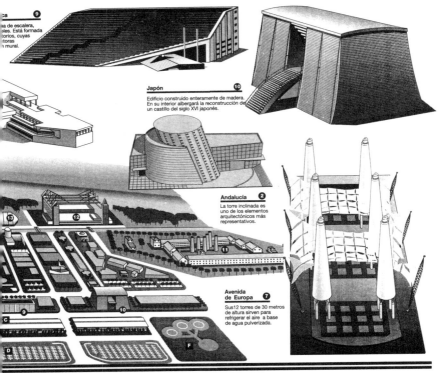

...ca **9**

...a de escalera,
...les. Está formada
...torios, cuyas
...toras
...n mural.

Japón **10**

Edificio construido enteramente de madera.
En su interior albergará la reconstrucción de
un castillo del siglo XVI japonés.

Andalucía **2**

La torre inclinada es
uno de los elementos
arquitectónicos más
representativos.

**Avenida
de Europa** **7**

Sus 12 torres de 30 metros
de altura sirven para
refrigerar el aire a base
de agua pulverizada.

1. Pabellón de España. **2.** Pabellón de Andalucía. **3.** Pabellones de las comunidades autónomas españolas. **4.** Hotel Príncipe de Asturias.
5. Plaza de América. **6.** Pabellón de México. **7.** Avenida de Europa. **8.** Avenida de las Palmeras. **9.** Pabellón de la URSS. **10.** Pabellón de Japón.
11. Cartuja de Santa María de las Cuevas. **12.** Auditorio. **13.** Pabellón del Futuro.
A. Puente de la Barqueta. **B.** Puente del Alamillo. **C.** Edificios de servicios. **D.** Aparcamiento. **E.** Terminal del AVE. **F.** Helipuerto.

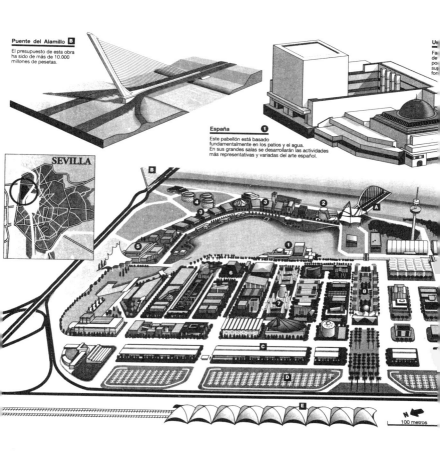

Puente del Alamillo **B**

El presupuesto de esta obra ha sido de más de 10.000 millones de pesetas.

España **①**

Este pabellón está basado fundamentalmente en los patios y el agua. En sus grandes salas se desarrollarán las actividades más representativas y variadas del arte español.

SEVILLA

100 metros

A Bit of History

Once the major city on the Iberian peninsula, Seville still retains much of its character from the early days of the sixteenth-century gold market. The popular image of Spain throughout the world — the orange trees, flower-filled patios, gypsies performing with castanets, and a relaxed pace of living — seems to find its origin in Seville more than any other Spanish city. The many legends, perpetuated in some of the world's most durable opera *(Don Giovanni, The Barber of Seville, Carmen),* would be unthinkable outside of the mystique of this southern city. Asked about Spain's capacity for music in a recent interview in Tribuna, Yehudi Menuhin directed his answer to the city of Seville: "Never has a city impressed me so much. It seemed to me that all its inhabitants had a gift for dancing, singing and reciting poetry. This to me is the pinnacle of civilization."

In Andalusia, the Muslim and Christian esthetics once found their greatest fruition and melding, are still visible in impressive structures such as Seville's Giralda Tower (built originally as a minaret for the Muslin call to prayer) and in romantic names such as the Guadalquivir, the expansive river that winds slowly through the center of the city and sets the graceful and dignified pace of things in the Andalusian capital.

Seville's paradox is the relative poverty of the region, juxtaposed with the awesome richness of its culture and history. All guide books single out Seville as the Spanish city with the highest incidence of pickpocketing. Seville, however, will reward you greatly if you visit it, living up to many of the fantasies of what Spain is supposed to feel like. Settling in Seville can be another matter, given the recent spasms in the real estate market due to Expo 92, and the critical lack of space affecting everything from housing to traffic. But, everything in Seville is possible, even relocating. In any case, if you're planning to get to know Spain as a country, you can't miss Seville as one of its most representative and lovely components.

Seville's geographic position near the Atlantic coast marked its character and history from the beginning. Phoenicians traded with the original population at Cádiz, just 150 kilometers away. Roman settlements nearby at Italica and Carmona were among the oldest in Europe, and Julius Caesar established a judicial district in the Seville region in about 45 B.C. The emperors Hadrian and Trajan were both born in Italica.

Conquered by Muslims in 712, the settlement received the name Izvilla, whence the present name of Seville. In 1248 the Christians retook the city under Fernando III, and later built important shipyards under Alfonso X.

After the discovery of America and of gold in the New World, Seville suddenly took on a whole new importance as the most important European port of the sixteenth and seventeenth centuries. Gold was brought in and weighed at the Golden Tower (Torre de Oro), originally built by Muslims and now serving as entry for Europe's major import. The city took on a new role not only as a major commercial and administrative center, but also as the cultural spawning ground of painters such as Zurbarán, Murillo, Valdés Leal and Velázquez, as well as home to Cervantes, Lope de Vega and Calderón.

Recent times brought the city to a less favored position, particularly following the defeat of the Spanish and French forces by Nelson at the naval battle of Trafalgar, off the coast at Cádiz. The following century brought down Seville in prominence. In the 1930s the city was a Nationalist stronghold under Franco and was later stigmatized by association with the dictatorship that followed. The current thrust to invest the area with growth and progress follows the largely successful effort in 1929 to do the same, at the Latin-American Exhibition; the placement of Expo 92 in Seville is a result of the conscious, stated policy of the present government to bring the region up to the standard of living enjoyed by the other provinces of the country.

Events

Processions *(pasos)* of religious pageantry pass through the streets at Holy Week time, in a celebration originated in the sixteenth century, depicting the Passion of Christ. Tourists from all over the world have made it a point of honor to get to Seville at that time; the processions are indeed impressive and moving, though more solemn than some tourists expect. It can be difficult, even impossible, to get accommodations in Seville during March and April.

Tuesday to Sunday two weeks after Easter is *Feria* time, with songs, dances and the color of local costume. Later in the spring the brotherhoods and horsemen make their way off to *el Rocío,* near Seville, during the feast of Corpus Christi.

In summer, small fairs are in every community known as velás, leading up to the 15th of August, when the patron saint of Seville, the *Virgen de los Reyes,* is celebrated.

Sites

• The Cathedral
Begun in the fourteenth century, it now ranks as one of the largest cathedrals in the world, the largest built in the Gothic style. Visits 10:30 to 1:00 p.m. and 4:30 to 6:30 p.m. Climb the Giralda Tower, which has a commanding view of the city.

• Giralda Tower
Seville's most famous landmark. Built in the twelth century as a minaret, later joined to the Cathedral after the Christians recaptured the region.

• The Alcázar
Built in the fourteenth century by Pedro the Cruel. Inhabited by Ferdinand and Isabel, as well as Carlos V. Built in the Mudéjar style as a Moorish fortress. Beautiful courtyards, gardens, handiworks.

• Hospital de la Santa Caridad
Seventeenth-century hospital, associated with the legend of Miguel Manara who retired from society after the death of his wife in 1661 and who devoted himself to helping the diseased and burying the dead.

• Tobacco Factory
Built from 1750-66, it was once the second largest building in Spain, after the Escorial. By 1850 it employed 10,000 workers. It served as the setting for Bizet's *Carmen;* now it

houses the university.

• Maria Luisa Park
Site of the 1929 Hispano-American Exhibition, and one of Spain's loveliest urban parks. If you are exploring the city by foot, the Park is a bit off the beaten track and necessitates some time set aside.

Museums

• Fine Arts Museum
Plaza del Museo
Tel. 422-1829
Works of Francisco Pacheco, Herrera el Viejo, Zurbarán, Valdés Leal, Murillo, Velázquez, El Greco, Alonso Cano, Rubens, Titian, Goya, etc.
• Bullfight Museum
Paseo Colón, 12
Tel. 422-4577
• Archaeological Museum
Plaza de América
Tel. 423-2405
One of Spain's major museums.
• Contemporary Art
Santo Tomás
Tel. 421-5830
• Folk Art and Costume
Plaza de América
Tel. 423-2576
• Maritime
Torre del Oro (Tower of Gold)
Tel. 422-2419

Bullfighting

March to October, at Real Maestranza bull ring.

Music

Throughout the year, at the Teatro Lope de Vega, the Cathedral, the Church of the Savior, the Music Conservatory and the Prado de San Sebastián. The newly formed Orchestra of Andalusia promises to be one of Spain's best.

Theater

• Imperial
Sierpes, 25
Tel. 421-7468.
• Lope de Vega
Avda. da María Luisa
Tel. 423-4546.
• Teatro de la Maestranza
Paseo de Colón.

Cinema

• Alameda
Alameda de Hércules, 9
Tel. 438-0157
• Avenida
Marqués de Paradas, 15
Tel. 422-1548
• Azul
La Florida, 15
Tel. 441-5309
• Florida
Menéndez y Pelayo, 31
Tel. 441-3553
• Corona Center
Between Salada and Paraíso
Tel. 427-8064
• Cristina
Cristina Gardens
Tel. 422-6680

Discotheques
- El Coto
Luis Montoto, 118
Tel. 425-1900
- Holiday
Jesús del Gran Poder, 71
Tel. 421-8877
- La Colina de las Fresas
Monte Carmelo, 12
Tel. 427-6677

Flamenco
Two establishments are Los Gallos (Plaza de Santa Cruz, 10, Tel. 421-2154) and Curro Velez (Rodo, 7).

Study Abroad Programs with Permanent Offices in Seville
Academic Year in Spain
Apartado 1084
41 Sevilla
Resident Director: Ana DeCicco
25 students/Sept.-May

The Center for Cross Cultural Study
Harinas, 18
41001 Sevilla
(954) 22-41-07
Resident Director: Daniel García
60 students/semester program
US Contact: Hudson Mohawk Association, 31 Maplewood Dr. Amherst, MA 01002

Cornell University & University of Michigan
Calle Harinas, 3-5, 2°
Apartado 554
41001 Sevilla
Tel: (95) 422-33-51
Resident Director: Frank Casas
US Contact: Center for Western European Studies, 5208 Angell Hall, Univ. of Michigan, Ann Arbor, MI 48109 or Cornell Abroad, 474 Uris Hall, Cornell Univ. Ithaca, NY 14853.

Council of International Educational Exchange (CIEE)
Facultad de Filología
Universidad de Sevilla
41004 Sevilla
Tel: (95) 422-20-53
Resident Director:
Dr. Jerry Johnson
113 students/semester program
US Contact: Academic Programs Dept. CIEE, 205 East 42nd St., New York, NY 10017

SUNY—New Paltz
Facultad de Filología
Maria de Padilla, s/n
41003 Sevilla
Tel: (95) 422-20-53
Resident Director:
Madeline Marfe
US Contact: Office of International Education, State University of New York, New Paltz, NY 12561

University of North Carolina at Seville
Facultad de Filología
Universidad de Sevilla
41003 Sevilla
Tel: (95) 422-20-53 ext. 22
Resident Director:
Cesareo Bandera
US. Contact: Dept. of Romance Languages, Univ. of North Carolina, Chapel Hill, NC 27514

Sweet Briar College Junior Year in Spain
Facultad de Filología
Universidad de Sevilla
41003 Sevilla
Tel: (95) 422-20-53 ext. 22
Resident Director:
Mary Ann Wilson
US Contact: Dr. Antonia M. Taylor, Box AP, Sweet Briar College, Sweet Briar, VA 24595

University of Seville

The University of Seville is located in the Tobacco Factory, scene of Bizet's Carmen. The campus resembles more the U.S. or UK model than the disparate conglomerations in other cities on the European continent. For complete information send for the *Guía del Estudiante,* Universidad de Sevilla, San Fernando, 4, 41 Sevilla. (Tel. 421-8600/08/09.)
The campus offers the full gamut of university courses, with a Language Institute (English, French, Italian, German, Russian, Spanish for beginners, Arabic, Japanese).
Instituto de Idiomas
Palos de la Fontera
41004 Sevilla
Tel. 421-8577

Other Universities in Andalusia

University of Cádiz
Plaza de Frágela
Cadiz
Tel. (956) 22.38.08

University of Cordoba
Alfonso XIII,19
Cordoba
Tel. (957) 47.31.25

University of Granada
Hospital Real
Avda del Hospicio
Granada
Tel. (958) 27.84.00

University of Málaga
Zona Universitario
Málaga
Tel. (952) 22.50.54

Language Institutes

Seville is endowed with no fewer than twenty private language institutes, each offering intensive Spanish to the newcomer. The University of Málaga also runs intensive summer language courses:

University of Málaga
Course for Foreigners
310 Apto de Correos
29080 Málaga
Tel. (952)21 40 07

Accommodations
Housing
This is the tricky part if you're planning to come for an extended stay or to live. Some recent settlers have found it difficult to get leases that run through 1992, as landlords hope to maximize their profits for this bumper year. But leases do exist, if you're persistent.

Points to Consider
• Avoid electric heat and bottled gas; don't expect to find central heating, but don't expect to be warm in the winter. Space heaters are necessary.
• Visit the neighborhood you're considering at night as well as in the daytime, as sections change character from one time of day to the other.
• Air-conditioning is a necessity.
• If the apartment you want is furnished or with kitchen, you'll have to pay a two-month security deposit plus the first month's rent up front (three months total). Apartments generally do not come with kitchen appliances.
• If you use a rental agency, expect to pay an additional six percent over your rent.
• Parking is difficult; reserved spaces cost 10,000 to 15,000 pesetas a month.
• If your personal effects arrive through the airport, be prepared to pay a refundable customs fee when picking them up (prior residency certificate from the police can avoid this).
• For repairs, call Multi-Asistencia, Tel: 421-3111.

Recommended Real Estate Agents
• Agencia Inmobiliaria Herrera
Córdoba, 5
Sevilla
Tel. 421-0265

• Agencia Inmobiliaria Torcal
Avda de la Constitución, 27-2
Sevilla
Tel. 422-6401/06

• Diagonal Agencia Inmobiliaria
Marqués de Paradas, 24
Sevilla
Tel. 422-1910

• Agencia Bermudo
Plaza Nueva, 13-1
Sevilla
Tel. 422-7612

Hotels

There are many dozen hotels in Seville; here are a representative few.

• Alfonso XIII: San Fernando, 2. Tel. 422-2850. One of the famous hotels of the Iberian peninsula, and one of the most expensive. At least wander in for a drink at the bar, which is an experience in itself.

• Los Lebreros: Luís Morales, 2. Tel. 457-9400. Considered more a business than tourist hotel, but endowed, in any case, with some of the most comfortable rooms in the city.

• Internacional: Aguilas, 17. Tel. 421-3207. A well-kept old building, located in a typical street of the old section near the Casa Pilatos Museum. Popular among Spanish tourists.

• Inglaterra: Plaza Nueva, 1. Tel. 422-4970. One of the best bargains in Seville. A particularly friendly staff, which can be important when you need information about the city. Centrally located but quiet.

• La Rábida: Castelar, 24. Tel. 422-0966. Between the bullring and the Plaza Nueva. Fine patio and well-maintained building.

• Doña María: Don Remondo, 19. Tel. 422-2990. Quiet elegance near the Giralda, thus at the core of the historic section of the city.

• Bécquer: Reyes Católicos, 4. Tel. 422-8900. A reasonably priced tourist hotel near the Plaza Nueva and Museum of Fine Arts.

• Murillo: Lope de Rueda, 7. Tel. 421-6095. In the middle of the Barrio Santa Cruz, along one of the walking streets (motor vehicles excluded). Though the rooms are rudimentary, the hotel is a fine sanctuary in the city's center.

Inexpensive Hostels

• Youth Hostel. Isaac Peral, 2. Tel. 461-3150.

• Atenas. Caballerizas, 1. Tel. 421-8047. Charming old house near the Internacional Hotel. No baths in the rooms, no meals served.

• Goya: Mateos Gagos, 31. Tel. 421-1170. A good bargain, if you can get a booking. Pretty patio, short walk to the Cathedral.

Cuisine
Tapas

Seville's tapas are Spain's most famous. You'll notice in cities like Madrid that some of the most earnest holes-in-the-wall are called Sevilla or Andalucía.

In scouring the landscape for good places, try the area around Triana, across the river on the airport side of the city —

particularly along its main street, San Jacinto; along the Triana side of the river, the calle Betis has a series of small *bodegas,* as do side streets such as Pagés del Corro. In the center of the city, try the Plaza Nueva for one of Seville's richest tapas areas; or the Barrio de Santa Cruz, the ancient, formerly Jewish section. Behind the Hotel Inglaterra is the Rincón del Gallo, specializing in Galician food. In addition, some of the major tapas establishments are the following:

• El Rinconcillo
Gerona, 40
Tel: 422-3183
One of Seville's most famous establishments, founded in 1670. Characteristic, decorative tiles and tasty dishes.

• La Alicantina
Plaza del Salvador, 2
Tel: 422-6122
Has a modern and undistinguished interior, but serves some of the best seafood tapas in Seville.

• José Luís
Plaza de Cuba, 3
Tel: 427-9649
An upscale cocktail bar with English décor.

Restaurants

If you're just out to wander, begin at the north and east sides of the Cathedral. Here you will find the touristy restaurants, but they're touristy for the good reason that they offer variety and reasonable prices. As for particular references, we offer a modest number of the better known restaurants:

• Bodegón Torre de Oro
Santander, 15
Tel: 421-3169
A rustic setting near the Tower of Gold.

• Enrique Becerra
Gamaza, 2
Tel: 421-3049
Small, requires reservation. One of Seville's best.

• La Isla
Arfe, 25
Tel: 421-5376
Seafood and paellas, crowded and popular.

• La Rayuala
Don Remondo, 1
Tel: 422-4352
The menu of the day is one of Seville's best bargains.

• El Burladero
Canalejas, 1
Tel: 422-2900
One of Seville's famous institution, decorated with motifs of the bullring. Frequented by Hemingway.

• La Judería
Cano y Cueto, 13
Tel: 441-2052
A starting place in the Barrio de

Santa Cruz. Traditional Spanish — gazpacho, suckling lamb, sea bass.

• Figón del Cabildo
Plaza del Cabildo
Tel: 422-0117
Traditional Spanish, near the Cathedral.

• Los Alcázares
Miguel de Mañara, 10
Tel: 421-3103
Near the Alcázar, caters mainly to tourists.

• El Bacalao
Ponce de León, 15
Tel: 421-6670
Near the Plaza Encarnación. Specializes in fish, particularly cod.

• El Mesón
Dos de Mayo, 26
Tel: 421-3075
Noticed by James Michener in Iberia, and John Fulton, the American artist and bullfighter whose paintings hang here.

• Río Grande
Betis, 70
Tel: 427-8371
A romantic setting on the Guadalquivir River. Fine Andalusian cuisine.

• Rincón de Curro
Virgen de Luján, 45
Tel: 454-0251
One of Seville's best.

• La Dorada
Virgen de Aguas Santas, 6
Tel: 445-5100
Fish, particularly in the light, Málaga style.

• Modesto
Cano y Cueto, 5
Considered the best pub by many. Dining upstairs.

Shopping
Special Boutiques

• Crafts: Artespaña. Plaza de la Concordia, 2.
• Suede & leather: Juan Foronda. Plaza Virgen de los Reyes, 3.
• Regional costumes: Lina. Lineros, 7.
• Flamenco costumes: Pardales. Cuna, 23.
• Shawl & mantilla: Feliciano Forunda. Alvarez Quintero, 52.
• Fans: Casa Rubio. Sierpes, 56.
• Embroidery: Bordados. Carcía de Vinuesa, 33.
• Castanets: Filigrana. León XIII, 73.
• Silver & gold: Matahacas, 14; Avda. Eduardo Dato, 2; Plaza Molviedro, 9; Santa Clara, 89.
• Ceramics: Cerámica de Sevilla. Pimienta, 9. Tel: 421-5749 (will ship abroad). Or Fábrica de Santa Ana in Triana (cheaper than the tourist places on the other side of the river).

Open Markets
- El Jueves. Feria (every Thursday).
- Alfalfa. Plaza de la Alfalfa. Sundays. Pets.
- Philatelic market. Plaza del Cabildo. Sundays.

- Tennis, swimming: Piscinas Sevilla. Avda. Ciudad Jardín.
- Horse riding: Pipica Puerta Príncipe. Ctra. de Sevilla-Utrera, km 11.5.
- Canoeing: The Guadalquivir River.
- Camping: Club de Campo. Airport road, 10 km. Open all year.
Camping Sevilla. Avda. de la Libertad, 13. Ctra. Sevilla-Dos Hermanas. Open all year.
Camping Villsom. Ctra. Sevilla-Cádiz. 8 km from Seville. Open February 1 to 31 November.

English Bookshops
- Pascual Lázaro. Sierpes 2-4.
- Libros Vértice. Matesos Gago, 24.

Consulates
- Belgium. Avda. San Francisco Javier, 20-3. Tel: 467-7061.
- Canada. Constitución, 30-2. Tel: 422-9413.
- Denmark. Avda. Reina Mercedes, 25-1. Tel: 461-1489.
- France. Plaza de Santa Cruz, 1. Tel: 422-2896.
- Germany. Avda. Ramón de Carranze, 22. Tel: 447-7811.
- Italy. Avda. de la Constitución, 36-1. Tel: 422-7774.
- Mexico. Martín Villa, 5. Tel: 422-2552.
- Norway. (See Denmark.)
- Netherlands. Gravina, 55. Tel: 422-8750.
- Portugal. Pabellón de Portugal. Avda del Cid. Tel: 423-1150.
- Sweden. (See Denmark.)
- UK. Plaza Nueva, 8. Tel: 422-8875.
- USA. Pabellón EE UU, Paseo de las Delicias, 7. Tel: 423-1885

Useful Numbers

(Area code 95, or 5 from outside of Spain)

Telephone information	Tel: 003
Emergencies (police)	Tel: 091
Guardia Civil	Tel: 462-8111

Tourist Information

Avda. de la Constitución, 21	Tel: 422-1404/421-8157
• Municipal	
Tourism Paseo de las Delicias, 9	Tel: 423-4465
• Regional Tourism	
Avda. de la Constitución, 24	Tel: 421-1091/422-5653
• Information Office of the Civil Government	
Plaza de España	Tel: 423-2270
• City Hall	
Plaza Nueva, 1	Tel: 421-2800
• San Pablo Airport (12 km from Seville.)	Tel: 451-6111
• Emergency clinic. Jesús del Gran Poder, 34.	Tel: 438-2461
• Post and Telegraph Office	
Avda. de la Constitución, 32	Tel: 422-8880
• Iberia Airlines	
Almiranet Lobo, 2	Tel: 422-8901
• Main Police Station. Plaza de la Gavidia	Tel: 422-8840
• Lost and Found. Almansa	Tel: 421-5694
• Royal Automobile Club of Andalusia	
Eduardo Dato, 22.	Tel: 463-1350
• RENFE (Spanish National Railroad)	
Zaragoza, 29	Tel: 441-4111
• Bus terminal	Tel: 441-7111
• Taxis	Tel: 458-0000/462-2222/435-9835
• Boat Trips (all depart from near the Tower of Gold)	
Barco Lola	Tel: 462-7448
Sevillana de Cruceros	Tel: 421-1396
• Guide service	Tel: 421-3894/422-4641/423-2930/422-2374
Bus tours of the city at García de Vinuesa, 39 (near the Cathedral)	
• American Express	
Viajes Alhambra, Teniente Colonel Segui, 3.	Tel: 422-4435
• Banks. Open from 9:00 to 2:00.	

Olympic Calendar of Competition

Opening ceremony: July 25, 1992

	July								August							
LIST OF SPORTS	Sa	S	M	T	W	Th	F	Sa	S	M	T	W	Th	F	Sa	S
Opening	•															
Track and Field						•	•	•	•		•	•	•	•	•	•
Badminton							•	•	•	•	•	•	•			
Basketball		•	•	•	•	•	•	•		•	•	•	•	•		
Handball		•	•	•	•	•	•	•	•	•	•		•			
Baseball		•	•	•	•	•	•	•	•	•	•		•			
Boxing		•	•	•	•	•	•	•	•	•	•	•	•		•	
Cycling		•			•	•	•	•	•		•					
Equitation			•		•		•		•		•	•	•	•		•
Fencing			•	•	•	•	•		•	•	•	•	•			
Football		•	•	•	•	•	•		•	•		•		•	•	
Gymnastics		•	•	•	•	•	•	•		•	•	•				
Weightlifting		•	•	•	•	•		•	•	•	•	•				
Field Hockey		•	•	•	•	•	•	•	•	•	•	•	•	•	•	
Judo							•	•	•	•	•	•	•	•	•	
Wrestling		•	•	•	•	•		•	•	•	•	•				
Swimming		•	•	•		•	•	•								
Jumping								•	•	•	•	•	•	•	•	
Synch. Swimming										•	•		•	•		
Waterpolo		•	•	•		•	•		•	•						
Pentathalon		•	•	•	•	•										
Canoeing					•				•	•	•	•	•	•		
Rowing		•	•	•	•	•		•	•							
Tennis		•	•	•	•	•	•	•	•	•	•	•	•			
Table Tennis		•	•	•	•	•	•	•	•							
Shooting		•	•	•	•	•	•	•								
Archery										•	•	•	•			
Sailing			•	•	•	•			•	•	•					
Volleyball		•	•	•	•	•	•	•	•	•	•	•		•	•	•
Closing																•
		17	18	18	20	19	16	18	18	18	19	17	15	12	8	3
		11	8	14	17	18	18	29	23	14	22	16	16	19	36	3

The 1992 Olympic Games

Of vast international importance in the Quincentennial celebrations are, of course, the Olympic Games, scheduled to be inaugurated on July 25 by King Juan Carlos I. Not an entirely new experience to this great Catalunian city, Barcelona hosted Universal Expositions in 1888 and 1929. The Games are costing Barcelona $4.3 billion and are expected to bring in $8 billion in tourism and investments. In the Games themselves, International Olympic Committee President Juan Antonio Samaranch has been determined to exclude grotesque commercialism and advertising, regardless of the profits that are coming in. Spain has high hopes for medals in swimming, sailing, fencing and gymnastics.

The Games are drawing participation from 92 countries and are staffed by 30,000 volunteers. The radio and television coverage alone is employing 10,000 workers. NBC has bought the American television rights for over 400 million dollars. SEAT, the national Spanish automobile company, is to inaugurate a new $5 billion plant in Barcelona the same month, under the sponsorship of Barcelona Mayor Pasqual Maragall. Investments have been kicked in from 113 corporations.

Ticket Information

The C.O.O.B. 92 Information Telephone Number for Ticket Sales is: (93) 414-1600

Tickets have been sold through branches of the Banesto Bank. Tickets are extremely difficult to come by, but here are the official outlets in various countries where inquiries can be made. In April 1992, all those people that have made successful reservations for tickets will be able to pay for and collect their tickets. Any unsold tickets will then go on sale or a period of one week. The last phase of ticket sales occurs during the the Games themeselves, when unsold tickets will be available at ticket offices at the Olympic venues.

Agents for the UK:
Sportworld Travel
New Abbey Court
Stert Street, Abington,
Oxon OX14 3JZ
Tel: (44) (235) 554844
Fax: (44) (235) 554841

For the US:
Olson Travel World (public)
100 North Sepulveda Bd.
Suite 1010
El Segundo, CA 90245
Tel: (1) (213) 615-0711
Fax: (1) (213) 640-2039
Jet Set Tours (sponsors)
260 Christophe Lane
Staten Island, NY 10314
Tel: (1) (718) 494-8522
Fax: (1) (718) 494-8493

For Canada:
Sportsworld Travel
2279 Towne Bd.
Oakville, Ontario L6H 5J9
Tel: (1) (416) 257-0059
Fax: (1) (416) 257-0059

For Australia:
Keith Prwse Expotel Travel
77 Alexander St.
Crows Nest NSW 2065
Tel: (61) (2) 906-11-44
Fax: (61) (2) 906-10-13

For France:
Sport Travel
23, rue d'Issy
92100 Boulogne
Tel: (33) (1) 47-61-99-11

Ticket Prices
In July 1991 there was a draw for tickets that had been oversubscribed. Ticket prices for the first heats range from 750 pesetas (baseball, fencing, handball, equestrian events, field hockey, modern pentathlon, canoeing, rowing, table tennis, archery) to 4500 pesetas (best seats). Prices for finals are subject to change. Here is a good indication:

Archery: 1000 ptas.
Badminton: 1000-3000 ptas.
Baseball: 1250-2250 ptas.
Basketball: 3500-9000 ptas.
Boxing: 3000-6000 ptas.
Canoeing: 1500 ptas.
Cycling: 1900-3800 ptas.
Diving: 7000 ptas.
Equestrian events: 2500-7000 ptas.
Fencing: 1000-2400 ptas.
Field hockey: 1400-2800 ptas.
Gymnastics: 3500- 7000 ptas.
Handball: 1500-3500 ptas.
Judo: 1500-3000 ptas.
Rowing: 900-1500 ptas.
Football/Soccer: 2500-6000 ptas.
Swimming: 2800-7000 ptas.
Shooting: 2000 ptas.
Synch. swimming: 2250-3500 ptas.
Table tennis: 1000-2000 ptas.
Track and field: 3000-8000 ptas.
Volleyball: 3500-6000 ptas.
Water polo: 2000-3000 ptas.
Weight-lifting: 1000 ptas.
Wrestling: 1800-2700 ptas.
(Source: Lookout Magazine, 1991)

Accommodations During the Olympics

For a list of hotels see General Tourist Information later in this chapter. You should note though that hotel reservations are all but impossible to obtain during the weeks of the Olympics and rooms have been booked for as much as $1000 US a night. Don't show up in Barcelona expecting to find accommodations.

Cultural Olympiad

Concurrent with the Games is the Cultural Olympiad in Barcelona which are to culminate in a film festival, various performances of opera, dance and theater and art exhibitions.

In addition, a Paralympics, for the handicapped, is scheduled from September 3-14, 1992, organized by Josep María Vila, Director General of the COOB (Barcelona Olympics Organizing Committee).

A Bit of History

The Iberian world is split between those who accept Madrid's takeover in the last two decades as the peninsula's major city, and those who consider Barcelona the real leader, with Madrid the usurper. The residents of both Madrid and Barcelona—fiercely competitive and proud—often resent even having both cities discussed in the same guide book. Be aware of the intensity of the Madrid-Barcelona/Castilian-Catalan rivalry. This is serious. To many, the city of Gaudi, Picasso, Casals and Miró will never be replaced as the aesthetic, cultural and commercial capital of Spain. Barcelona breathes a special flavor and likely always will — fiercely independent, staunchly egalitarian in defiance of the stratified Castilian tastes, and imbued with artistic proportion and a deep sense of public justice. Writing in 1632, Lope de Vega said of Catalans, "...to preserve their rights, they'll die a thousand deaths." (La Dorotea, IV,1). Three and a half centuries later, the principle holds true.

For centuries Barcelona has been Spain's most inter-nation-alist city, with direct links to France and the Mediterranean basin denied by nature to landlocked Madrid. Since early Phoenician settle-ments and the Carthaginian occupation of 237 B.C., Barcelona has been the point of entry for empires from the east. Romans, Goths, Moors, and Franks vied for the area until the Counts of Barcelona established its independence in 874. Today still, German, American, French and Japanese companies hoping to make inroads on the Peninsula see Barcelona as the best foothold for their Spanish headquarters. They seek a part of the action in a region which has outstripped the Spanish average yearly growth since 1986, and whose present five percent soars above the EC average of three and a half.

Whatever the final outcome, 1992 is leaving a profound effect on Barcelona, producing the swiftest, deepest urban renewal of any modern city in recent memory. Road and infra-structure improvements, hotel additions and public works modernizations have leapt forward, changing the face of the city dramatically for the better, in preparation for the Olympic Games. Beyond the three-week extravaganza, the improvements will remain in one of western Europe's most positive developments. While prices of lodging have become exorbitant in preparation for the climactic events of July, 1992, they are expected to stabilize in the following months with things returning to normal. In the meantime, visit, study, take in the events, but don't plan to settle there without an ingenious plan on how to handle the dizzying inflation.

Official Holidays in Catalunia

January 1	New Year's
Friday before Easter	Holy Friday
Monday after Easter	Easter Monday
May 1	Labor Day *(Fiesta del Trabajo)*
(Last Monday in May)	*La Pascua Granada*
June 24	Pentecost *(Pentecostes)*
August 15	Assumption *(Asunción de la Virgen)*
September 11	*La Diada* (Catalan National Holiday)
September 24	*La Merce* (Patron Saint of Barcelona)
October 12	Spanish National Holiday
November 1	All Saints *(Todos los Santos)*
December 6	Constitution Day *(Día de la Constitución)*
December 25	Christmas *(Navidad)*
December 26	Saint Stephen *(San Esteban)*

Accommodations

Here is a list of Barcelona's major hotels organized alphabetically and by category. Note that the number of hotels is constantly growing as the city continues to develop. Prices, highly susceptible to price variations, have not been quoted here.

Avenida Palace *****
Gran Vía Corts Catalanes, 605
Tel: 301-9600

Alexandra****
Mallorca, 351
Tel: 215-3052

Almirante****
Vía Layatena 42
08003 Barcelona
Tel: 319-9500

Apartamentos Victoria****
Avda. Pedralbes, 16
Tel: 204-2754

Barcelona Hilton*****
Av. Diagonal, 589
Tel: 419-2233

Belagua***
Via Augusta, 89-91
Tel: 237-3940

Calderon****
Rambla de Catalunya, 26
Tel: 301-0000

Casal del Medico**
Tapineria, 10
Tel: 319-7812

Colon****
Av. Catedral, 7
Tel: 301-1404

Condes de Barcelona****
Paseo de Gracia, 75
Tel: 215-0616

Hesperia****
Los Vergos, 27
Tel: 204-5551

Diplomatic*****
Pau Claris, 122
Tel: 317-3100

Gotico***
Jaime I, 14
Tel: 315-2211

Majestic****
Paseo de Gracia, 70
Tel: 215-4512

Presidente*****
Diagonal, 570
Tel: 200-2111

Princesa Sofia*****
Plaza Papa P/o XII, s/n
Tel: 330-7111

Ramada Renaissance*****
Ramblas, 111
Tel: 318-6200

Ritz*****
Gran Via Corts Catalanes, 668
Tel: 318-5200

Rivoli****
Rambla del Estudis, 128
Tel: 302-6643

Royal****
Ramblas, 117
Tel: 301-9400

Sarria Sol*****
Avda. Sarria, 50
Tel: 410-6060

Suizo***
Plaza del Angel, 12
Tel: 315-4111

Tres Torres***
C/Calatrava, 32
Tel: 417-7300

Youth Hostels
Alberg Municipal Pujades
Passeig de Pujades, 29
Tel: 300-3104

Alberg Verge de Montserrat
Ntra. Sra. del Coll, 41-45
Tel: 213-8633

Kabul Hostel
Plaça Reial, 17
Tel: 318-5190

Restaurants
Here is a starters list of Barcelona's best loved eateries.

Luxury
Beltxenea
Mallorca 275, entlo.
Tel: 215-3848

Ara Cata
Dr. Ferran 33
Tel: 204-1053

Azulete
Via Augusta 281
Tel: 203-5943

Botafumeiro
Mayor de Gracia 81
Tel: 218-4230

Finisterre
Avda. Diagonal 469
Tel: 239-5576

Guria
Casanova 97
Tel: 253-6325

Eldorado Petit
Dolors Monserda 57
Tel: 204-5506

La Balsa
Infanta Isabel 4
Tel: 211-5048

La Dorada
Travesera de Gracia 44
Tel: 200-6322

Neichel
Avda. Pedralbes 16bis
Tel: 203-8408

Orotava
Consejo de Ciento 335
Tel: 302-3128

Reno
Tuset 27
Tel: 200-9129

Via Veneto
Ganduxer 10
Tel: 200-7024

Quality
Agut d'Avignon
Trinidad 3
Tel: 302-6034

Café de l'Academia
Llado (Pl. Sant Just)
Tel: 315-0026

Carballeira
Reina Cristina 3
Tel: 310-1006

Del Teatre
Montseny 47
Tel: 218-6738

El Gran Café
Avinyo, 9
Tel: 318-7986

El Tunel de Muntaner
San Mario 22
Tel: 212-6074

L'Olivé
Muntaner 171
Tel: 230-9027

Los Caracoles
Escudillers 14
Tel: 302-3185

Siete Puertas
Paseo Isabel II 14
Tel: 319-3033

Senyor de Parellada
Argenteria 37
Tel: 315-4010

Modest
Agut
Cignas 16
Tel: 315-1709

Pescallunes
Magdalenas 23
Tel: 318-5483

English Language Bookstore
Come In Bookshop
Calle Provença, 203
08036 Barcelona
Tel: 253-1806 or 253-1204

Sites

• Montjuich Park

Situated at the southeast corner of the city, Montjuich offers a variety of Palaces and Museums such as the Palacio Nacional, Fundacion Joan Miro and the Pueblo Espanol. In the latter, one may visit Spain in miniature and purchase artifacts from the various provinces.

• Gothic Quarter

The Gothic Quarter is located in the area between Plaza San Jaime and the Cathedral. There are good restaurants and interesting shops where one can purchase souvenirs and stop for coffee along the way. There are also museums with treasures that go back many centuries.

• Ramblas

This is one of Europe's most talked about avenues. It is located between Plaza de Cataluna and Puerta de la Paz. One may purchase flowers, artcraft and birds along its walkway.

• Gaudi Architecture

Antonio Gaudi who died in 1926, was one of Spain's most famous architects. His works, with their fairytale shapes, give evidence of an artist ahead of his time. Some of his most famous works are Guell Park and Sagrada Familia Church located in Plaza Sagrada Familia.

Study Abroad Programs

Brethren College
Program in Barcelona
Office: Illusa, 11
Tel: 330-1703
Resident Director:
Robert Anderson
US Contact: Brethren Colleges Abroad, 604 College Ave., North Manchester, Indiana 46962

Centro de Estudios de la Universidades de California e Illinois
Gran Vía, 585
Universidad de Barcelona
Facultad de Filología
Tel: 317-5018
Resident Director:
James D. Compton
US Contact: Education Abroad Program, University of California, Santa Barbara, CA 93106

Knox College Program in Spain
Bigay, 19
Resident Director:
Isabel Livosky
Tel: 211-7218
US Contact: CIEE, 205 E. 42nd St., New York, NY 10017

Schools

The American School of Barcelona
Balmes, 7
Tel. 371-4016

Kensington School
Carretera de Esplugas, 86 bis
Tel. 204-1579

The Anglo-American School
Castelldefels
Tel. 665-1584

Benjamin Franklin
International School
Avda. Pearson, 34
Tel: 204-1271

Institute of American Studies
Via Augusta, 123
Tel: 209-2711

Cursos de Verano

(summer courses)
University of Barcelona
Plaza de la Universidad
Tel: 318-4266
Housing available in the student residence for summer courses: San Jordi, Maestro Nicolau, 13, 08021 Barcelona. Tel: 201-6600.

Eurolingua
Calle Prats de Mollo
08021 Barcelona
Tel: 201-3307

Houses of Worship

St. George's Church
San Juan de la Salle, 41
Tel: 417-8867
Parroquia Francesca
English Catholic Mass
Angli, 15
Tel: 204-4962

Salvation Army
Rubi, 18
Tel: 237-0447

Catalan

The relationship between Spanish and Catalan is a complicated linguistic, political, and cultural question covered widely in texts and guides. You will see Spanish words crossed out with graffitti and replaced with the Catalan. Up until Franco's death, it had been illegal for Catalan words to be used in public signs, store fronts, and billboards. A systematic cultural repression was inforced. So, be aware of the charged history and question of identity that comes with the language. As a foreigner, you may feel free to speak Spanish in Barcelona; everyone will understand and not judge you poorly. Remember though that Catalan is its own language and is gaining a greater identity as more and more foreign works are being translated into the language. Catalan is a romance language with a relationship to Spanish, much like what Provençal is to French. Here is a short lexicon on common Catalan words for your use. Note: X is pronounced SH, as in Portuguese).

Lexicon

un 1
dos 2
tres 3
quatre 4
cinc 5
sis 6
set 7
vuit 8
nou 9
deu 10
onze 11
dotze 12
tretze 13
catorze 14
quinze 15
setze 16
disset 17
divuit 18
dinou 19
vint 20
trenta 30
quaranta 40
cinquanta 50
xeixanta 60
setanta 70
vitanta 80
nourante 90
cent 100

accident - accident
adéu - goodbye
aeroport - airport
això - that
autobús - bus
bitllet - ticket
cambrer - waiter
carrer - street
ciutat - city
comprar - buy
el compte - the bill
el cotxe - car

darrera - behind
devant - in front of
diners - money
dispensi - excuse me
dona - woman
dreta - (to the) right
escolti! - Hello (to get someone's attention)
gracies - thank you
esquerra - (to the) left
habitació (hi ha habitació?) - room (is there a room available?)
hola - hello (greeting in the street)
home - man
hotel - hotel
lliure - free, available
llogar - rent
moll, port - pier, port
em permet...si us plau - please
quant val? - how much does (it) cost?
recte - straight
serveis - service (toilet)
si us plau - please
sortida - exit
taxi - taxi
telefon - telephone
tren - train
tu - you
urgent - urgent
vaixell - boat

Quant val? - How much is...?
Bon dia - Good morning.
Bona tarda - Good afternoon.
Bona nit - Good night.
Aon es - Where is...?
Ajuda - Help

Nightclubs

La Belle Epoque
Muntaner 246
Tel: 209-7385

Los Tarantos
Flamenco Dancing
Plaza Real 17
Tel: 317-8098

La Salsa
Traditional Dancing
Pau Claris 122
Tel: 317-3100

Up & Down
Discoteque
Numancia 179
Tel: 204-8809

No
Discoteque
Aribau 242
Tel: 201-8150

Bikini
Diagonal 571
Tel: 322-7254

Department Stores

El Corte Ingles
Diagonal 617
or
Plaza Cataluna 14

Galerias Preciados
Diagonal 471
or
Puerta de Angel 19

Consulates

• Canada
Via Augusta, 125
Tel: 209-0634
• Denmark
Via Laietana, 5
Tel: 310-2091
• United States
Via Laietana, 33
Tel: 319-9550
• France
Passeig de Gracia, 11
Tel: 317-8150
• Great Britain
Avda. Diagonal, 477
Tel: 322-2151
• Netherlands
Passeig de Gracia, 111
Tel: 217-3700
• Ireland
Gran Via Carles III, 94
Tel: 330-9652
• Japan
Avda. Diagonal, 662-64
Tel: 204-7224
• Norway
Provença, 284
Tel: 215-0094
• Sweden
Corsega, 289-91
Tel: 218-1566

Useful Numbers

(Note: Barcelona's area code is 93 within Spain, just 3 when calling from outside. For operator assisted long-distance calls in Europe, dial 008; for outside Europe, 005; in Spain, 009).

Telephone repairs	Tel: 002
Information	Tel: 003
National Police	Tel: 091
Municipal Police	Tel: 092
Fire Service	Tel: 080
Weather	Tel: 094
Time	Tel: 093
Highway conditions	Tel: 212-5666
Town Hall	Tel: 302-4200
Catalonia Autonomous government	Tel: 302-4700
Catalonia Parliament	Tel: 300-6263
Post Office	Tel: 318-3831
Telegrams by telephone	Tel: 322-2000
Lost and Found	Tel: 301-3923
Hotel Association	Tel: 301-6240
Restaurant Association	Tel: 301-6740
Travel Agents Association	Tel: 321-9729
Tourist Guide Association	Tel: 255-1355
City Information	Tel: 318-2525 or 010
Ambulance	Tel: 302-3333/256-6666
	Tel: 329-7766/323-4372
	Tel: 323-4376

Hospitals

Hospital Clínico - Villarroel, 170	Tel: 323-1414
Clínica Quirón - Virgen de Montserrat, 5	Tel: 284-1200
Instituto Dexeus - Pas. de la Bonanova, 67	Tel: 212-4600
Doctors - house calls	Tel: 200-2924/ 317-1717
Camping Association	Tel: 317-4416
RENFE (train)	Tel: 322-4142
Urban transport	Tel: 336-0000
Plaça Pau Neruda	Tel: 245-7621
Monumento a Colón	Tel: 302-5224
Gran Vía	Tel: 301-7443

Post Offices

Plaza Antonio López	Tel: 318-3831
Paseo de la Bonanova, 117	Tel: 203-1421
Telegrams by phone	Tel: 322-2000

Travel Related Numbers

Central train station (Sants)	Tel: 322-4142
(airport train departs Sants station every 20 minutes)	
Iberia	Tel: 325-4304
British Air	Tel: 487-2112
American Airlines	Tel: 410-7760
TWA	Tel: 215-8486
Flight arrivals	Tel: 301-3993
Road conditions in Catalonia	Tel: 204-2247
in rest of Spain	Tel: 254-5005

Car Rentals

Europcar	Tel: 239-8401
Totcar	Tel: 321-3754
Real Automovil Club	Tel: 200-3311

Taxis   Tel: 300-3811/322-2222/330-0804/300-3905/387 1000/358-1111/490-2222/490-3958

Airport	Tel: 325-5829
Agons Lits Travel	Tel: 317-5500

Credit Cards

American Express	Tel: 217-0070/450-9061
Diners Club	Tel: 302-1428
Master Charge	Tel: 315-2512
Visa	Tel: 302-3200

Currency Exchange

Exact Change, 130 Ramblas

Home Repairs

Multi Asistencia	Tel: 325-9511
ENHER (electricity)	Tel: 214-4337
FECSA (electricity)	Tel: 241-5200
HECSA (electricity)	Tel: 309-5108
	Tel: 309-5104
Water	Tel: 231-9211/ 231-9100/ 231-9000
Gas	Tel: 319-4705/ 310-6308/ 310-6304
Butane	Tel: 410-5500
U.S. Chamber of Commerce	Tel: 321-8595/Fax 321-8197

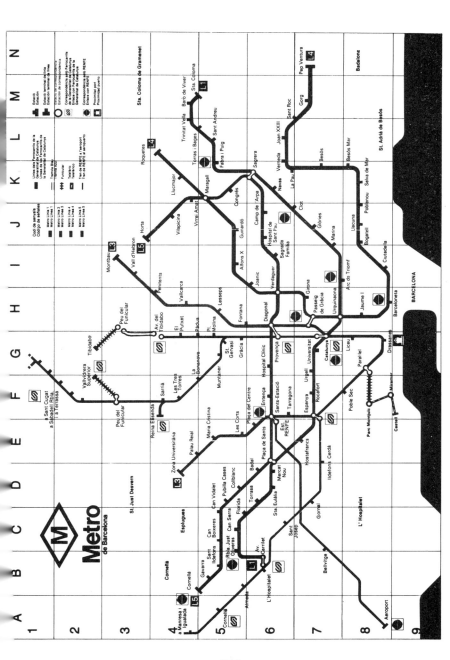

Metro de Barcelona

Gaudi's lamp post
Plaça Reial
Barcelona 13-9-86

Academic Year Abroad. Institute of International Education, 1989.

Atkinson, William C. *A History of Spain and Portugal.* London: Penguin, 1960.

Atlas de Madrid. Madrid: Almax (Indispensable map and listing of all streets, bus routes, hospitals, etc., updated every year.)

Borrow, George. *The Bible in Spain.* London: John Murray, 1843. One of the best primary sources on Spain in the nineteenth century. Borrow, an eccentric English linguistic genius, toured Spain performing the only job anyone was willing to pay him for: propagating the Protestant Bible in Catholic Spain.

Bear Facts about Madrid. Women's Club of Madrid. A good settling-in guide edited by spouses of American diplomats in Madrid. Oriented towards families with Embassy privileges.

Berlitz Travel Guide, Madrid. Lausanne. An amazingly compact guide to living and survival in the Spanish capital, updated every year.

Besas, Peter. *The Written Road to Spain.* Madrid, 1988. (A lively study of the writers who wrote about Spain from 1820 to 1850.)

Blackshaw, Ina. *Doing Business in Spain.* London: Oyez, 1980.

Brenan, Gerald. *The Face of Spain.* London: Penguin, 1965. City by city travelogue.

Brenan, Gerald. *The Literature of the Spanish People.* London: Peregrine, 1963. A survey of the history of Spanish literature.

Cervantes, Miguel de, Saavedra. *Don Quixote.* Trying to live in Spain without a basic knowledge of this great and funny work is like trying to live in Los Angeles without a car.

Cities of Fashion. Promostyl, Vincennes: Frank Books, 1991. An Insider's Guide to Shopping in Nine Cities. With an excellent and up-to-date section on Barcelona.

Debelius, Harry. *Collins Guide to Spain.* London: Collins, 1988. A good overall guide to the country with a strong section on history, but a bit sketchy on each individual city, including Madrid.

Dumas, Alexandre. *Adventures in Spain.* New York: Chilton Co.,1959.

Fodor's Madrid. New York and London: Fodor's, updated yearly. Excellent sections on culture, history, wines, bullfight, etc. An uneven performance, but unsurpassed in its strong areas.

Ford, Richard. *Gatherings from Spain.* London: John Murray, 1846.

Ford, Richard. *A Hand-Book for Travellers in Spain and Readers at Home.* Centaur Press, London: 1966.

Fraser, Ronald. *Blood of Spain: an Oral History of the Spanish Civil War.* Gordon Press, 1976.

Gautier, Théophile. *Voyage en Espagne.* Paris: Gallimard, 1981.

Gudiol, José. *The Arts of Spain.* London: Thames & Hudson, 1964. Complete history of Spain through its artists' eyes.

Guía de Madrid. El País, Madrid: Aguilar, 1990. (A complete tourist guide with photos, and some useful lists of theaters, hotels, fiestas, etc.)

Guía de Madrid. Colegio Oficial de Arquitectas de Madrid, 1984. (An architectural guide to the newer and older sections of the city, ideal for self-instructional walking tours.)

Hooper, John. *The Spaniards.* London: Penguin, 1987 (an award-winning study of contemporary Spanish society).

Hugo Spanish Phrase Book. Essex: Hugo's, 1986. (The most compact and practical phrase book one comes across.)

Irving, Washington. *Diary in Spain.* New York: Hispanic Society of America, 1926.

Irving, Washington. *Tales of the Alhambra.* Philadelphia: Carey & Lea, 1926. Also Sanchez, Granada, 1990. One of the most Romantic works ever written about Spain. Penned after Irving's stay in the Alhambra itself during his stint as U.S. Ambassador to Spain. Filled with local lore and legend collected in the 1830s.

Jackson, Gabriel. *A Concise History of the Spanish Civil War.* London: Thames Hudson, 1980.

Kite, Cynthia and Ralph. *Spanish Country Inns and Paradors.* London: Harrap Columbus, 1987 (attractive, hand-wrought illustrations and lively text describing 70 of Spain's most charming hotels).

Longfellow, Henry Wadsworth. *Outre-Mer: a Pilgrimage Beyond the Sea.* New York: Harper, 1835.

Madrid. Insight City Guides, Lucinda Evans, Ed., Singapour: APA Publications, 1991. Excellently researched, written, and lavishly presented general tourist guide on Madrid.

Michelin: Spain and Portugal. Paris, updated every year. The most definitive (but not complete) listing of restaurants and hotels in Madrid and other Spanish cities.

Michener, James. *Iberia.* New York: Random House, 1968, a rambling, narcissistic work, not one of Michener's better efforts.

Morisson, Jan. *The Way of Spain.* New York, 1985. (The masterful Jan Morisson at her very best, and most succinct.)

Morton, H.V. *A Stranger in Spain.* Methuen, 1955, with many reprints (lively English travelogue from the 1950s — a favorite).

Orwell, George. *Homage to Catalonia.* London: Penguin, 1966. Orwell's famous reflec-tions on the Civil War written in 1938.

Porter, Darwin. *Frommer's Spain and Morocco on $40 a Day.* New York: Simon and Schuster, 1990. The best tourist guide book currently available on Spain. A treasure of anecdotal and descriptive material, with no sugar-coating except where it is really called for.

Pritchett, V.S. *The Spanish Temper.* London: Hogarth, 1984. A classic from this master writer.

Reay-Smith, John. *Living in Spain.* London: Hale, 1983. A good legal and economic guide.

Rough Guide to Spain. London: Harrap-Columbus, 1988. A good adjunct to the Frommer's, but secondary to it.

Searl, David. *You and the Law in Spain.* Fuengirola, Spain: Lookout Publications, 1990. The best English-language guide to explain local laws dealing with taxes, work permits, cars, buying property, etc.

Thomas, Hugh. *The Spanish Civil War.* London: Penguin, 1977. The most respected work on this topic, devoured by Spaniards with admiration, illegally, during the end of the Franco period and still the most authoritative.

Todo Madrid. Arnao, Madrid, 1989, the most detailed Spanish-language guide to actual living in the capital. Strongest on its guide to night life.

Williams, Mark. *The Story of Spain.* Fuengirola, Spain: Lookout Publications, 1990. Strong on anecdotal and political history. Makes a strong case (daringly) for the Spanish empire as "one of history's most humane."